Globalization and Nationalism

Globalization and Nationalism

The Changing Balance in
India's Economic Policy, 1950–2000

Baldev Raj Nayar

Sage Publications
New Delhi • Thousand Oaks • London

First published in 2001 by

Sage Publications India Pvt Ltd
Second Printing 2003   M-32 Market, Greater Kailash-I
New Delhi 110 048

Sage Publications Inc.   Sage Publications
2455 Teller Road   6 Bonhill Street
Thousand Oaks, California 91320   London EC2A 4PU

Published by Tejeshwar Singh for Sage Publications India Pvt Ltd, typeset in 10 pt Classical Garamond by Line Arts, Pondicherry and printed at Chaman Enterprises, Delhi.

Library of Congress Cataloging-in-Publication Data
Nayar, Baldev Raj.
    Globalization and nationalism: the changing balance in India's economic policy, 1950–2000/Baldev Raj Nayar.
        p. cm.
    Includes bibliographical references (p.) and index.
        1. India—Economic policy—1974– 2. India—Economic conditions—1947– . I. Title.
    HC435.2.N346 338.954—dc21 2001 00-067638

ISBN: 0–7619–9536–6 (US-Hb)   81–7829–015–4 (India-Hb)

Sage Production Team: Nomita Jain, Arpita Das, N.K. Negi and Santosh Rawat

To the memory of my parents,
Jamna Das Nayar, 1905–1948, and
Jaswant Kaur (nee Durga Devi Marwah), 1911–99

Contents

List of Abbreviations

AITUC	All India Trade Union Congress
Assocham	Associated Chambers of Commerce and Industry
ATF	aviation turbine fuel
BJP	Bharatiya Janata Party
BMS	Bharatiya Mazdoor Sangh
CII	Confederation of Indian Industry
CITU	Centre of Indian Trade Unions
CMP	Common Minimum Programme
CPI	Communist Party of India
CPI(M)	Communist Party of India (Marxist)
DMK	Dravida Munnetra Kazhagam
EU	European Union
FDI	foreign direct investment
FERA	Foreign Exchange Regulation Act, 1973
FICCI	Federation of Indian Chambers of Commerce and Industry
FII	foreign institutional investor
FIPB	Foreign Investment Promotion Board
FIRA	Foreign Investment Review Agency (Canada)
FPI	foreign portfolio investment
GATT	General Agreement on Trade and Tariffs
GDP	Gross Domestic Product
GOI	Government of India
ICICI	Industrial Credit and Investment Corporation of India
IDBI	Industrial Development Bank of India
IFIs	international financial institutions
IMF	International Monetary Fund
IRA	Insurance Regulatory Authority
ISI	import substitution industrialization
LDC	less developed country

LPG	liquid petroleum gas
M&As	mergers and acquisitions
MITI	Ministry of International Trade and Industry (Japan)
MNC	multinational corporation
MP	Member of Parliament
MRTP	Monopolies and Restrictive Trade Practices [Act]
NAFTA	North American Free Trade Area
NIC	newly industrialized country
NRI	non-resident Indian
OBCs	other backward classes
OECD	Organization for Economic Cooperation and Development
OPEC	Organization of the Petroleum Exporting Countries
PFI	public financial institution
PSEs	public sector enterprises
POWs	prisoners of war
R&D	research and development
RBI	Reserve Bank of India
SDRs	Special Drawing Rights
RSS	Rashtriya Swayamsevak Sangh
SJM	Swadeshi Jagran Manch
TMC	Tamil Maanila Congress
UF	United Front
US	United States
VSF	viscose staple fibre
WTO	World Trade Organization

Set against the larger canvas of the historic interaction between economic globalization and economic nationalism, this study examines the successive attempts over the half-century from 1950 to 2000 to change the roles of the state and market in the management of the Indian economy. No single piece of research seeks to attack all problems at once but tends to examine limited areas, as does this study. It looks at economic policy reform, not economic development as such, though the two are not unrelated; indeed, the very purpose of reform is to accelerate development or overcome crises of development. What lies at the heart of such reform are the respective roles of the state and market in the conduct of economic affairs.

Given that economic policy reform has to do with the roles of both the state and market, the study necessarily takes a broader, more encompassing view of reform than that of the economist. Economic policy reform goes beyond economics and inherently involves extra-economic dimensions. In this more architectural view of reform, the Indian state occupies a central place in the analysis. As elsewhere in the world, the state as the locus of nationalism confronts new challenges in the face of the acceleration of globalization. Intensified globalization is assumed to decree a wider role for markets and greater openness of the economy, and thus a shrinking role for the state. Since the Indian state is located in a representative democracy and is therefore intimately linked to society, the study necessarily also takes account of society in the analysis. Because no state is an economic island, the international system occupies an important place in the analysis; particularly relevant in this connection is the state leadership's perception of that system, especially in the early years of economic planning. In brief, the state, society and the international system constitute the basic explanatory framework. Of course, it can be validly objected that such a framework is bound to explain everything since nothing remains excluded from it. However, the real question is—what is the priority among the variables of state, society and international system. Even then, no single hierarchy of priority among these variables can explain economic policy over the entire period of a half-century; different variables emerge as more or less important in different reform episodes.

In the more recent period of economic liberalization in the 1990s, the democratic structure of the Indian state emerges as a key explanatory variable; it made for the economic crisis that provoked the reform episode, it led to an incremental reform approach as against shock therapy, and it allowed for the consolidation of the reforms once they were instituted. Regardless, the state has not been rendered helpless by the more recent phase of intensive globalization; it remains the master actor in determining the nature, scope, pace and sequencing of economic policy reform. However, the unfinished agenda for reform is vast. Given the critical role of the state in reform, that agenda ought also to include enhancing the regulative and transformative capacity of the state to cope with the challenges arising from globalization.

The overarching interaction between the two mighty social forces of globalization and nationalism, which have moulded and continue to mould the modern world, serves as the overall organizing framework for the study. Accordingly, Chapter 1 looks at the fundamental issues that emerge from this interaction for economic policy reform. Subsequent chapters examine the national vision that forged the basic Indian development model (Chapter 2) and the attempts to reform it in the context of the contention between globalization and nationalism (Chapters 3–4 and 6–7). Chapter 5 discusses the response of business to the reforms; labour may seem slighted in the process, but no separate treatment is indicated since the Indian trade unions are largely the labour fronts of political parties.

I would like to thank the *Asian Survey, Economic & Political Weekly, Indian Economic Review, Journal of Commonwealth and Comparative Politics*, and *Pacific Affairs* for permission to use materials from articles originally published in them. Much is owed to my colleagues, Professors John Hall, Jagdish Handa, S.J. Noumoff, Philip Oxhorn and T.V. Paul; they have been extraordinarily generous in giving of their time and effort in reading parts of the study, discussing the issues raised in it, and offering criticisms and suggestions for improvement. Professor Yogendra Malik brought his innate wisdom to his review of Chapter 7. Nandita Jaishankar was most helpful in preparing the bibliography. I am very indebted to the Social Sciences and Humanities Research Council of Canada for funding my research for this project and many others over the last three decades and more. My greatest debt is to my wife for her support and forbearance.

1

Globalization, Nationalism and Economic Reform: The Fundamental Issues

The last quarter of the twentieth century has seen a wave of economic policy reform in the developing world, with one country after another taking the liberalization cure, often imposed by the international financial institutions. This wave of reform had been preceded by a quarter-century of state-directed effort at economic development, during which time the goals of economic self-reliance and import substitution industrialization (ISI) were the hallmarks of development strategies in the less developed countries. These goals seemed particularly justified, given the long experience of these countries with colonialism and the agricultural nature of their economies. There was, besides, intellectual support for them from Keynesianism and the new discipline of development economics, especially in view of the historical memories of the massive market failures of the Depression years. However, all this seemed to be overtaken by the subsequent surge of liberalization.

Economic liberalization covers many aspects of policy, but the central issue at stake is the relative role of the state and market in the operation and management of the national economy. The contemporary movement in economic policy reform has involved the retreat of the state and the shedding of many of its economic functions in favour of the market, which has been accorded a wider and increasingly important role. An interesting question pertains to whether there are limits to the shrinking of the state, or whether the process is destined to lead to the withering away of the state. Equally important is the question as to what ought to be the appropriate relationship between the state and market for purposes of effective economic performance. One way to investigate these questions is to carry out narrowly-delimited, empirically-based studies of one or more specific episodes of economic policy reform in one or more specific countries. That is what the present work seeks to do through an examination of India's economic policies over the half-century from 1950 to 2000. However, there is also some intellectual merit in examining the questions more broadly and holistically—so as not to miss the forest for the trees—from the perspective of the different logics of the state and market and, in the process, in defining the fundamental issues they raise for economic policy reform, and in setting out the ways in which they place limits on the complete triumph of one or the other in the economic arena.

The recent wave of economic policy reform in the developing world has been seen as a necessary consequence of a changed world economic system. The key feature of the changed world economy is the element of heightened *economic globalization*, which provides new external challenges as well as opportunities for development. As globalization has accelerated, it has come to loom large in the perceptions of policy-makers, and adjustment to it in the form of economic liberalization and the shrinking of the state has moved to the forefront of their economic agenda, even when not imposed on them. The phenomenon of economic globalization provides the widest possible context for the examination of economic policy reform. However, as a concept in contemporary social science, it appears in many variants. In one strong version, globalization refers to the presumed emergence of a 'supra-national', borderless global economy with its own laws of motion, encompassing and subordinating the various local economies in a single worldwide division of labour, rendering national governments into municipalities. A softer version of the concept, which informs the present study, treats globalization less as an end-stage and more as a process in which the 'international' economy becomes more closely integrated, with domestic economic agents increasingly oriented to the global market rather than to particular national markets, even as the state continues to remain central to national economic advancement (Hirst and Thompson 1996: 7–16). Regardless, economic globalization represents only one part of the equation. Equally necessary to the understanding of economic policy reform is the opposing social force in the form of *economic nationalism*. While diverse meanings go with the term, economic nationalism's core is constituted by the paramountcy of national economic interest against the claims of other nations (Burnell 1986: ch. 1).

Economic globalization and economic nationalism are, then, the two fundamental forces that have been shaping the world's economic terrain over the last few centuries. The two forces are obviously related to each other, with globalization both opposing and provoking economic nationalism as well as transforming and transcending it, even as its own apparently inexorable path of expansion and possible eventual triumph has been continually interrupted and redirected by nationalism. Both contending forces are integrally linked with *markets* and *states*, for both have been fundamentally rooted in the rise of markets and states in the modern era. Indeed, economic globalization is simply a fuller expression of the expansion of one or more markets to world scale, while economic nationalism is nothing but the manifestation in the economic arena of the consolidation of states in the international system. They thus simply represent another level of the working of markets and states. At the same time, each by itself as well as in interaction with the other generates pressures for economic policy reform which, in turn, has principally to do with the roles of states and markets in economic affairs. One of the vital questions for the developing world at the dawn of a new century, therefore, becomes precisely the relationship of globalization and nationalism to economic policy reform.

The central argument of this chapter is that economic globalization has been on the rise, but it has not necessarily meant the weakening of economic nationalism, which tends to find new incarnations. In the interaction between these two social forces, new balances are arrived at and effort needs to be directed towards studying how they influence economic policy reform. At the same time, in economic policy reform, the state and market need not be seen as adversaries in a zero-sum game but as partners in economic development; however, this partnership tends to be facilitated more by some types of regimes than by others.

In exploring the fundamentals of the interaction of globalization and nationalism and its relationship to the agenda of economic policy reform in the developing world, this chapter looks at (1) the rise and expansion of globalization; (2) the nationalist shaping of markets by states in their external role in relation to other states, with particular emphasis on national security and economic autonomy; (3) the continuing centrality of economic nationalism, especially among the developed countries, in the context of the post-war deepening of globalization; and (4) the nationalist shaping of markets by states in their internal role within society, highlighting the need for legitimacy and the relationship of the structural characteristics of states to the potential for effective economic policy reform.

The Rise and Expansion of Globalization

Economic globalization can be said to have originated in the development of a regional international market in Europe as foreign trade increased following the commercialization of agriculture and national specialization in agricultural activities after the Middle Ages (Wallerstein 1974). Meanwhile, in a process which can be fairly characterized as imperialism, several European states as they consolidated themselves during the course of the 'long' sixteenth century began bringing other vast geographic regions of the world under their political control and domination. In this manner, many of what had been earlier largely autonomous and self-sufficient economies of these regions were subordinated to the European economies. Thus, the origins of economic globalization lie in the rise of capitalism in Europe and the penetration by capitalism from that economic core into the regional economies of the periphery around the world. The process of penetration across the globe was not accomplished all at once but took place in a succession of expanding concentric circles.

This process was reinforced by the rise of industrialization, which arose as a spontaneous development in Great Britain, though definitely aided directly and indirectly by the state (Weiss and Hobson 1995: ch. 4). After having achieved its own industrialization under mercantilistic auspices, Britain turned to liberalism in the nineteenth century, for as the most advanced industrial power it now perceived greater economic advantage for itself in the operation of freer trade. However, it has received more credit for its liberalism than was deserved, since in practice its trade policies towards other states were invariably affected by geopolitical or strategic considerations (Gowa 1994: ch. 5). More particularly, in relation to the less developed world, while Britain preached the virtues of liberalism, it also insisted, through political and military coercion, on other nations opening their doors to economic penetration by it. Economic globalization thus developed not simply through the operation of some autonomous economic forces, but with military power serving as its necessary midwife. Consequently, its first challenge to economically backward and politically weak areas was invariably a military challenge to their security.

The rise of industrialization in Britain, because of the radical difference it made to the acquisition of wealth and power, and therefore to economic welfare and military security, forcefully persuaded other European powers and European colonial settlements around the globe to launch their own programmes of industrialization under strongly protectionist or mercantilist policy regimes, intellectually legitimized by Alexander Hamilton in the United States (US) and Friedrich List in Germany. However, this option of economic nationalism was firmly closed for most countries in Asia and Africa because they were overwhelmed militarily by the North Atlantic powers and rendered into colonies or semi-colonies. The only exception during the nineteenth century was Japan, both because of the perspicacity of its leadership and the geopolitical fact that, situated at the northeastern edge of the Eurasian continent, it was far removed as a prey from the industrial powers. Interestingly, the goal of industrialization was integrally linked to the search for national security through military power in Japan's development as it was in that of virtually every major North Atlantic power.

Although economic globalization has thus been under way for long, there is an essential difference nonetheless between the earlier 'extensive' or 'widening' phase of globalization, which linked the entire world economically, and the more contemporary 'intensive' or 'deepening' phase. The extensive phase can be said to have been completed by World War I. The North Atlantic states had been especially active in extending globalization in this phase during the course of the long period between the end of the Napoleonic wars and World War I. The period largely saw internal peace among the North Atlantic powers while they were engaged in the enterprise of extending, forcibly or otherwise, their economic and political sway over the entire world. Indeed, it was Lenin's (1974) profound insight that the origins of World War I lay precisely in the completion of the imperialist enterprise of bringing the entire world under the domination of the North Atlantic powers and dividing it up among themselves, at which point they turned—as they were bound to—against each other over the question as to who should preside over the newly-created world economy and international system. That question remained unresolved until the end of World War II, which explains the economic and political turmoil of the inter-war period. The outcome of that war, however, placed most of the world, though not all of it, under the military, political and economic hegemony of the US.

It is with the end of World War II that the intensive or deepening phase of globalization began. Until then, the economic integration of the world was largely confined to international trade between national economies, with underdeveloped areas in the periphery tied in a colonial economic relationship, serving as sites for the extraction of natural resources, often as tribute, and as kept markets for the manufactures of the North Atlantic powers. Industrial production in the world economy was largely organized in national systems, which were largely though not exclusively responsive to their internal markets. In the post-war period after World War II, the United States as the new hegemon reorganized the world's economic institutions, chiefly in the form of GATT and the Bretton Woods system, to establish what has been characterized as a liberal international economic order, but one that was clearly designed to serve the interests of the advanced industrial powers, more particularly the US.

Under the protective framework of the political and economic hegemony of the US across the world, powerful American corporations, looking for new markets in their search for larger private profits, spearheaded the setting up of production centres in many countries, especially in Europe, organized and coordinated from their headquarters in the US. So vigorous was the new thrust of expansion abroad by them—transformed in the process into multinational corporations (MNCs)—that cries about the spectre of American domination went up in Europe, particularly in France. However, in due course American MNCs were joined by MNCs from among the allies of the US in the OECD, and the expansionary thrust under their joint aegis accelerated from the mid-1970s onwards. While reflecting the heightened globalization, these MNCs, in turn, became the key agents in its intensification. Meanwhile, they grew ever more powerful so that many 'now dwarf some governments in economic power' (UNDP 1999: 32).

The deepening of international economic integration by the end of the twentieth century is evident in several new developments. For one thing, international trade has seen a dramatic acceleration. In absolute terms, the value of world exports (in 1990 dollars) multiplied nearly five times from $700 billion in 1960 to $3,432 billion in 1990 (Maddison 1995: 239); it stood at $5,115 billion in 1995 (UNCTAD 1998: 28). As a percentage of world GDP, merchandise exports almost doubled from 7.0 per cent in 1950 to a historic high of 13.5 per cent in 1992 (Baker et al. 1998: 5). The expansion of world merchandise trade at a rate higher than that of world output—twice as much in the second half of the 1980s and three times in the first half of the 1990s (Kumar 1998: 3)—is a significant indicator of the heightening of globalization. Such expansion in international trade was also accompanied by significant structural changes, with the proportion of manufactures in world exports rising from 60.9 per cent to 74.7 per cent between 1970 and 1994 (Baker et al. 1998: 7).

Second, and more profoundly, economic production has come to be increasingly organized on a global basis. This is manifest in the fact that one-third of the world trade takes place within the MNCs. It is evident also in the spectacular increase in foreign direct investment (FDI). In 1997, FDI flows were over $400 billion, having increased seven-fold from the level of the 1970s (UNDP 1999: 25). Wholly or partly foreign owned corporations were responsible for more than one-third of the world economic product. Meanwhile, increased globalization has resulted in new patterns of cooperation and competition among the MNCs. While greater globalization has made for fierce competition, it has also brought about a pattern of 'strategic alliances' among MNCs, because of the tremendous R&D costs of new technology, and as well a frenzy of mergers and acquisitions. Third, there has occurred the rapid internationalization of money markets, with instant computer-based satellite communications making for a global capital market that functions round the clock. The international movement of capital has acquired an independent life of its own, unrelated to the needs of international trade. There has been an explosion in portfolio investments and short-term capital flows. In 1997, these amounted to $2 trillion in gross terms, having grown about three-fold from the level of the 1980s. The daily turnover in foreign exchange markets in 1998 was $1.5 trillion as against about $10–20 billion in the 1970s, while international bank lending multiplied about 16 times from $265 billion in 1975 to $4.2 trillion in 1994 (UNDP 1999: 25). Fourth, globalization has generated a common world culture of consumerism, albeit nascent. The same brand name products, such as those from Coca-Cola, Colgate, or Sony, dominate in markets across the world.

These developments are said to have created a new world, a world characterized by deeper economic interdependence—no doubt, unevenly spread, but interdependence nonetheless. Given such interdependence, the question arises as to what are the implications of this phenomenon for the making of economic policy in the less developed world. It is necessary to explore this question against the larger canvas of the interaction between states and markets, which as social organizations underlie the phenomena of economic nationalism and economic globalization.

States and the Shaping of Markets: The External Dimension

Politics and economics as specialized activities for the pursuit of power and wealth, respectively, have been evident in human society since the development of social differentiation in human groups beyond the level of tribes or folk societies. But the unique organizational expressions of these two activities in the modern era—indeed, they are key to the very definition of the era as modern—are states and markets (Gilpin 1987: chs 1–2). These two mighty innovations came to define European civilization over the last three centuries or so. Besides, they enabled Europe to overpower physically the rest of the globe, and in turn diffuse the two social institutions across it either by force or by example. That process of building states and markets in areas outside Europe, and even in some parts of Europe, is a process that is still going on. Indeed, that is the very heart of the contemporary challenge of development for the less developed world.

The two mighty social innovations of Europe began their development in the sixteenth century. Although some interpretations, as in Marx, see the economy as the primary determinant, with the modern state viewed as an outgrowth of markets, others see the state as prior and determining. In the latter view (Tilly 1975: ch. 1), conflict among kingdoms led to the formation of the modern state, with war activities between states and the consequent need for mobilizing greater economic resources leading to the development of markets. Besides, in line with their prior and determining status, states have always attempted to keep markets subordinate to the higher interests of the state. Given the ambiguity of social facts, the dispute between these two contending views is unlikely to be resolved, but it is sufficient to note that, in the broad sweep of history, states and markets arose about the same time. Their rise was part of the birth of modernity in the world, while it in turn pushed modernity further. Having arisen together, the two social organizations, even as they have their separate spheres, are interacting forces, affecting each other. They are dialectically connected, even as they have their separate logics.[1]

The market is a coordination mechanism for the exchange of goods and services on the basis of relative prices. Ideally, it is a self-regulating mechanism that brings together buyers and sellers on a competitive basis. Driven by the motive force of maximizing private gain, the market orders the overall productive system on the basis of demand and supply, determining the allocation of resources among various economic activities. Its key feature of competition between buyers and sellers serves as the driving force behind the noted efficiency of the system. The competition determines which economic actors will survive or flourish on the basis of their efficiency. Survival in competition on the basis of efficiency often rests on innovation in technique, in production and distribution; indeed, technology has become an independent factor in production besides land, labour and capital, and a potent source of economic and political power in the world. The characteristic efficiency of the market system is believed to advance the absolute welfare of society, since everyone gains from it, at least over the long term, even if not in the same measure. This absolute advancement of economic welfare is based on the law of comparative advantage, where everyone contributes on the basis of one's endowment and benefits accordingly. The law, of course, entails a division of labour among economic actors, with specialization based on their capabilities.

Absolute gain for all, obtained through the market system resting on a division of labour, implies that there is a basic and ultimate harmony of interests among economic actors, and that the market system should accordingly be allowed to expand since all would gain—eventually even if not immediately. Similarly, it suggests that political boundaries ought not to be allowed to stand in the way of such market expansion, and that different political units ought to be brought within the compass of a single market economic system. That at least has been the liberal creed since Adam Smith, who saw markets, if left alone, to be self-regulating and socially beneficial. In *liberalism*, absolute gain emergent from the market system has priority (as against relative gain which is critical to states) while political boundaries are seen as an obstacle to the efficiency of markets (as against their being regarded as constituting the very definition of states). Yet, instead of proceeding on the assumption of such absolute harmony in the long run, states have constantly intervened in their external markets or their economic relations with other states. Why that should have been so takes us to the nature of states.

The modern state exists in a world of other states, which are demarcated from each other territorially with defined boundaries, with each state sovereign over its people and claiming exclusive loyalty, monopoly of the legitimate use of violence, and sole responsibility for the protection of its territory and the welfare of its people. The key concerns of the state are fundamentally two: *security* in relation to other states and *legitimacy* in relation to its population, at least the important groups within it. Each concern has a critical bearing on markets and the economic system. Here, attention is first directed to national security and the associated need for economic autonomy.

National Security

Security is the primal interest of states, it is their very raison d'être, situated as they are in an anarchical inter-state system. Security, in turn, requires power or capabilities, regardless of whether they are sought independently or in alliance. Such capabilities pertain, in the first instance, to the military arena—the size and preparedness of the armed forces and the size and lethality of their weaponry. But such military power, in the ultimate analysis, rests on economic capabilities. Paul Kennedy (1988: xvi) succinctly articulates the connection: 'It sounds crudely mercantilistic to express it this way, but wealth is usually needed to underpin military power, and military power is usually needed to acquire and protect wealth'. There is a caveat, however, for there is a tension between the two elements, which complicates the task of decision-makers who are charged with the responsibility for formulating national policy. If too much is spent on security, less will be available for investment and the likely result would be economic weakness—and therefore military weakness—in the long term; if too little is spent, the likely consequence would be vulnerability to security threats from others in the short term. The historical conclusion is nonetheless compelling: 'The history of the rise and later fall of the leading countries in the Great Power system since the advance of western Europe in the sixteenth century ... shows a very significant correlation *over the longer term* between productive and revenue-raising capacities on the one hand and military strength on the other.'

It can thus easily be seen why states intervene in markets, both domestic and foreign. They do so in the first instance in order to make sure that they have the economic capabilities to undergird military power. Economic development or capital accumulation is patently essential for security; indeed, it is taken to be an 'imperative' by the developing countries no less than it is by the developed countries (Nayar 1972, 1974). It is noteworthy that it was national security that made economic development the first priority of the state in Japan, South Korea and Taiwan. Given the close relationship between capital accumulation and security, economic issues are not always, and cannot therefore be, evaluated in terms of economic criteria alone. Strategic interests of the state are, and have to be, taken into account in the formulation of economic policy; indeed, they usually form the ordering framework, even if not always made explicit, for such policy. To take a narrow technical view only of economic issues, as economists normally tend to do, and to ignore the larger geopolitical architecture associated with states is myopic and likely to put national security at risk. Importantly, in respect of security, the reference point for any particular state with regard to capabilities is always other states; in other words, the state's view of capabilities is fundamentally relative. States are interested not just in absolute capabilities but, critically, *relative capabilities*. For, relative capabilities are essential to the reduction of vulnerabilities in relation to other states, both military and economic. Accordingly, states intervene in markets to ensure that their capabilities relative to other states improve and not deteriorate. But this task has to be accomplished with some prudence and delicacy, so that excessive intervention does not undermine the very condition that is desired.

Economic Autonomy

Apart from national security, there is, however, another external dimension to the intervention by states in markets to assure both wealth and power, a keener understanding of which requires a little backtracking in history. As states and markets arose in the sixteenth century, they had somewhat contrary effects on the political and economic organization of the world. States tended to politically fragment the world, organized as they were on the basis of territoriality, legal sovereignty, and exclusive domestic jurisdiction. On the other hand, markets as they expanded tended to encompass several states within a single division of labour. As noted earlier, they further tended to promote integration between several regional economies of the world. Though over a considerable period of time the integration of the world economy took place through physical force, many countries also took part in it willingly as they saw economic advantage in it, in absolute if not relative terms. They continue to participate in it, because there is economic advantage or, put another way, because there is some economic penalty in not participating in it.

Even as it may have the potential to advance human welfare, economic globalization also results in the transfer of disturbances from one part of the world economic system to other parts of that system, as abundantly conveyed by the oil shocks of 1973 and 1979 and also by the market crash of 1987. Further, as UNCTAD (1999: v) has pointed out: 'The humbling of the Asian tigers since 1997 has revealed the vulnerability of even the strongest developing economies to the powerful forces unleashed by globalization.' It also generates disturbances in national markets as the entry of economic agents from outside, such as MNCs, affects the fortunes of local economic actors. While the deeper economic integration of the world provides an apparent autonomy to the working of the global economic system, with its own laws of motion, it at the same time exercises an overpowering impact on national economies. National economies are increasingly buffeted by world economic forces which are not always amenable to effective national control. For example, 'financial volatility is a permanent feature of today's globally integrated financial markets' (UNDP 1999: 40). The consequence can be serious economic dislocations.

Such economic dislocations may eventually make for economic advancement and strengthening of economic capabilities through encouraging entrepreneurship and forcing the pace of innovation, but they can also result in the weakening and erosion of capabilities, marginalization, and de-industrialization. Regardless, they invariably make for gainers and losers. There is, therefore, an inevitable tension between globalization and social cohesion, raising the spectre of social disintegration (Rodrik 1997: 2, 4, 85). Indeed, 'international integration can lead to national disintegration. National disintegration may manifest itself in growing unemployment, poverty, exclusion or marginalization' (Streeten 1998: 4). In its social impact, globalization can thus let loose struggles over shares in the economic product, which necessarily pull states into them. The struggles are then carried out within and between states. Such struggles necessarily feed into economic nationalism, for states are loath to lose control over their national economies when the consequences can be disruptive for them and their societies. While willing to accommodate globalization for the economic benefits it may bring, all states prefer to maintain a certain level of national autonomy in economic affairs vis-à-vis other states.

There is, however, a more structured aspect to the impact of globalization—beyond the cyclical and episodic disruptions that may accompany it—that has implications for economic nationalism. The economic integration of the world has been based on economic specialization, which has tended to place countries in a hierarchical order. It has resulted in dividing the economies into 'core' and 'periphery', often through economic and military coercion during the successive stages of an expanding world economic system. Even though the distinction between the two categories may be blurred at the margins, the core economies have been the centres of autonomous growth and expansion, more advanced in technology and research, specializing in capital and skill-intensive manufacturing and producing complex and higher-value goods. The rich economies of the core have thus been the dynamic centres of economic power. In contrast, the poor and marginalized economies of the periphery have stood at the other pole, largely rendered into a source of raw materials and cheap labour or labour-intensive products as also a market for the higher-value manufactures of the core. The periphery economies were also made dependent on the core, with the core having the ability to transfer its economic disturbances to them or to dominate them politically, and thus to condition their development. Indeed, in some cases, the economic agents of the core—the MNCs in the post-war period—came to exercise dominant control over periphery economies. Globalization, in this perspective, appears then not as a neutral universal force exerting itself uniformly around the world, but rather as representing the pressures of the economically advanced part of the world on the less developed part in an asymmetrically interdependent and hierarchically organized international economic system. In this system, the actors in the less developed part lack economic autonomy and are simply the objects of the decisions of the advanced part.

While impressive aggregate statistics can be easily reeled out to underline the deepening of globalization, in actual fact a slight probing and disaggregation reveal how partial the phenomenon is. For example, almost all the world's 37,000 MNCs belong to the OECD countries. Further, 'they retain a clear national home base; they are subject to the national regulation of the mother country, and by and large they are effectively policed by that home country' (Hirst and Thompson 1996: 9); and they limit the R&D function to the home base. Again, about 80 per cent of world trade in the early 1990s took place among the OECD countries (ibid.: 196). Similarly, there is high concentration of FDI; about 75 per cent of FDI stock and 60 per cent of FDI flows were in the early 1990s confined to the 'triad' of North America, Europe and Japan, while 'the Third World remains marginal in both investment and trade'. What is described as globalization is thus simply 'triadization'; indeed, 'for all intents and purposes it is the advanced industrial economies that constitute the membership of the 'global' economy'. The extremely unequal distribution of FDI underlines, not international economic integration, but the lack of it. Integration remains partial and truncated, for 'nearly two-thirds of the world is virtually written off the map as far as any benefits from this form of investment are concerned' (ibid.: 2, 51–69, 196).

What is more, behind the proffered promise of prosperity for all through globalization lies the present ugly reality of global inequality (though not necessarily of increase in absolute poverty). The top fifth of the world's people living in the richest countries had 86 per cent of the world GDP in 1997, while the bottom fifth had only 1 per cent and the middle 60 per cent had 13 per cent; the same top fifth had a share of 82 per cent in the export of goods and services, and a share of 68 per cent in FDI. There has also been an intensification of inequality, evidencing a 'race to the bottom' rather than a 'climb to the top' or convergence; the ratio between the shares of the top fifth and the bottom fifth in world GDP, which was 30 to 1 in 1960 and 60 to 1 in 1990, had increased to 74 to 1 in 1997. As the UNDP (1999: 3, 7–8, 31) noted:

> Competitive markets may be the best guarantee of efficiency, but not necessarily of equity.... Some have predicted convergence [as a result of globalization]. Yet the past decade has shown increasing concentration of income, resources and wealth among people, corporations and countries. [Indeed, the consequence has been] pernicious trends—growing marginalization, growing human insecurity, growing inequality.... The collapse of space, time and borders may be creating a global village, but not everyone can be a citizen.

It has been the abiding contribution of dependency theory, rising in revolt against modernization theory, to link the location of societies in the hierarchy of the international economic system with the possibilities of national development. Dependency theory was deeply pessimistic about the prospects for development of the periphery as long as it was integrated into the world economic system, which drained its economic surplus. It, therefore, recommended breaking away from the world system in the cause of development. Of course, this radical recommendation masked an a priori preference of the theory's proponents, often unstated, for socialism. In its determinative prognosis, dependency theory was subsequently discredited with the rapid industrialization of South Korea and Taiwan and their breaking out of the periphery, like Japan earlier in the first couple of decades of the post-war period, deepening their integration with the international economic system by way of a strategy of export-propelled growth. However, while dependency theory as a theory is no longer viable, its emphasis on the international system as a factor in national development is enduring. Although dependency theory tended to emphasize the economic aspects of the system, the strategic aspects are no less important in development. It is not without significance that all the three aforementioned countries made their industrial transition under the political and military umbrella of the US, while South Korea and Japan additionally had a substantial physical presence of American armed forces on their soil. Interestingly, China's adoption of an 'open door' economic policy in the post-Mao period was based on a prior de facto strategic alliance with the US against the Soviet Union and on an understanding over access to the American market. Furthermore, the discrediting of dependency theory does not dissolve the fact of dependence or the lack of national autonomy as a major aspect of existential reality in an asymmetrically divided world.

Economic dependence in a hierarchical world economy has implications for the economic capabilities and well-being of the populations of the periphery states. If the economy is conditioned by outside forces, disturbances that are likely to be transferred to them from the more powerful economic centres would affect local populations adversely, in turn bringing the legitimacy of the wielders of state power into question. Again, dependence within a global system of economic specialization makes periphery countries vulnerable in the world, not only economically but also politically, since to be less advanced and weak economically means to be weak and vulnerable politically in the inter-state system. What matters for states is not simply absolute gain within a world economic system but also relative gain in an inter-state political system—relative gain as between core and periphery, but also as between different gradations of core and periphery. Known as 'political realism' in international politics, this perspective, when translated into the economic sphere, has been referred to as *mercantilism*, and has historically served as the action framework for countries that are less advanced and, therefore, less autonomous. Against this, the core states, with the advantage of being economically advanced, have often insisted on liberalism as the disciplining framework for the world economic system which they dominate and benefit from. Indeed, one can quite legitimately maintain that liberalism is the economic policy of the strong and is at base the mercantilism of the more advanced economic powers!

From the very dawn of the differentiation between the core and periphery in an increasingly integrating world economy, dependent states have intervened to modify their integration into the world economy and to develop greater economic autonomy so as to advance their national interests, whether in terms of their relative economic and political position in the international system, or the welfare of the local population. They have intervened to replicate, in whole or in part, in their own economies the economic structures of the core countries. Thus was inaugurated in one country after another 'catch-up' industrialization, as if in a ripple effect. As against the core countries which, because of their initial economic head start and therefore economic advantage, believed in free or liberal trade, or 'outward orientation', the late industrializers adopted mercantilistic or protectionist policies to foster economic growth and development. In this fashion, they tended to cut down their integration in the world economy, for a shorter or longer period, at times with a view to subsequent re-insertion into the world economy on a more equal basis with the core countries, that is, coordinate with them rather than subordinate to them. In other words, they tried to disengage themselves from the world economy or to disassociate, or to delink from it, that is, they chose an economic strategy of 'inward orientation' or 'self-reliance'. They did this in varying measure and through various techniques—tariffs, quantitative restrictions on imports, and non-tariff barriers. Some carried mercantilism to an extreme so as to set up national autarkic economies, as in the case of the Soviet Union and Maoist China. It is nonetheless clear that markets do not exist as creatures given by the forces of nature but are constantly shaped by states in considerable measure because of the very international economic and political order in which they are located.

Justified as excessive inward orientation may be in terms of national security and dependency-reversal or economic autonomy, there are costs to it also. Countries adopting this economic strategy fail to take advantage of the opportunities and advantages that participation in the larger world economy provides. This specific strategy can, moreover, introduce serious economic distortions and therefore inefficiencies and heavy economic costs. For, in attempting to simply replicate the economic structures of the core, it limits taking adequate, if not the fullest, advantage of the particular endowment of the country. One consequence is the setting up of high-cost economies that produce goods of low quality that no one on the outside wants, making for serious balance of payments problems. By the same token, it results in the smuggling in of goods and currency and the setting up of a parallel black economy. States are consequently led to weigh carefully the relative advantages and disadvantages of participation in and withdrawal from the world economic system. The principal issue in economic policy reform for states on the external dimension, therefore, becomes the orientation of the national economy to the world economy. Should the posture be one of inward orientation or outward orientation, disassociation or association, delinkage or linkage, 'closed door' or 'open door', or some combination of the two?

This is an issue that cannot have a single answer for all time and for all countries. The answer would depend on the size of the economy, the nature of its endowment, its stage of development, the capacity of its institutions, and its geopolitical location in the interstate system. Nor can there be a single answer of national scope. The issue would need to be constantly evaluated for various economic sectors in terms of costs and benefits. Perhaps the issue itself should not be either-or, but to what extent. The response would also need to take into account the specific features of the international economy. Here, the stage of intensive globalization seems to raise profound questions both for social science and for the protection of domestic industry.

Intensive Globalization and the Role of the State

The intensive phase of globalization after World War II has made for increased interdependence in the world, especially in contrast to the situation during the 1930s when stridently mercantilistic 'beggar-thy-neighbour' policies were dominant among the advanced industrial powers. Indeed, the increasing pace of interdependence and its political ramifications have since the early 1970s led to the development of a new school of thought in the discipline of international politics, variously described as liberal institutionalism, globalism, or transnationalism (Sullivan 1990: ch. 1), in an endeavour to replace the traditional state-centric view that political realism represents.

The new school's posture on the traditional perspective is well expressed in the title of Raymond Vernon's book *Sovereignty at Bay* (1971) and in Walter Wriston's *The Twilight of Sovereignty* (1992), as also in such statements as: 'The nation-state is just about through as an economic unit [Charles Kindleberger]' and 'the nation state is a very old-fashioned idea and badly adapted to serve the needs of our present complex world [George Ball]' (Gilpin 1975: 20, 220). More elaborately, Sullivan (1990: 9–11) underlines four decisive ways in which the new school is said to differ from realism in its perceptual universe. First, there has occurred the diminution in the role and function of the state in international affairs, following the rise of other governmental and non-governmental international organizations, particularly MNCs, which exercise leverage on internal politics as well as external relations of states. Moreover, states are no longer the unitary actors of old but consist of large bureaucracies that are internally divided and subject to influence not only by domestic forces but also external actors. In sum, the state's traditional role has been drastically reduced.

Second, there has been a change in the nature of the dominant issues in international politics. Military-security issues have become downgraded in the face of the rising critical issues of population explosion, food security, and threats to the world's ecology. Being global in nature, these new issues cannot be addressed by any one nation alone or in alliance with a small group of nations as was the case with military-security issues. On the contrary, they compel co-operation among states rather than rivalry as had been the pattern in the past. Third, this requirement of cooperation has been reinforced by the intense interdependence that has come to characterize the international system not only in economic areas but also in communications and transportation. Finally, the nature of military technology itself, with the development of nuclear weapons, places constraints on states to resort to the traditional means of statecraft centring, in the final analysis, around war. In brief, these developments are said to have made the traditional state obsolete and realism outmoded.

While the institutionalist perspective has an air of intellectual novelty about it, it is really only a new incarnation of an old challenge to realism. The history of the discipline of international politics has, indeed, been marked by several successive outbreaks of debate between realism and its challengers. The issue is controversial, but this much can be said with certainty that predictions about the demise of the state have been made before, most particularly in the years prior to World War I. Though the state as a political institution cannot ever be presumed to be permanent, so far each time that the predictions have been made they have proven to be exaggerated and premature, pointing to the continued robustness of realism. True, there is evident increased interdependence today compared to that during the inter-war period, and it may well lead to a nascent international community, but there is some question about whether there is more interdependence today than at the end of the

nineteenth century in terms of the share of trade or foreign investment in world output (Hirst and Thompson 1996: 26–31; Sullivan
1990: 43–52).

Moreover, the state, whether as existing fact or aspiration, continues to be the focus of loyalties of peoples, and the world has actually
seen a vast expansion in the number of states in the post-war period.
Political legitimacy is invariably organized on the basis of states, notwithstanding greater economic interdependence. Furthermore, state
behaviour in the inter-state system continues to revolve around the
expectation of war. The post-war period has seen no end to war,
though the theatre of war has undoubtedly shifted to outside the
North Atlantic area. The contemporary era has, indeed, witnessed
wars with massive casualties among both civilians and combatants,
such as in Korea and Vietnam, the most recent ones being those in
the Persian Gulf in 1991 and Yugoslavia in 1999. The major states
continue to maintain large armies for combat, while the American
military girdles the globe with numerous bases. Besides, the absence
of war over a given period of time does not mean the irrelevance of
power, for the world continues to be structured by power, which at
its deepest level is constituted by military power. The nuclear powers have endeavoured mightily to see that their military advantage is
not eroded by the diffusion of nuclear weaponry to others, while the
power oligarchy at the United Nations does not aim to give up any
of its statutory privileges. Even the liberal institutionalists perforce
acknowledge that the strategic arena lies outside their claims about
the cooperation-inducing impact of interdependence, which is then
said to pertain chiefly to the economic and social arenas.

Realism versus Liberal Institutionalism

Outside the strategic arena, a strong case was made by liberal
institutionalists from the 1970s onwards for the constraints on states
emergent from interdependence and for the enhanced possibilities
of international cooperation. In due course, the school came to
place much store in the concept of *international regime*, which was
claimed to constrain the self-regarding behaviour of states.
Developed within the discipline of international political economy,
the concept referred to the overall framework of rules and norms
governing activity carried out between states in a given sector

(Krasner 1983: 1–21). Liberal institutionalists saw, notwithstanding the pervasive inter-state conflict, the gradual but parallel emergence in the world of an international society centring on cooperation among states. In an increasingly interdependent world where elites are compelled to interact repeatedly, the institutionalists maintained that social practices or regularized patterns of behaviour develop. As these persist, they acquire a normative aura and come to act as constraints on the behaviour of leaders. A variation on this approach, while taking the state to be a rational, egoistic, utility-maximizing actor, held cooperation between states to be both necessary and possible. Utility maximization was not seen as a bar to cooperation but rather required and induced it, for in the absence of cooperation the result would be suboptimal outcomes for most parties. Once patterns of cooperation are thus established to coordinate state behaviour, they tend to persist because of the functions they perform and in turn come to influence state behaviour.

The notion of international regime in liberal institutionalism conveys the impression that it is an element that stands above the interests of individual states, something that is supra-national and neutral in respect of their particular interests. In contrast, political realism takes an entirely different position, holding international regimes to be simply an epiphenomenal reflection of the underlying distribution of power (Krasner 1983: 1–21). In other words, at the base of the apparent consensual framework of norms and rules of an international regime lies a particular structure of power that determines and upholds that framework. That is to say, a dominant state or set of dominant states in a given configuration of power usually finds a particular normative framework more appropriate to serve its interests and is able, through coercion or consensus, to make it prevail in the international system. In this interpretation, then, international regimes last as long as the given balance of power lasts, only to be replaced by a new international regime consonant with the changed balance of power. Here, Gilpin (1975) showed that the very phenomenon of the post-war expansionary thrust of American MNCs was grounded in the provision by the US of an overarching international political framework under its hegemony, while Cox (1993: 150) underlined that 'ultimately the security of globalization depends upon military force with a territorial basis', that is, the military force of the hegemonic power. In addition, a series of authors demonstrated the continuing and paramount relevance of power and national interests in what superficially seemed instances of operative international regimes: Grieco (1990) and Gowa (1994) in trade, Krasner (1991) in communications, Cafruny (1987) in shipping, and Nayar (1995) in aviation. In matters which bore on distribution of relative gains or losses, as distinguished from technical coordination, these studies showed that state behaviour was guided by national interests and power.

Power has been similarly manifest in economic governance at the world level, which enhances the capacity of the powerful to manage disturbances from the international economy. Liberalism has been generally taken to be the distinctive principle underlying the American design for the post-war international order. However, even an admirer of the American economic design (Ruggie 1983: 195–231) has underlined the conditional nature of the commitment to that principle by calling it 'embedded liberalism', in so far as it reserved for the powerful states the right to transfer adjustment costs to the international system (read: weaker states) in case of conflict between liberalism and domestic welfare. Besides, the advanced industrial states structured the decision-making arrangements in the Bretton Woods institutions, such as the IMF and World Bank, to assure a dominant and determining role for themselves. Later, the G-7 summits were organized as an oligarchical arrangement of these same states to make decisions on the management of the world economy to the exclusion of the rest of the globe. As the UNDP (1999: 8, 34) underlined: 'Intergovernmental policy-making in today's global economy is in the hands of the major industrial powers and the international institutions they control' and 'the key economic structures—the IMF, World Bank, G-7, G-10, G-22, OECD, WTO—are dominated by the large and rich countries, leaving poor countries and poor people with little influence and little voice.'

Occupying the dominant position in the international institutions of economic governance, the advanced industrial states have established international economic arrangements that primarily serve their interests. Even if globalization places some constraints on their options, they are able to limit them by virtue of their dominant position. In contrast, attempts on the part of the less developed countries to change the system to favour their interests, as in the case of the new international economic order movement, have been sternly derailed. There is thus a vicious circle here: economic weakness requires but thwarts change in the international economic order, which in turn perpetuates economic weakness. As a consequence, often the sole alternative left for the weaker states is to work within the confines of the existing order which has been fostered and is sustained by the economically powerful states and serves their interests. The only choice for them is thus to restructure their own economies internally to fit in with the existing order, barred as they are from changing it by their weakness. State elites in the developing world may go into sociological rage over this compulsion but that is how the world works.

The advanced industrial states have been in the forefront of advising and, indeed, pressuring the less developed countries (LDCs) to liberalize their economies and to become integrated into the world political economy over which they preside. However, while preaching the virtues of globalization and liberalization to others, these same states have not been above practising protectionism themselves. In trade, this has been obvious for so long in regard to non-tariff barriers that such barriers have been made into a part of the accepted international economic order. GATT had originally permitted developed countries to undertake measures to allow their economies and industries time to adjust to cheaper LDC imports. This provision was, however, meant only for application over the short term, but the industrial powers instead turned it into a virtually permanent feature of the trade landscape.

Even as they establish quotas on LDC imports, the developed countries proclaim their commitment to free trade. They are able to maintain the myth in respect of free trade because the quotas are ostensibly part of the so-called 'voluntary export restraint' arrangements adopted by LDCs, but which are in actual fact imposed on them. Again, the advanced industrial states articulate strongly the advantages of openness for their multinationals and urge the LDCs to adopt policies to welcome them. What is noteworthy, however, is their actual protectionist stance when it comes to the presence of foreign multinationals on their own soil. The disparity between the rhetoric broadcast abroad and practice at home is particularly striking. This is over and beyond the earlier fostering of their own industrialization invariably under mercantilist auspices.

The Developed Countries and Foreign MNCs

Japan's capacity to frustrate entry of foreign MNCs, through restrictive controls, until its own firms are strong enough to prevail in competition in any sector is legendary. In relation to their domestic market, the Japanese have not seen foreign MNCs in their self-proclaimed role of advancing economic growth but rather as holding the threat of domination over the local economy, the stunting of the growth of domestic entrepreneurship, as well as retarding technical progress since MNCs preferred to do their R&D at home. Similarly, Germany, despite its liberal image, has had mechanisms in place to thwart threatened takeovers by foreign MNCs of its important firms in key sectors. These mechanisms were strengthened in the wake of increased inflow of OPEC money after the early 1970s. Again, France has remained vigilant, shrewd and innovative in safeguarding the interests of French firms, and looked for a 'French solution' in the first instance when they were threatened by foreign MNCs. The US, rhetorically always in the forefront of preaching the virtues of foreign investment, is no exception to this pattern. As one study (Bailey et al. 1994) convincingly demonstrated, protectionism in relation to foreign takeovers has been equally characteristic of the US, especially in the wake of the entry of Japanese MNCs.

An analysis in the early 1980s by Canada's Foreign Investment Review Agency (FIRA) underlined that the US followed an active policy to prevent investments that it did not consider desirable. Besides the 'plethora of laws, regulations, agencies, hearings, programmes and ordinances at both state and federal levels', there was the very ambiguity in the rules—as if by design to deter—as well as the undue delays and the prospect of one or more of a score of regulatory agencies, such as the Interstate Commerce Commission, the Civil Aeronautics Board or the Securities and Exchange Commission, going beyond their mandates to scrutinize and block investment 'precisely because it is not US controlled'. In addition, FIRA believed, in the words of one authority, that 'a number of sectors were explicitly protected from foreign investment: shipping, aviation, aeronautics, communications, nuclear and hydro-electric power, banks, insurance, real estate, mining, maritime activities and defence—which in itself encompassed a whole range of industries' (Bailey et al. 1994: 127). And, above all, there hung the uncertainty emanating from anti-trust legislation.

What is noteworthy is that not only has there been a consensus in the US Congress over blocking takeovers by foreign MNCs in sectors considered important by the US, but there was before the economic boom of the 1990s a groundswell of sentiment in the country

about the threat of such takeovers. The reaction to foreign investment featured two chief characteristics: worry about loss of control
over the country's destiny, and injury to national pride (Kanter
1995: 119–34). Interestingly, these reactions were similar to those
expressed in the LDCs during the 1960s and 1970s towards American investment abroad. They were then dismissed as unwarranted
chauvinism and xenophobia by both government representatives
and scholars in the US. However, it seems that the American cosmo-
politanism of the time was simply misunderstood. For, the US has, in
fact, been a stridently nationalistic country, only its nationalism has
had a global scope; its very globalism is, indeed, an expression of its
nationalism. Every president in the post-war period has affirmed
American resolve and determination to remain number one in the
world. That is simply taken to be the manifest destiny of the US,
expressed in the title of a book by one authority: *Bound to Lead*
(Nye 1990). It is interesting, however, to note the American reaction
when the tables seemed turned on the US, prior to the Japanese economic crisis of the 1990s, in terms of economic power and foreign
investment. The resulting mood of anger affected not just the populace or the politicians but also otherwise sober-minded scholars.

Important insights into the relationship of economic power to
economic well-being and national security were made evident in the
writings of one of America's foremost intellectuals, Samuel Huntington. Favourably quoting the statement 'economics is the continuation of war by other means', Huntington (1993: 68–83) made a
shrill case for the continued economic primacy of the US in the
world, which was taken to be under siege by Japan through a deliberate strategy of economic warfare. 'Japan', he said, 'has accepted all
the assumptions of realism but applied them purely in the economic
realm.... Japanese strategy is a strategy of economic warfare.... Japanese strategy, behaviour, and declarations all posit the existence of
an economic cold war between Japan and the United States.' The
consequences for the US of this new cold war were considered very
serious and potentially dangerous, given the increasing American
dependence on Japan for technology and money and as well the rising Japanese penetration not only of the American economy but also
of its polity and society. Huntington then asked for decisive measures for the US to triumph in this economic cold war much as it had
done in the strategic cold war with the Soviet Union.

What the foregoing review demonstrates is that the phenomenon of mercantilism or economic nationalism is not just a passing phase peculiar to the stage of industrialization but is of continuing relevance in state behaviour, manifesting itself in new incarnations corresponding to changing phases in the international environment. Indeed, the latest incarnation has been the formation of economic blocs, such as the European Union (EU) and the North American Free Trade Area (NAFTA), which are liberal only within but protectionist without. As the internationally-renowned economist Jagdish Bhagwati (1997: 21–23) pointed out:

When President Clinton argued that NAFTA would help American firms to compete better with their (excluded) Japanese competitors, he was explicitly appealing to the trade-diverting aspects of the agreements—that is, to the welfare-reducing aspects. True, he was also exploiting the Japanophobia that his first term had fanned. In the main, however, he was simply deploying the most powerful special-interest incentive to choose PTAs [preferential trade agreements] over non-discriminatory trade liberalization.

The US was not alone in this, for in his view 'the EU is simply the greater culprit in the game of trade discrimination'. Economic globalization has evidently not erased or ousted economic nationalism, only made it assume newer forms. If nationalism thus continues to inform economic policy in the already affluent developed countries, should it occasion surprise if it arises in the LDCs, given their more serious concerns about penetration, control and domination by powerful outside economic forces on a much larger scale. What is surprising is that the developed countries despite their own protectionist behaviour tend to be dismissive, as they can well afford to be, of LDC concerns.

The conclusion for the LDCs cannot, of course, be that they close their doors to globalization, for that path of economic self-ghettoization imposes serious costs. The experience of the Soviet bloc and China is vivid testimony about both the difficulties and disadvantages of economic insulation as well as the advantages of participation in the global economy. That said, however, participation does not mean 'open door' across the board and surrendering of national control to economic forces from the outside, or allowing national assets to be swallowed up by foreign MNCs. Rather, new balances have to be worked out between states and markets, between economic nationalism and globalization. The watchword has to be *selectivity*, just as it is in the developed countries. With the national interest kept paramount, policy on the relationship between states and markets, both national and international, needs to take into account changing circumstance rather than be a prisoner of dogma or routine. To be sure, the content of national economic interest is not susceptible to precise description, but the behaviour of the advanced industrial states leaves little doubt about the general ends that inform it—national security, economic autonomy and mass welfare.

States and the Shaping of Markets: The Internal Dimension

It is not only the relationship of the state to its external setting, political and economic, that leads to efforts on the part of states at the shaping of markets, national and international; similar consequences follow from the internal compulsions of states. Just as security is the central concern of states in relation to other states, *legitimacy* is the key concern of states in relation to their societies. Legitimacy refers to the tacit or explicit support of key groups in society to the core institutions of the state. Such support may be obtained by a state in return for the protection accorded to groups or for the advancement of their interests, or for both. Since advancement of group interests revolves primarily around material concerns, legitimacy also compels the acquisition of capacity on the part of states to assure delivery of economic goods and services. Thus, like national security, legitimacy also requires economic development or capital accumulation, so that there would be resources available in society to satisfy material concerns. States therefore cannot be indifferent to the economy, for it has direct implications for legitimacy.

Given that both states and markets are concerned with the economy, a principal issue for both research and policy has been as to what are the appropriate roles for markets and states in the economy. The issue arises because, even as states and markets have their separate logics, their operations affect each other and therefore are not likely to be left alone. Markets determine gainers and losers, and they decide the economic fate of different classes of producers, such as capitalists and workers. They do so not only in times of growth and expansion, but especially in times of economic crisis. Indeed, Marx saw social conflict arising out of crises of overproduction and immiserization of workers to be structurally built into markets under capitalism, inevitably leading to economic collapse. Unlike Adam Smith, Marx saw not harmony but class struggle as the inherent consequence of markets under capitalism. The notion of conflict among classes as an unavoidable feature of capitalism became the intellectual hallmark of Marxism. Regardless, through the differential impact they have on various societal groups, markets have a crucial impact on political power. Their operations affect the material interests and welfare of different groups and classes, and therefore the legitimacy of government.

No state can, therefore, leave markets completely alone. After all, markets exist for human groups, not the other way around. As Polanyi (1957: 128–33, 141–50) recognized, even as the market advances economic efficiency and innovation, it is destructive of social solidarity and therefore needs to be embedded in society and regulated by the state. Accordingly, states intervene to protect key groups in society that are important to their legitimacy, and therefore endeavour to regulate the economy in order to overcome 'market failures'. Keynes had provided the theoretical rationale in the 1930s for state intervention and regulation of the economy, holding that, contrary to Marx, capitalism was fixable through these mechanisms rather than being fated for irreparable breakdown and self-destruction. However, state intervention in markets, whether stemming from legitimacy or from national security, may make for economic inefficiency, but the logic of states imposes its own political compulsions. Success in the endeavour, of course, would depend on national consensus over goals and the coherence of state institutions in economic management.

However, states may intervene in markets not just to overcome market failures, or for the mercantilistic protection of national interests, but for other reasons as well. They may take over some of the functions that the market performs in order simply to pre-empt the resources that markets provide. Indeed, some states may be predatory or kleptocratic in relation to the economy, unmindful of the damage inflicted on the economy over the long run. Or, states may, for reasons of ideology, appropriate entirely the functions that markets perform, as was the case with the Soviet Union. In such bureaucratic coordination of the economy, or 'command economy', the economy assumes the form of a single firm run on the basis of superordinate-subordinate relations, with the state at the head of the firm issuing orders to those below as to how to carry out their functions in the productive and distributive processes. In other economies, the state may impose thoroughgoing licensing in respect of production and distribution, determining who shall produce or distribute what and how much and at what price.

Given the separate logics of economics and politics, such heavy intervention by the state often results in severe distortions in the allocation of the factors of production, and thus onerous costs, even if such costs do not become immediately apparent. Take, for example, the former Soviet Union, where Soviet planners had to decide administratively on some 20 million prices (Lindblom 1977: 304), which would otherwise have been determined by the market on the basis of demand and supply. It has, however, simply not been within the competence of any group of planners so far to do such price determination effectively. The inevitable consequence of such market displacement is the generation of allocative distortions which make for economic inefficiency, and may even grind the economy to a halt. State intervention, often designed to overcome 'market failures', can thus end up in massive 'government failures'.

Market economy and 'command' bureaucratic economy are ideal types. Even among the advanced industrialized democracies what exists is not an unregulated market system, but a 'mixed economy'. Note, for example, the many controls that exist in the US and Canada in agriculture, financial markets, and inter-state commerce. State intervention in many of the advanced states has gone beyond regulation of the market to encompass public ownership of firms as well as industrial policy and economic planning. The very rise of such a mixed economy has been a result of the operation of politics within the modern state, especially the democratic state. In view of the political compulsions engendered by electoral politics, the modern state has intervened to protect vulnerable sections, to provide a welfare net for weaker groups, and to cope with the periodic disturbances that emerge from the functioning of markets, both internal and external. It is this profound modification of liberalism in practice, both domestically and internationally, inspired by the requirements of the state for the maintenance of social and political stability, that has come to be conceptually characterized, following a distinction made by Polanyi, as 'embedded liberalism' (Ruggie 1983: 195–231). It is a matter of no mean importance that the period of intensive globalization has been accompanied by an increased share of government expenditures in the GDP of the advanced industrial states; it rose from 28.3 per cent in 1960 to 40.5 per cent in 1980 and 43.8 per cent in 1998 (*The Economist*, 31 July 1999: 3–16). Significantly, the openness of economies in terms of the share of trade in GDP is positively correlated with the scope of government in terms of government expenditure in GDP (Streeten 1998: 41).

What is striking about the 'mixed economy' or 'embedded liberalism' of the advanced industrial democracies is that, despite state intervention, a delicate balance—no doubt, always in tension—has been kept between the state and market in economic management. The state has restrained itself from excessive intervention even as it has, in a process of constant and continuous readjustment, modulated this intervention on analyzing what its effects are on the economy, now deepening it, now withdrawing from it. Economic policy reform, therefore, remains a perpetual item on the agenda of the modern state, and it has to do centrally with the respective roles of state and market in the running of the economy. At one time, it may mean greater state intervention to overcome 'market failures'. At other times, it may mean limiting or shrinking the area of state interference in the economy, to remove restrictions imposed on the operation of the market and the private sector, to deregulate, to privatize the public sector, to shed its role as the owner and manager of economic enterprises—all this in an endeavour to correct 'government failures'.

Regardless of whether the state plays an expanded or shrunken role, it remains central to the functioning of the market. Indeed, the very functioning of the market presupposes political authority. Simply, no market can exist without an encompassing political framework. As a public good, the market requires a public authority outside of itself to enforce the rules of the game according to which it must function. Even economic policy reform aiming to reduce the role of the state raises the 'orthodox paradox', whereby it is the state that may need to take the initiative and reform itself, which may mean strengthening it, so as to facilitate a greater role for the market (Haggard and Kaufman 1992b: 222). Economic theory or doctrine is no sure guide in the matter, for it may often have a faddish quality about it. As Krugman (1996: 717–32) pointed out, measures endorsed by economic doctrine seem to go in cycles, where the prescriptions of the 1990s to counter the supposedly harmful effects of state interventionism of the 1950s and 1960s are similar to the practices of the 1930s, to avoid the grievous results of which the very state activism of the 1950s and 1960s had initially been adopted. What is certain is that even the most unreconstructed liberal therefore admits, following Adam Smith, that the market requires the performance of the following minimal functions by the state: the overall constitutional and legal framework for the operation of the market, the specification of property rights, and public investment in the social and economic infrastructure. In other words, the state undertakes or must undertake the provision of public goods that the private sector cannot or would not provide adequately—education, health, and the transportation network. Beyond that, states vary in their degree of intervention in the market, both across time and space. Nonetheless, it is clear again that markets are no creature given by the forces of nature, but are shaped by states, in turn influenced by their different locations in the international hierarchy and their varied internal circumstances.

For the LDCs, the most impressive phenomenon since the 1960s—even when due note is taken of the economic crisis in the region in the late 1990s—has been the dramatic transformation of several economies of East and Southeast Asia, most particularly South Korea and Taiwan, enabling them to graduate to the status of newly-industrialized countries (NICs). This development led to a search among both policy-makers and social scientists for the causes of their success. Given the paucity of natural resources in these NICs, the key explanation was seen to lie in the nature of policy followed by them. Here, liberals in the academia as well as the international financial institutions (IMF and World Bank) right away saw a vindication of their neoclassical prescription of giving the markets full play and getting the prices right, a prescription incorporated in what is known as the 'Washington consensus' (Williamson 1990, 1994). The success of the NICs was seen as lying externally in their reliance on a policy of outward orientation or export-propelled growth rather than the misguided ISI policies typical among other LDCs. A consensus soon developed over the importance of outward orientation for the efficiency it spurred as a result of competing in international markets. Similarly, the NIC achievement was attributed internally to the reduced role of the state in favour of the market.

This pattern of state abstention was held to contrast dramatically with that of other LDCs which had resorted to excessive state intervention. However, empirical research soon showed the assumption about the reduced role of the state among the NICs to be a mistaken one. Amsden (1989) on South Korea and Wade (1990) on East Asia revealed the presence of the heavy and visible hand of state intervention in the effort to boost exports, not simply through exploiting existing comparative advantage but creating new sectors of dynamic comparative advantage precisely by, as it were, 'getting the prices wrong'. The view of the shrunken state was thus shown to be in serious error, for economic growth in East Asia was state-led while the states themselves were fundamentally anti-liberal.

This turn in the assessment of the experience of the NICs only led to investigating the specific nature of the state that had made for intervention to assume a benign form as against the malign state intervention elsewhere in the developing world. The neoclassical resurgence after the 1960s had focused on the 'rent-seeking' inherent in state bureaucracies to be the cause of economic retardation in the LDCs and, therefore, argued for the shrunken state for the sake of economic growth. However, scholarship on the NICs showed that rent-seeking was not inherent in all bureaucracies or all branches of a bureaucracy; rather, rent-seeking depended on the particular configuration of institutions in states. Already, on the basis of the Japanese experience, Johnson (1982: 305–24) had advanced a model of the 'developmental state', which was then taken to be typical as well of the NICs in East Asia. Such a state was noteworthy for having economic development as its first priority; development was viewed as a prerequisite to everything else and made for its very characterization as a developmental state. Its focus was on savings and production as against consumption and distribution. Structurally, the Japanese model consisted of several elements: (1) a small cohesive bureaucracy consisting of 'the best managerial talent available in the system'; (2) a political system that gave this bureaucracy sufficient scope to function and exercise initiative in the management of the economy, with the other branches of government primarily serving to deflect pressures from interest groups so as to safeguard the priority for development; (3) the adoption of market-conforming methods of state intervention for the fostering of industry, chief among them being 'administrative guidance'; and (4) 'a pilot organization' like the Japanese MITI, mandated to implement industrial policy even as it was endowed with sufficient control of funds, think-tank functions and a mix of powers that would make it effective without becoming too powerful.

This empirical reassessment of the East Asian experience coincided with a theoretical reorientation in the discipline of comparative politics in a statist or state-centric direction, in which the notion of state strength or state power vis-à-vis society was articulated (Evans et al. 1985; Katzenstein 1977; Krasner 1978). Two concepts emerged as having particular importance in this new direction: state autonomy, which referred to the ability of the state to establish policy unconstrained by society; and state capacity, which referred to the ability to implement such policy. Subsequently, Evans (1995) put forward the concept of 'embedded autonomy' of the state—reminiscent of embedded liberalism—which, with its combination of the two structural features of an internally coherent Weberian-style bureaucracy and the simultaneous external embeddedness of the bureaucracy in society, was offered as a powerful explanation specifically for the rapid industrialization of the NICs in East Asia, more particularly South Korea. Both features were considered essential to performance; autonomy empowers the bureaucracy to set and pursue national goals, unencumbered by particularistic societal pressures; embeddedness, on the other hand, through its network of institutionalized links with the corporate sector, enables the bureaucracy to mobilize relevant information, develop and implement realistic policy, assess policy impact, and revise policy.

Evans held the East Asian model of embedded autonomy as of great potential value for other LDCs. It is noteworthy, however, that, for a scholar who had made his initial reputation on the basis of a trenchant critique of the Brazilian model of dependent development because of its exclusionary and repressive features, Evans now evidenced little concern over military rule or labour repression in respect of either South Korea or Taiwan. When he talked of embeddedness in society, it curiously referred only to the corporate sector, ignoring the labour sector. Evans thus neatly sidestepped the issue of authoritarianism and democracy in relation to economic performance. Seemingly, success compels admiration, regardless of the methods employed to achieve it. Autonomy, embedded or not, emerges in the process as a mere euphemism for authoritarianism, especially as it centres on a Weberian bureaucracy, with politics and political leadership simply erased from consideration.

The defining characteristic of an authoritarian regime is that it is based on coercion as against the consent of society, which is central to the definition of democracy. It is apparent that an authoritarian regime alone is likely to have the potential for autonomy of the kind prescribed as essential for rapid industrialization. However, there are strict limits to autonomy in a democratic regime precisely since its authority is based on consent and the representation of societal interests; such a regime is simply a mirror of society rather than autonomous from it. To shift the basis of authority to coercion within a democratic regime in the pursuit of autonomy would be to change the nature of the regime itself. If autonomy is indeed essential for industrial transformation, the logic of its necessary connection with authoritarianism finds powerful empirical support in the experience of South Korea and Taiwan, for it is undeniable that these countries endured several decades of authoritarian rule while the pace of industrialization was being forced by the state.

Of course, there is divergence of opinion among social scientists about the relationship of economic performance, variously defined, and the nature of political regime. Bates and Krueger (1993: 459) assert that 'We found little evidence for a relationship between economic reform and political authoritarianism. Nor have others who have also conducted comparative case studies'. The latter part of the statement is not entirely correct, however. Quite the contrary, Haggard and Kaufman (1992b: 221–40) hold the debate over the relationship to be 'the most heated and long-standing'. What is more, on the basis of their sample of case studies they conclude that 'the most comprehensive structural adjustment initiatives have generally come under the auspices of authoritarian regimes'.

The dissonance in the debate is partly explicable by what is included under economic policy reform. It is one thing to merely enact reform and quite another to implement it, particularly on a sustained basis. Further, if the reference to reform is only to short-term episodes of stabilization, or even of some structural adjustment, certainly democracies have the capacity to execute such programmes, for they also can rally a consensus in crisis situations to which these programmes are addressed. However, sustaining programmes of deep economic policy reform over several decades is another matter; it would require a degree of coercion that would transform the very nature of the political regime. Thus, it is understandable that industrialization in the contemporary industrialized states was achieved under non-democratic or pre-democratic auspices. Similarly, in the post-war period *rapid* industrialization has occurred or is in the process of occurring also under authoritarian auspices; the relevant sample of NICs along these lines in East and Southeast Asia would include, besides South Korea and Taiwan, China, Indonesia and Thailand, and in Latin America it would encompass Brazil, Chile and Mexico. It is hard to think of a democracy that would deserve inclusion in this list. This much is clear then that authoritarianism and rapid industrialization have gone together. It may well be that 'theoretically, democracies are not intrinsically less capable of generating these foundations of growth' (Diamond and Plattner 1995: xxii), but there is little empirical support so far for that proposition. Even if correlation is not causation, the association between authoritarianism and rapid industrialization is too powerful to ignore. To be sure, authoritarianism has not been sufficient for either economic policy reform or economic performance. Other authoritarian regimes were not always successful. No doubt, South Korea and Taiwan benefited from the greater equality inherited from the destruction of the oligarchical landed elites as a result of war and occupation, so that the authorities were not distracted by issues of distribution. But such benefits could easily have been dissipated under democratic auspices as the experience of South Korea during the 1950s illustrates. On present evidence, then, while not sufficient, authoritarianism seems almost necessary.

The conclusion, of course, is not that LDCs that are democratic should shift to authoritarianism for the sake of industrial transformation, but rather that expectations for sustained rapid economic growth would need to be moderated. The issue is linked to legitimacy, which can be of two kinds. One type is instrumental legitimacy, where governments must be effective in order to merit support. The other can be called constitutive legitimacy, where certain political institutions are desired for their own sake, regardless— no doubt, within limits—of their implications for economic performance. A society may well prefer to opt for democracy for its particular mix of liberty and order, consent and coercion, even if it is at some cost to economic performance. Indeed, it may deliberately avoid rapid industrialization, even if it were capable of it, considering it to be destabilizing for democratic institutions. On the other hand, where neighbouring states in a given region advance more rapidly, the resultant regional power imbalances may threaten national security, and as a consequence place legitimacy in jeopardy. Clearly, there are no easy choices for policy-makers in balancing the requirements of states and markets in economic policy reform.

Summary and Conclusions

The two historical forces of economic globalization and economic nationalism have been at work over the last few centuries in shaping the economic landscape of the world and of the states within it. As before, they have generated pressures for economic policy reform, the agenda for which fundamentally revolves around the roles of states and markets in economic processes. With the end of World War II, globalization entered an intensive phase as its pace quickened. Undergirded by a resurgent neoclassical doctrine, its pressures had by the last quarter of the twentieth century started a chain reaction of economic liberalization across a broad segment of countries in the developing and communist worlds, both internally and externally, allowing fuller play to markets and, correspondingly, reducing the economic role of states. However, globalization's apparent triumph is bound to be limited.

Although the liberalization cure is justified where serious economic distortions exist, as a wholesale prescription it is likely to encounter obstacles if it fails to take into account the legitimate role of states in the economy. States are compelled to intervene in markets, because markets exist for human groups, and not human groups for markets. Human groups are prior to markets and they organize themselves into political entities, called states in the modern era, for important and compelling reasons. With their two key concerns of national security in relation to the outside world and legitimacy in relation to domestic society, states have a paramount interest in the economy and therefore intervene in it. Capital may be internationally mobile, but legitimacy is rooted in states. Accordingly, for states to surrender entirely to markets, whether external or internal, would be to destroy the very basis of states. It is, therefore, no surprise that economic nationalism continues to be very much alive, not least in the developed countries. Globalization thus does not altogether do away with economic nationalism; it only spurs it to new forms and to the working out of new balances between the two. As a consequence, the research enterprise in respect of countries undertaking economic policy reform should be precisely the examination of how older balances are modified or replaced by new ones, and of the interplay of world-system, state and societal variables in causing such change (Gereffi and Wyman 1990: chs 1, 14).

While globalization has limits, so does economic nationalism. While some state protection of the national economy may be justified in relation to external markets, excessive amounts of it can forestall taking advantage of the growth-inducing impulses that the international economy may provide. Similarly, excessive state intervention internally is likely to lead to serious economic distortions. The two situations, singly or jointly, may undermine the very purposes for which state intervention is undertaken—national security and legitimacy. No doubt, the spheres of states and markets overlap, and doctrines that set up an absolute partition between the two or set them against each other are mistaken. However, excessive encroachment of one upon the other that undermines the very logic of their separate functioning is also likely to prove counter-productive. What is called for is a collaborative relationship between the two that respects their separate spheres of operation. The policy content of such a collaborative relationship would, of course, vary with the nature of each country's situation. In general, it would include placing primary reliance on markets, externally and internally. Within that ordering framework, the state would intervene to overcome market failures, to serve as a coordination mechanism, and to provide 'administrative guidance' but only selectively in specific sectors and specific aspects, always taking into consideration its own institutional capacity. The state is pivotal in all these respects, for there is no other institution to take the initiative for them. To perform these tasks adequately, however, it must develop and enhance its own adaptive and transformative capacity (Weiss 1998).

Notes

1. Gilpin (1987: 10). The attempt to reduce the inter-state system to the single logic of the world capitalist system is challenged by Rapkin (1983: 241–68).

2

Planning for Autarky and State Hegemony: Nationalist Development Strategy under Nehru

For several years after independence in 1947, the Indian state under Prime Minister Jawaharlal Nehru was intensely absorbed in the problems of coping with a general breakdown of law and order as well as of administration in north India in the wake of the partition of the subcontinent, war with Pakistan over Jammu & Kashmir, the rehabilitation of six million refugees, the assassination of Mahatma Gandhi, the establishment of a constitutional order, the conducting of the founding national elections based on universal adult franchise, and overcoming factional strife withing the ruling Congress Party. It is only in the mid-1950s, after the consolidation of political power and the rehabilitation of the economy from the ravages of World War II and partition, that India made a sharp break with the inherited colonial economic policy of laissez-faire. That break in economic policy—with economic planning, autarky and building socialism as its centrepiece—is of historic importance, at least for India. All three elements also lie at the core of economic nationalism.

Autarky, of course, is equated with economic nationalism by definition and is used interchangeably with it as well as with economic independence and economic self-sufficiency, involving 'a deliberate rejection of external relationships than simply manifesting indifference or ignorance of their possibilities'. But no less important is the connection of planning and socialism with economic nationalism. It has been rightly claimed that planning is 'an assertion of economic nationalism', 'a formal expression of sovereignty by the state, and of an intention to exert ultimate direction and control. It is a symbol of independence'. Similarly, 'a fairly well-defined position purports that the practical success of economic nationalism is inconceivable without the presence of key components of socialism'. Indeed, such a position has been pushed even further to maintain that 'in the absence of an appropriate socialist commitment, no claim to be nationalistic can be accepted as valid. Economic nationalism is, then, in some versions and some accounts actually subsumed under socialism' (Burnell 1986: 37, 78, 209). As a general proposition, however, this statement suffers from obvious limitations since countries can subscribe to economic nationalism without going socialist, as is evident in the case of Meiji Japan. Still, it has the merit of underlining the link between socialism and economic nationalism.

Setting aside for the moment the controversies surrounding the question whether the Indian endeavour at policy change was rigorous or authentic enough so as to be dignified by using the terms economic planning, autarky and, particularly, building socialism, these three features can nonetheless be said to define, in some measure, the *Indian development pattern* until the beginning of the 1990s. A 'development pattern' has been considered to have three dimensions: (1) the kind of industries accorded prominence; (2) the orientation of these industries to the world economy (whether they are oriented inward or outward); and (3) the economic agents chosen for development (Gereffi and Wyman 1990: 17). In the Indian development pattern, firstly, the emphasis was placed on capital goods, metal-making and heavy engineering industries, also referred to as heavy, basic or investment goods industries in Indian planning; secondly, these industries were inward-oriented and were expected to make the Indian economy self-sufficient as well as self-reliant for future sustained growth; and, finally, they were to be both owned and managed by the state. While this development pattern was executed with full force only between 1956 and 1965, it can be considered to have lasted in its broader dimensions, at times in intensified form and at others in attenuated form, until 1985 and indeed until 1991. That much is clear. The important question is: what led to the change in economic policy as a historic rupture that resulted in this development pattern. That issue relating to the origins of the particular policy change forms the central focus of this chapter.

There are two major interpretations in the literature, with the proponents of both referred to here being only illustrative and not exhaustive. One interpretation focuses on economic theory or economic ideas of the time as being influential in the policy change, or at least as theoretically validating the policy stance adopted by Indian economic planners. A key proponent of this view has been the distinguished internationally-renowned economist as well as noted economic planner, the late Sukhamoy Chakravarty. The immediate intellectual basis for the economic strategy that led to the Indian development pattern had been the 'plan-frame' for the Second Five-Year Plan (1956–61) and the underlying economic model, both having been put forward by the eminent economic planner P.C. Mahalanobis, and accordingly characterized as the Mahalanobis model. Chakravarty (1987, 1993) justifies the Mahalanobis model by reference to contemporaneous economic theory and economic ideas, referring in different contexts to Harrod and Domar, Hicks, Lewis, Nurkse, Prebisch, and Rosenstein-Rodan. Similarly, another economist and economic administrator with a long record of service in high economic positions in the government, Bimal Jalan (1991), also refers to the prevailing economic ideas of the time as influential in determining the economic strategy set out in the Second Plan. These authorities may additionally refer to other factors in justification of the strategy, but the primary thrust of their argument is to place reliance on what may be called 'the power of theory', that is, economic theory.

The other interpretation, which is held by Marxist activists and scholars, debunks any claims to building socialism and forthrightly proclaims the intent in the economic strategy as building, instead, capitalism on behalf of the bourgeoisie or capitalist class. The late communist leader E.M.S. Namboodiripad (1988: 2, 226) thus declares that Nehru 'represented, and acted as the spokesman of a particular class—the Indian bourgeoisie' and that his economic plans 'were all in line with the objectives of the bourgeoisie as a class'. Similarly, the Marxist scholar Prabhat Patnaik (1994) states that 'the class-configuration which prevailed, upon which industrial capitalism was to develop, dictated in broad terms a certain course of action, and the Mahalanobis strategy fitted in with this'.

As against the first of these two interpretations, the position taken in the story as it unfolds here is that, while in a proximate sense a case can be made, no doubt, about the affinity between the Mahalanobis model and the then prevailing economic theory, that argument establishes what is only a surface relationship, serving merely to detract from a deeper analysis into the origins of the model. In a more profound sense, the Mahalanobis model was founded on the historical commitment of the freedom movement to economic nationalism. Without in any way minimizing the theoretical merits of the Mahalanobis model, or its conjunctural importance in the formalizing of the Indian economic strategy, or its intellectual affinity with contemporaneous economy theory, it would be no exaggeration to say that the model simply provided a theoretical scaffolding as it were for an economic architecture already determined on political grounds, without the benefit of or any reference to economic theory. In this perspective, a more appropriate explanation for the strategy is a 'theory of power', as will be demonstrated here, instead of the power of theory.

As for the second interpretation, it would seem that it errs in making a mechanical application of the Marxist theory of state power and class agency, derived from the single model of the industrialization of Britain, to the entirely different situation of India. As a consequence, it neglects the specificity of India's class structure, power configuration, and ideological currents. As against this interpretation, the argument here will emphasize the importance of the ideological commitment of certain strategically placed political leaders to socialism in the context of a different balance of class forces that essentially excluded the capitalist class from state power. It is curious why Marxist activists and scholars, who are themselves convinced of the merits of the Marxist mode of analysis and are committed to the ideal of socialism notwithstanding their own petit bourgeois background, deny or fail to see the impact of ideology in the case of others. In the discussion that follows, the first and second sections critically examine each of the preceding two interpretations in that order.

The Mahalanobis Model and its Origins

The Mahalanobis model belongs to the general family of economic models encompassed under the rubric of what is known as the Harrod-Domar model. The latter model had already been employed in the formulation of the First Five-Year Plan (1951–56) though only redundantly, for the First Plan had in essence little to do with serious economic planning since it was essentially an aggregation of projects already under way or readily available on the shelf. As a renowned statistician of world eminence, but initially without familiarity with the economic literature, Mahalanobis had developed the conceptual foundations of his model independently without any awareness of the Harrod-Domar model, but when the latter was brought to his attention he graciously acknowledged its temporal priority. The Harrod-Domar model is focused on capital accumulation as the engine of economic growth; its aim was to determine for developed economies the rate of investment necessary to assure such increase in national income as to provide full employment. The Mahalanobis model went further, however; going beyond the aggregate requirements of investment, it specified the various sectors within the economy in which investment ought to take place and in what measure in order to make the structural leap from an agricultural underdeveloped economy to an industrial developed economy. The model was nonetheless focused on the operational requirements specifically of the Indian case without any larger claim of contribution to economic theory. It had arrived at that stage not in one blow, but had evolved in several steps.

In 1952, Mahalanobis had developed a model which treated the entire economy as a single sector and, on the basis of empirical data on the growth experience of the US (S. Kuznets) and of the UK (A.R. Prest and L.H. Lenfant), he suggested—in the fashion of Arthur Lewis (1954) later in his article on 'Economic Development with Unlimited Supplies of Labour'—that India needed to increase its annual rate of investment as a proportion of national income from 5 per cent to 10 or 11 per cent if it wished to double its per capita income in 35 years.[1] In 1953, he went on to elaborate the single-sector model into a two-sector one, differentiating the two sectors on the basis of whether they produced investment goods or consumer goods, along with making the implicit assumption of a closed economy. His distinction between the two sectors paralleled, though it did not completely follow, Marx's division between Department I and Department II.

The two-sector model was crucial to the formulation of the final Mahalanobis model; its main conclusion, based on a set of mathematical equations, was that

in the initial stage of development, the larger the percentage [of] investment on consumer goods industries, the larger will be the income generated. But there is a critical range of time and as soon as this is passed, the larger the investment in investment goods industries the larger will be the income generated. Hence, it would be desirable to invest relatively more on the consumer goods industries: provided we are interested in the immediate future. If, on the other hand, we are interested in the more distant future, relatively larger investment on investment goods industries would give distinctly better results (Mahalanobis 1953: 309).

This stance on investment became of elemental importance in the evolution of India's economic strategy, which had—as had Mahalanobis himself—considerations of long-term development as its foremost aim. The model, with its preference for the investment goods industries sector, was similar to the Feldman model developed in the Soviet Union in 1928.[2]

The final Mahalanobis model—as conceptualized in 1955 in 'The Approach of Operational Research to Planning in India' (Mahalanobis 1963), and applied in the 'plan-frame' under the prosaic title of 'Draft Recommendations for the Formulation of the Second Five Year Plan 1956–1961' (GOI 1962: 29–55)—was, unlike his previous two contributions which revolved around growth models, an allocation model intended to determine the broad sectoral outlays. For its time, it was a marvel of ingenuity, sophistication and precision in development planning. For purposes of allocation, the two-sector model was now further elaborated, so that while (1) the basic investment goods industries sector was retained as such, the consumer goods sector was divided into three sectors: (2) factory consumer goods industries; (3) household industries, including agriculture; and (4) services. In this final model, the basic task for the Second Plan was set by the two objectives of (a) an annual increase of 5 per cent in national income, and (b) additional employment for 11 million persons over the plan period (ibid.: 31). Not all the allocations were generated by the variables within the analytical model, however. The process of allocation was initiated with the exogenous injection of a well-reasoned, though in the final analysis arbitrarily determined, allocation of one-third of total investment to sector 1, as against the existing share in investment of one-tenth, 'broadly from considerations of long period development' (Mahalanobis 1963: 30, 37–38, 40, 47). The allocations for sector 2 (17 per cent), sector 3 (21 per cent), and sector 4 (29 per cent) were figured out on the basis of both the expected productivity of investment and the employment generation potential of investment in each sector, in order to arrive at—in combination with the allocation for sector 1— the annual growth of national income of 5 per cent and additional employment for 11 million persons.

The logic of the differential allocations within the consumer goods sector can be illustrated with reference to the competing claims of factory consumer goods industries and household industries. The former were far more consumptive of capital even as they were far less labour-intensive in comparison to the latter. Accordingly, in order to assure increased employment, Mahalanobis (1963: 23) was led to place constraints on the factory production of consumer goods. He was emphatic in his negative and restrictive posture on such pro- duction. Until the problem of unemployment was solved, he wanted no new investment in factories that would compete with small-scale industry; indeed, he favoured a temporary ban on expansion of pro- duction by such factories. He accepted with equanimity any surplus factory capacity thus becoming idle, for the employment of human beings commanded higher priority. Going further, he recommended the imposition of a higher excise duty on factory-made goods that competed with goods of comparable quality from the small-scale sector.

In the final analysis, the entire economic strategy of the Maha- lanobis model rested on a single fulcrum, on the one side of which lay what were believed to be strategically required investments for heavy industries—but which in the interim led to new demands— while on the other side were investments on small and household industries that were deemed necessary precisely to satisfy the new demand, with the essential aim of the strategy being to balance the two sides. If in the process the factory consumption goods industries sector—which lay between the state-owned heavy industries sector and the privately-owned small industries sector—was squeezed to meet the requirements of maintaining that balance, no tears needed to be shed since restrictions on it, stemming from the technical re- quirements of the model, additionally met other socially-motivated goals of the planners from the viewpoint of limiting concentration of wealth and power.

In making the case for small-scale and household industries, Mahalanobis did not mean to plan for a technologically dualistic economic structure. His larger objective of achieving a universally modern economy was clear, with the small industry sector meant only for a transitional phase. Mahalanobis (1963: 71) set for India the long-term aim of employing the most technologically-advanced means to produce both investment and consumer goods. Since this was, in the absence of a local heavy industry base, not feasible in the immediate future, Mahalanobis envisaged 'a transition phase' during which labour-intensive small-scale and household industries would be favoured for the sake of higher employment while capital resources would be husbanded carefully for heavy industry. Over time, with the expansion of the local capital goods industry and the growth of employment, the balance of preference would shift from labour-intensive and low-efficiency production to more efficient production employing power-driven machinery.

The Mahalanobis model was critical to the determination of India's economic strategy, for it not only settled the contours of the Second Plan but more generally for the Indian approach to economic development over the long term; in addition, it by and large determined the final outlays of the Second Plan. Of the three components constituting a development pattern, the Mahalanobis model definitively determined (1) the inward orientation of the economy and (2) the powerful thrust for the basic investment goods industries. In so far as the former was concerned, the closed nature of the economy was simply assumed. No balance of payments considerations entered into the calculations of the model. There was some reference to foreign trade but foreign trade as such did not figure in either the architecture of the model or in its details. More importantly, one aim in the thrust for investment goods industries was not just to assure long-term development but also to cut down, indeed eliminate, dependence on the outside world in the future. This stance of attempted autarky has been attributed to what has come to be characterized as *export pessimism* or export fatalism on the part of Indian planners. In this view, the markets of the developed world were assumed not to hold any improved prospects for commodities or products produced by India at that stage in its development. In turn, the resultant poor prospects for exports would have constrained development, because of the consequent inability to obtain capital goods in exchange. Accordingly, India needed to develop its own investment goods industries in order to avoid the trade constraint on its future development.

The third component (3) of the Indian development pattern of state ownership and management of major industry, with the public sector seizing the 'commanding heights' of the economy, stood on a different footing as it did not necessarily stem from the Mahalanobis model. As Mahalanobis (1963: 51, 65–67) stated it, the model was a technical model and was neutral in regard to ownership. The issue of ownership, he said, was a matter of choice for party and government policy, which had by the time of the formulation of the 'planframe' already ruled in favour of state ownership of heavy industry. However, Mahalanobis (ibid.: 69–70) himself endorsed that choice, and indeed advanced instrumental economic reasons for placing the heavy industries in the public sector, maintaining:

> The heavy machinery industry should be in the public sector. For rapid industrialization of an under-developed country it would be desirable to keep the cost of capital goods as low as possible. The further removed the type of capital goods under consideration is from the production of final consumer goods the greater is the need of keeping the price low. Heavy machinery which would manufacture machinery to produce investment goods is the furthest removed from the consumption end. It is essential, therefore, that Government should have complete control over the heavy machinery industry so as to be able to fix prices to suit national needs. Such control would enable Government to shape the future pattern of industrialization through a properly planned programme of production of heavy machinery.

Economic Theory and the Mahalanobis Model

What was the bearing of economic theory and economic thinking on the conceptualization of the Mahalanobis model? Neither Chakravarty nor Jalan necessarily trace a direct lineal descent from contemporaneous economic theorists or their thinking to the Mahalanobis model. Nor do they maintain that Mahalanobis was necessarily influenced directly by such economists or their ideas, but what they do demonstrate is that the profound ideas incorporated in the model were widely shared among economists of the time, that indeed there was a consensus over these ideas in development economics, and that Indian economists and planners partook of this consensus. In other words, the Mahalanobis model had a sound basis in the economic theory of the time. However, the direct influence of economists, including foreign economists, cannot be altogether excluded. After all, the Indian Statistical Institute, which had been founded in 1931 by Mahalanobis and had been mandated by the government to develop the plan-frame, had seen a stream of eminent foreign economists, though mostly of the progressive kind, visit it in connection with the development of the plan-frame. Among them during the winter of 1954–55 were: Ragnar Frisch (Norway); Oskar Lange (Poland); Charles Bettelheim (France); Richard Goodwin (UK); and D.D. Degtyar (Soviet Union) who headed a team of Soviet economists and statisticians. Mahalanobis (1963: 4–7) himself acknowledged that these visitors 'helped us to think clearly; they made constructive criticisms about the logical basis of our thinking' and that the visit of Bettelheim was 'particularly stimulating and helpful'.

While the relationship of economic theory or ideas can be related to many aspects of the Mahalanobis model, here attention will be focused on the assumption of (1) the closed economy with its inward orientation, and (2) the heavy industry strategy. The two were, of course, related and were joined in the assumption of export pessimism. Chakravarty and Jalan differ in their approach to tackling this element, with the former quite sharply focused on the Mahalanobis model while Jalan pays little attention, indeed none, specifically to Mahalanobis. Further, both often advance a multiplicity of factors in the choice of the economic strategy, which makes it difficult to determine what weight they really accord to economic thinking in the choice. However, there is certainly a greater emphasis on the importance of theory in Chakravarty.

In his survey of the Indian planning experience, Chakravarty (1987: 1–2) states his objective to be 'to ascertain and evaluate the type of reasoning that has gone into the formulation of Indian plans', and goes on to discuss 'the economic theory underlying Indian plans', and indeed figures that *Economic Theory and Indian Planning* could also be a possible title for the book.[3] He goes on to delineate an interactive pattern of influence between early development economics and Indian planning. Not only was Indian planning 'in the formulation of its theory, far more self-conscious than that attempted in many third world countries' but most major economists with an interest in development interacted with Indian planners and policy-makers in the 1950s and 1960s. There was, as a consequence, a two-way exchange: 'Dominant ideas of contemporary development economics influenced the logic of India's plans, and correspondingly, development theory was for a while greatly influenced by the Indian case'.

While acknowledging that the Second Five-Year Plan 'was heavily influenced by the work of Mahalanobis', Chakravarty characterizes the Second Plan's strategy as lacking 'neither a theoretical rationale nor a measure of empirical plausibility', and underlines—as he approaches the issue of relationship between economic theory and Indian planning—several perceptions then prevalent about the underlying causes of structural backwardness. Chief among these perceptions were: (1) the extreme shortage of material capital as the basic constraint on development; (2) the low level of savings as a factor retarding capital accumulation; (3) the presence of structural limitations on converting savings into investment even if savings could be raised; and (4) the necessity of industrialization in order to employ underemployed rural labour, since agriculture faced long-term diminishing returns. Chakravarty then sees a direct link between these perceptions and planning through the medium of economic theory: 'Given all these perceptions, it was felt that economic theory indicated that the basic questions relating to how much to save, where to invest, and in what forms to invest could be best handled with the help of a plan'. At the same time, he emphasizes the wide consensus then prevalent on these perceptions:

> It will be noted that the economics profession in the fifties, especially during the early and middle part of the decade, subscribed to most of the perceptions presented above. It is enough to recall Arthur Lewis's famous dictum that the central issue for development economics was to understand how a country which saves 5 per cent of its income is transformed into one which saves 20 per cent of its income. The same view was expressed by A.K. Das Gupta, a prominent Indian economist with a classical bent of mind, who defined India's problem as one of 'primary accumulation of capital'.... On the third proposition, agreement was not so universal. While structuralists like Prebisch would have endorsed it, for most economists it was an empirical question. However, quite a few would have subscribed to Nurkse's *export lag* thesis, especially because of the heavy weight of primary products in India's export basket. Furthermore, the sharp fall in commodity

prices after the Korean War also added to the plausibility of that proposition.

Chakravarty avers that 'Indian planners operated on the assumption of *a low elasticity of export demand* accompanied by a system of strict import allocation. Thus they were in reality operating on the assumption of a nearly closed economy'. However, he underlines the importance of eluding the savings constraint in the choice of the heavy industry strategy. For, if the economy was closed and savings had to be increased from about 5 per cent to 20 per cent over a 25-year period, then 'inter-sectoral consistency over time would demand that the productive capacity of the capital goods sector would have to rise at an accelerated rate to convert growing savings into additional real investment. It was therefore the need to raise the real savings rate that led Indian planners to accord primacy to a faster rate of growth in the capital goods sector'. He then speculatively adds: 'Doubtless there could have been other considerations such as building up defence capability'. Similarly, he attributes the reluctance of the Indian state to take to an export strategy, based on India's considerable strength in textiles, to the political factor of not being forced to support a particular region-based group of industrialists.

In sum, the choice of the Indian heavy industry strategy at the time of the Second Plan reflected the thinking in the economics profession, and the key element that led to that choice was apparently export pessimism. Chakravarty cites in support the perception in the Second Plan to the effect that export earnings would increase only after industrialization has gone some distance, but does not enlighten us as to the opinion of Mahalanobis on the issue. That opinion should have been important since the strategy had already been determined in the Mahalanobis model, through a rigorously developed rationale, rather than in the Plan document.

In his attempt at understanding the origins of India's economic strategy, Jalan focuses on several aspects: the emphasis on industrialization and the corresponding neglect of agriculture, the inward orientation of the strategy and its relationship to export pessimism, and the activist role of the state as entrepreneur. His multifold explanation is that 'the initial choice of the strategy was a response to the prevailing intellectual perception of the initial conditions and the role of the state in development. India's own political and social history also supported the case for an inward-looking strategy of industrialization, with the state in command' (Jalan 1991: 13).[4] Importantly, he underlines that foreign trade had only a small place in Indian planning, because it was believed that the trade regime had a built-in bias against underdeveloped countries 'and partly because of the intellectual conviction that *export prospects were severely limited*'.

Jalan then links Indian perception to economic thinking, stating: 'The intellectual basis for *pessimism about exports*, which was widely shared by development economists of the time, was broadly the same as that articulated by Nurkse in his "*export lag*" *thesis*'. He repeats the theme by saying:

> The conclusions of Prebisch (1950) and Singer (1950)—on the secular tendency of the terms of trade turning against countries exporting primary products and importing manufactures—had *an important impact* on the thinking of planners in developing countries.... Equally influential was Lewis's paper.... Singer, Prebisch and Lewis's works thus provided a powerful case for import substitution and protection.

He then adds: 'These perceptions were widely shared by political leaders and Indian intellectuals of the time, and the business of choosing an *economic strategy responded to these perceptions*'. Having thus emphasized the impact of these economic thinkers on Indian planners, or at least the affinity between the ideas of the two, Jalan refers to several other factors as strengthening India's determination to build a self-reliant industrial base:

> The colonial experience was sufficient *to reinforce* the belief that the free-trade regime was biased against India and other developing countries and could not be relied upon to generate growth and improve living standards. The call for Swadeshi therefore became an important element in the political struggle against colonial rule. It was inevitable that, after independence, the building of an indigenous manufacturing base should become an important objective of economic policy. This strategy was also an aspect of the struggle for economic and political independence from the UK and other Western powers. The apparent success of the Soviet Union in building up a strong manufacturing base, and its emergence as a superpower within a relatively short period of time,

strengthened belief in the efficacy of the state as the primary agent of accumulation.

Since Jalan employs the notion that the colonial experience served 'to reinforce', and again reiterates that 'these powerful economic arguments were *buttressed by* political perceptions and the ideas of political and intellectual leaders in developing countries', it would be fair to infer that for him it is the economic theory of distinguished thinkers such as Prebisch, Singer, and Lewis that was influential in the determination of Indian economic strategy.

Export Pessimism and the Mahalanobis Model

In view of the subsequent strong emphasis placed on the link between export pessimism and the heavy industry strategy, it comes as a surprise that there is no reference to such a link in the Mahalanobis model itself. Certainly, such an important premise which would have constituted as it were the very foundation of the model would have merited some reference somewhere in the lengthy documentation of the 'plan-frame' or the Mahalanobis model. Curiously, Chakravarty had, in an earlier article, written jointly with Bhagwati, maintained that the planners gave very cursory attention to the question of the prospective stagnation in external demand for Indian goods, that the subsequent justification of the strategy in terms of stagnant world demand came 'somewhat close to a ex post facto rationalization', and that 'such a *crucial* assumption, if made, would surely have been examined more intensively!' (Bhagwati and Chakravarty 1969: 7). Interestingly, Rosen (1966: 126) had already pointed out that exports were not a serious problem at the time of the preparation of the Second Plan and that the theoretical argument on export pessimism was essentially post facto.[5] It is noteworthy that Mahalanobis himself articulated five possible limiting factors that could undercut the achievement of the goals of the Second Plan— inadequacy of consumer goods production; inadequacy, equally, of capital goods production; lack of trained manpower; poor mobilization of financial resources; and rigidities of the administrative structure—but none pertained to the external sector.

Indeed, it is evident that the case for the heavy industry strategy was made, not on the basis of a prevailing export pessimism, but on the basis of viewing economic development in the light of a long-term 'perspective' of 20 or 30 years. Here the crux of the issue for Mahalanobis (1963: 26) was that in the single structural weakness of India's national economy—by way of the lack of capacity to produce capital goods, despite the country's abundant resources—lay the explanation for the vast and persistent unemployment; as he saw it:

> India has plenty of iron ore, coal and other natural resources. The long-term aim should, therefore, be to manufacture capital goods within the country rather than to import them. The proper strategy would be to bring about a rapid development of the industries producing investment goods in the beginning by increasing appreciably the proportion of investment in the basic heavy industries. As the capacity to manufacture both heavy and light machinery and other capital goods increases, the capacity to invest (by using home-produced capital goods) would also increase steadily and India would become more and more independent of the import of foreign machinery and capital goods.

The argument for the heavy industry strategy rested, not on a negative and reactive posture towards export pessimism, but on more positive foundations, where the foremost interest of long-term development was further conjoined with the related policy-engendered aim of *economic independence*. Early on, on the basis of the two-sector model of 1952, Mahalanobis (ibid.: 35) had 'assumed that, with the progress of planning, the domestic supply of investment goods would become more and more important'. Rather than evincing any immediate concern over export pessimism, he simply added: 'That is, although in the beginning India will, no doubt, have to depend on imports of capital goods, the policy would be to make India *independent* of such imports as soon as possible. In the present model I have, therefore, assumed that there would be no imports or exports of investment goods' (emphasis in the original). In the 'plan-frame', Mahalanobis (GOI 1962: 36) had asserted:

> In the long run, the rate of industrialization and the growth of national economy would depend on the increasing production of coal, electricity, iron and steel, heavy machinery, heavy chemicals, and the heavy industries generally which would increase the capacity for capital formation.

He then continued:

> One important aim is to make India independent, as quickly as possible, of foreign imports of producer goods so that the accumulation of capital would not be hampered by difficulties in securing supplies of essential producer goods from other countries. The heavy industries must, therefore, be expanded with all possible speed.

Seemingly, then, economic independence had its own intrinsic value for Mahalanobis, without being justified by instrumental reasons such as export pessimism. Not that he was insensitive to external constraints but they belonged to a whole range of possibilities, not immediate pressures and not particularly focused on foreign trade. In a footnote to one statement on economic independence, Mahalanobis (1963: 35) explained:

> This does not mean that India would not purchase capital goods from other countries. India would make such purchases but India would also manufacture and export capital goods. Secondly, if for any reason (such as lack of foreign currency, shortage of supply or high prices in the world market, state of blockade or war, etc.) there is difficulty in securing essential investment goods from abroad, India should be able to manufacture such goods within the country.

Throughout, Mahalanobis placed emphasis, consistently and persistently, on the long range, asking as to what would advance development over the long term, without any reference to export pessimism. Interestingly, his position on the heavy industry strategy, which constituted the heart of the model—with the aim of making India self-sufficient in capital goods industries—had firmed up before any possible adverse consequences from the end of the Korean war for exports were visible, as is evident from the two-sector model that had been developed by 1952. That position had to do with enhancing the capacity for long-term growth, indeed making India economically independent over the long run, and not with any syndrome of export pessimism. And here there is no hiding his penchant for self-sufficiency and independence from the world economy. As Mahalanobis (ibid.: 69) put it:

India's present dependence on imports of capital goods is a fundamental structural weakness which must be corrected as quickly as possible. It would be obviously more economical from the national point of view to produce in India as much heavy machinery as possible because this would ensure a supply of capital goods which would make India increasingly independent of imports and would strengthen India's position in the world market. In my opinion, the development of the heavy machine building industry is so important that, if necessary, targets of even steel, coal, or transport should be reduced to give higher priority to heavy machines because this would facilitate a much quicker rate of industrialization after four or five years.

The penchant for independence emerges also in the discussion on individual industries. Thus, for example, in relation to aluminium, Mahalanobis (1963: 28) argued:

The Plan-frame has recommended that the production of aluminium should be progressively increased with a view to replacing copper by aluminium to the largest extent possible. This would be a wise decision because it would increase production through the utilization of Indian resources; and would also make India progressively independent of imports of copper in future. This is the kind of thinking which made us give so much emphasis to the rapid development of the basic industries.

Mahalanobis (ibid.: 70) did not necessarily advocate the necessity or desirability of India becoming 'completely self-sufficient in the production of machinery'. Nonetheless, he maintained:

India should, however, acquire both the means of production and technical knowledge to be able, if and when necessary, to manufacture essential investment goods within the country. This is necessary for economic independence.

As he continued, Mahalanobis took a position which was emphatically contrary to expectations of export pessimism:

But under normal conditions India should continue to purchase abroad such machinery and capital goods as it would not be economic from a national point of view to manufacture in India. On the other hand, India should also develop in the course of time the production of specialized machinery for which there would be an external market. The policy should be to encourage both imports and exports of machinery and capital goods which would be of mutual benefit to India and other countries.

It is obvious that prevailing economic theory or more generally the thinking of economists as regards export pessimism had little to do with the heavy industry strategy as articulated in the Mahalanobis model. Equally, there is no doubt that the model was, in a proximate sense, immensely influential in determining the shape of India's economic strategy and, hence, its development pattern. The question arises whether Mahalanobis was the original fountainhead of the heavy industry strategy—with its associated underlying aim of economic independence—on the basis of mathematical model-building, or whether he was simply the agent of other larger social forces emergent on the Indian scene. An answer to that question requires recourse to an exploration of recent history leading up to the formulation of the Second Plan.

The Nationalist Movement and Economic Planning

The aim of industrialization goes back to the beginnings of the nationalist movement in India, the organizational expression of which was the Indian National Congress, more commonly referred to as the Congress Party. During the liberal or moderate phase of the movement, from 1885 to 1905, the goal of industrialization through large-scale industries was taken to be a self-evident proposition. Indeed, 'by the end of the 19th century, the demand for rapid industrialization of the country along modern industries had assumed national proportions' (Chandra 1966: 65–89). The Congress leadership deemed such industrialization as essential for a variety of reasons: removing poverty and unemployment, eliminating the exclusive dependence on agriculture, developing the productive powers of the nation, achieving a higher level of civilization, and promoting national integration. Toward that end, the moderate leadership endorsed the prescriptions of List for state intervention in the economy for purposes of development, refusing to buy the laissez-faire logic proffered by the British colonial authorities.

By the first decade of the twentieth century, the moderate phase of nationalism had been overtaken by extremism and militancy. In one interpretation, this turn in the course of the nationalist movement sprang in part from the failure of colonial authorities to introduce political reform to meet Indian aspirations, but also importantly in part from the feeling that the authorities had betrayed the trust placed in them about bringing industrialization to India. What is more, it was felt that Britain did not simply fail in actively helping with industrialization, but that in actual fact it thwarted industrialization as a matter of deliberate state policy (Sheel 1986).

Subsequently, after World War I, Mahatma Gandhi transformed the nationalist struggle into a mass movement of the new middle classes and the rich and middle peasantry, and similarly forged the Congress Party into a mass organization. In the process, new leaders rose to the first ranks of the party, among them none more important than Jawaharlal Nehru, second only to Gandhi who later also designated him as his successor. Nehru, however, differed radically from Gandhi on economic policy. Gandhi was against industrialization out of philosophical conviction, believing it to be destructive of traditional civilization and its values. Instead, he wanted a society based on limited wants and organized in self-sufficient villages, relying on agriculture and household or cottage industries. Nehru as a modernizer, however, favoured nothing less than a full-dress industrialization of the country. In his presidential address to the Congress Party at Lucknow in 1936, Nehru declared: 'I believe in the rapid industrialization of the country; and only thus, I think will the standards of the people rise substantially and poverty be combated' (Norman 1965: 434).

Nehru thereafter repeatedly advocated the case for industrialization and underscored the importance of economic planning. At his urging, the Congress Party established in 1938 a National Planning Committee, with Nehru as chairman. With that, Nehru devoted a lot of effort to working with industrialists, economists and political leaders on the committee in order to evolve a plan for India's future economic development. In the end, the effort proved abortive because of the drastic change in the political situation following the outbreak of World War II, soon to be followed by his own departure for jail. However, in the meantime, Nehru had already begun to underscore the importance of heavy industry. In a significant article he wrote before the Quit India movement of August 1942, which took him again to jail, Nehru set out the framework for an economic strategy that has an uncanny resemblance with that subsequently associated with the Second Plan. All the key features of the 'plan-frame' are present here: the pre-eminent place accorded to heavy industry; the reliance on cottage industries for consumption goods; and the restraint on factory-made consumer goods. What is more, in its reasoning or economic logic for advocating the adoption of these measures, the text reads astoundingly like the Mahalanobis model document, though preceding it by more than a decade. Nehru (1943: 26) stated:

The objective aimed at should be maximum production, equitable distribution and no unemployment. With India's vast population this cannot be achieved by having big industry only, or cottage industry only. The former will certainly result in much greater production of some commodities, but the unemployment problem will remain more or less as it is, and it will be difficult to have equitable distribution. It is also likely that our total production will be far below our potential because of the wastage of labour power. With cottage industries only, there will be more equitable distribution but the total production will remain at a low level and hence standards will not rise. In the present state of India, of course, even widespread cottage industry can raise standards considerably above the existing level. Nevertheless they will remain low. There are other factors also which make it almost impossible for any country to depend entirely on cottage industry. No modern nation can exist without certain essential articles which can be produced only by big industry. Not to produce these is to rely on imports from abroad and thus to be subservient to the economy of foreign countries. It means economic bondage and probably also political subjection.

Therefore it seems essential to have both big industries and cottage industries in India and to plan them in such a way as to avoid conflict. Big industry must be encouraged and developed as rapidly as possible, but the type of industry thus encouraged should be chosen with care. It should be heavy and basic industry, which is the foundation of a nation's economic strength and on which other industries can gradually be built up. The development of electric power is the prerequisite for industrial growth. Machine-making, shipbuilding, chemicals, locomotives, automobiles and the like should follow. All these, and others like them, are wealth-producing industries and work-producing industries which do not create unemployment elsewhere. Lighter industries should not be encouraged to begin with, partly because the capital at our disposal is limited and required for heavy industry, partly because they are likely to come into conflict with cottage industries and thus create unemployment.

It is manifest that the roots of India's economic strategy clearly lie here in the ideas of a man who later as prime minister and chairman of the Planning Commission presided over the launching of that strategy. Coming as this article did in the midst of World War II, it could not have been influenced by export pessimism in relation to the less developed countries, for economic theory then paid no attention to them. Nor could it have been influenced specifically by scholars such as Lewis, Nurkse, Prebisch, or Singer, for Nehru's developmental framework had a substantial chronological priority over their work.

What is impressive about Nehru at this time, however, is not only that he had worked out India's economic strategy this early on and had provided a cogent economic rationale for it, but that his rationale was grounded in a profound understanding of its relationship to power and international politics. An insight into this understanding is provided by his dispute with Gandhi over the relevance of cottage industries to mass welfare. Nehru readily accepted the need for cottage industries as a transitional measure to cope with unemployment; much as Mahalanobis was to express it later, he stated in 1936: 'I look upon them more as temporary expedients of a transition stage than as solutions of our vital problems' (Norman 1965: 435). However, he absolutely would not countenance making them the sole mechanism of growth in his economic strategy. His reasoning for that posture combined both an economic and a political rationale; in a letter in 1939, he explained:

But I cannot conceive of the world or of any progressive country doing away with the big machine. Even if this was possible, this would result in lowering production tremendously and thus in reducing standards of life greatly. For a country to try to do away with industrialization would lead to that country falling a prey, economically and otherwise, to other more industrialized countries, which would exploit it. For the development of cottage industries on a widespread scale, it is obvious that political and economic power is necessary. It is unlikely that a country entirely devoted to cottage industries will ever get this political or economic power, and so in effect it will not even be able to push cottage industries as it wants to (Norman 1965: 697).

While in jail during World War II, Nehru thought further about the relationship between cottage industries and modern factory industry, and declared that 'I am convinced that the rapid industrialization of India is essential to relieve the pressure on land, to combat poverty and raise standards of living, for defence, and a variety of other purposes'. Then in a remarkably incisive passage, Nehru (1946: 411–13) laid bare the political logic for his attachment to heavy industry:

It can hardly be challenged that, in the context of the modern world, no country can be politically and economically independent, even within the framework of international interdependence, unless it is highly industrialized and has developed its power resources to the utmost. Nor can it achieve or maintain high standards of living and liquidate poverty without the aid of modern technology in almost every sphere of life. An industrially backward country will continually upset the world equilibrium and encourage the aggressive tendencies of more developed countries. Even if it retains its political independence, this will be nominal only and economic control will tend to pass to others. This control will inevitably upset its own small-scale economy which it has sought to preserve in pursuit of its own view of life. Thus an attempt to build up a country's economy largely on the basis of cottage and small-scale industries is doomed to failure. It will not solve the basic problems of the country or maintain freedom, nor will it fit in with the world framework, except as a colonial appendage.

What thus underlay the economic strategy of the Second Plan was not the power of economic theory, for Nehru could not have had access to it before it had been formulated for the underdeveloped countries, but a theory of power, to which he gave the fullest expression. Further, the economic nationalism embodied in the strategy

was not simply negatively aimed at preventing domination by foreign powers, which India had experienced for some hundreds of
years, but also more positively for assuring India a role in the future
in the international community commensurate with its perceived
importance stemming from its territorial and population size, geographic location and its past as a centre of civilization. These themes
continued to be articulated by Nehru before and after the adoption
of the economic strategy in the mid-1950s.

The Mahalanobis model was subjected to considerable scrutiny by
economists and others immediately after its presentation. Critics
called attention to its unrealism in respect of the neglect of agriculture and the wage goods constraint as well as the excessive reliance
on the household sector to deliver on consumer goods; its irresponsibility in depending on deficit financing to a large extent and in
neglecting balance of payments considerations; and its courting
political risks by implanting a Soviet-style economic strategy in a
representative political system (Shenoy 1962: 15–26; Vakil and
Brahmananda 1962: 114–19). One critic found it full of inadequa-
cies and asserted that it made sense only in the light of 'what you
are after. If you are asked (by, say, Pandit Nehru or Khrushchev)
whether a particular target, which the government for some reason
wants to achieve, can be achieved, you can answer the question with
a model of Professor Mahalanobis' sort' (Sen 1958). This would
seem to be a harsh and uncharitable judgement. What is closer to
reality is that both Nehru and Mahalanobis shared the same larger
orientation in regard to economic strategy, rather than that Mahalanobis simply provided an economic rationale for Nehru's direc-
tives. Indeed, it could be argued that this orientation was by and
large shared by most Indian intellectuals, either on their own or they
had been brought up on it by the constant advocacy by Nehru over
the years. As part of the same intellectual classes, most economists in
India shared the same value orientation also. So did, in good measure, the capitalist class as well as the right wing of the Congress
Party, though they would have preferred to follow a strategy mod-
eled after that of the Meiji regime in relying on the private sector
rather than state ownership. It is precisely the foundation of the
strategy in economic nationalism that explains why when, soon after
the Second Plan was launched, many of the economic strains and
dislocations that had been predicted for the strategy emerged, India
persisted with it even as it made some modifications to cope with the
crises.

Even though there developed a widely shared consensus around the strategy, Nehru was the most crucial actor in relation to the strategy since, not only had he first suggested the strategy and propagated it and mobilized support for it, he also held the reins of power in both party and government that implemented the strategy. Of course, in developing his notions about the appropriate economic strategy for India, Nehru was himself powerfully influenced by the economic achievements of the Soviet Union precisely through a similar strategy. But the Soviet Union and more importantly the socialist ideology, which purportedly lay at the foundation of the Soviet Union and its economic strategy, were no less influential in the third element of India's development pattern—state ownership and management of the heavy industries. Indeed, even though for purposes of analysis and discussion, the two elements of the heavy industry strategy and its inward orientation have been separated from state ownership here, for Nehru himself all three elements along with some others constituted a single seamless ensemble encompassed in his vision of a route to an eventually socialist society.

The Ideological Foundations of the Public Sector

The Marxist case on Nehru's planning as having been intended for building capitalism, rather than socialism, rests on the assertion that the state in India is a capitalist state in which state power is held essentially by a coalition of the bourgeoisie and landlords. In this view, the weakness of the bourgeoisie in the context of an economically backward society and the threat to it from western imperialism results in the reliance by the bourgeoisie on the state—which it controls—to launch a programme of industrialization, particularly in the area of heavy industry, for which it does not have the organizational capacity or the resources to meet the large requirements for investment (Kurian 1975). It still must remain a mystery, however, how a class too weak to undertake industrialization on its own was strong enough to seize control of the state.

A particularly strong piece of evidence often advanced on behalf of the Marxist case is the extraordinarily ambitious Bombay or Tata-Birla Plan—and Patnaik specifically refers to it—which a group of eminent industrialists developed in 1945, a decade prior to the Mahalanobis plan-frame and model. That plan resembles the Mahalanobis

effort in several respects: high ambition in terms of rapid industrialization, recognition of the necessity of centralized planning, emphasis on heavy industry for the explicit purpose of making India
economically independent, the reliance on the state for the mobilization of resources, particularly through heavy deficit financing, and
the need for strong state interventionism by way of regulation and
controls as also for state ownership in certain sectors (Thakurdas et
al. 1945). Although, as should be evident, Nehru's ideas on planning
had preceded the Bombay Plan, the resemblance between the Bombay Plan and the Mahalanobis model is taken as sufficient evidence
of the state acting on behalf, even if not at the behest, of the capitalist class.

In this argument, state ownership of heavy industries is seen as
particularly advantageous for the capitalist class because, apart from
the large outlays required for them which are beyond the capacity of
private capitalists, such industries have a long gestation period during which no profits accrue and also because of their supposedly low
profitability even subsequently, while they would provide state-
subsidized inputs for the privately-owned consumer goods industries (Kurian 1975). Of course, the hypothesis of reliance on state
ownership because of the weakness of the capitalist class is held
more widely than just by Marxists. Thus, for example, Jalan (1991:
22) states matter-of-factly: 'Since the investment requirements in
these sectors were high, largely beyond the capability of the private
sector, and the financial profitability was low, it followed that such
investments would have to be undertaken by the state'.

The issue, however, is beset with ironies. When the plan-frame
document was released, the representative organization of the capitalist class, FICCI (Federation of Indian Chambers of Commerce
and Industry) opposed the kind of economic strategy that was advocated in it. FICCI (1955) found it to be disturbing because of 'differences of a basic character' in approaches to planning by government
and business, and it took umbrage at 'total comprehensive planning'. More specifically, FICCI's concern was centred on the plan-
frame's near-exclusion of the private sector from large-scale modern
industry through the strategy of reliance on cottage and small-scale
industry for consumer goods and on the public sector for producer
goods. For its part, it advocated pushing forward with large-scale
consumer goods industry, and rejected the artificial propping up
of village industries 'at the cost of organized industry'. FICCI was

dismayed at the diminished role given to the private sector, and challenged the assumption that the private sector did not have the resources for the kinds of projects envisaged in the public sector. It asked the planners 'to avoid a doctrinaire approach embodying the prejudices of a few and resulting in viewing the private sector with suspicion or antipathy'. However, the government did not budge from its determination to go ahead with the strategy, and the business class had to reconcile itself to the situation.

Of course, it has been suggested by some Marxist scholars that even when the state opposed what the capitalist class wanted and imposed its own programmes on it, the state still reflected the true interests of that class which the class itself was incapable of discerning! Thus, for example, one scholar (Rudra 1985) states:

> how to explain the Government of India adopting a strategy which turned out to be one for building State Capitalism in the name of Socialism but which was initially opposed by the bourgeoisie itself?... This is one more instance in history of leaders of a ruling class being much more farsighted than individual members of the same class. The distance between the understanding of ruling class interests as perceived by ordinary individual members of the class and their representatives in the state can be so big that the former may actually oppose the actions of the state until they come to understand the real motive behind the state policies.... Nehru and his closest cabinet colleagues were alone crystal clear about what was happening—they alone did not suffer from any delusions.

It would really be futile to attempt to dispute this statement, for framed in the manner that it has been the statement lifts the argument beyond empirical social science.

There is, however, a further irony. As against the strong opposition of the capitalist class to the emphasis in the plan-frame on the public sector and the heavy industry strategy, the Communist Party of India (1977) endorsed the key features of the proposals embodied in the plan-frame, despite its having been the handiwork of a supposedly capitalist state:

> The proposals to build basic industries, if implemented, would reduce the dependence of India on foreign countries in respect of capital goods, strengthen the relative position of industry inside

India and strengthen our economic position and national independence. The party, therefore, supports these proposals and also the proposal that these industries should be mainly developed in the public sector. It supports the proposal that the demand for consumer goods should be met, as far as possible, by better utilization of the existing capacity and by development of small-scale and cottage industries so that jobs are provided for an increasing number of people and maximum possible resources are available for the development of basic industries. The party not only supports these proposals but will *expose and combat* those who want them to be modified in a reactionary direction [emphasis added].

It is clear then that the capitalist class opposed the thrust of the plan-frame, while the Communist Party as the representative of the working class supported it. However, the reasons for opposition by one and support by the other were fundamentally the same. Both opponents and supporters saw the public sector as excluding important arenas of the economy from private accumulation. More fundamentally, both saw it as reducing the economic and political power of the capitalist class. Again, both saw it as effectively facilitating—to be dreaded by one side and welcomed by the other—the prospect eventually of abolition of capitalism and the capitalist class altogether. Such an outcome would occur either in a unilinear but peaceful fashion through the ever-increasing absolute and relative role of the public sector (as envisaged by Nehru and socialists of his persuasion), or in a dialectical fashion through the eruption of violent conflict between a weakened capitalist class and the strengthened socialist forces cohering around a potent public sector (as envisaged by the communists). What emerges plainly from the entire episode is the fact that, despite the difference in rhetoric and even more in strategy over the question of the mode of transition to socialism, Nehru and the communists essentially shared the same vision of the end of capitalism and the same calculations about the role of an expanding public sector in achieving it.

Contrary to what Marxists asserted, Nehru in the post-independence period was really not taken in by the argument that the Indian capitalist class was incapable of fostering industrialization. Rather, his ideologically-driven aim was to contain, undercut and eventually marginalize the power of the private sector. When he was attacked for excluding the private sector from the basic industries sector,

Nehru (1968: 130) noted that the private sector already had some basic industries, and then added sharply that private business wanted more of such industries because 'not only they might prove to be very profitable but because it gives them economic power'. To Nehru that was unacceptable; he found it 'highly objectionable that economic power should be in the hands of a small group of persons, however able or good they might be', and he was emphatic that 'such a thing must be prevented'. It is instructive that Nehru, if he were truly building capitalism, did not say to the business community in respect of basic industries: 'Look, friends, here is a field which is not profitable for business, you should therefore let the state carry the burden on your behalf'. Rather, he declared that this is a field which is apt to add to the economic power of business, and precisely for that reason he meant to preempt it for the public sector and to see that business stayed deprived of it.

Nehru, Socialism, and the Mixed Economy

Fundamentally, Nehru's vision of the public sector stood on a different footing from that of the Bombay Plan, in relation to which there really exists a profound misunderstanding or misrepresentation. For the Bombay planners, the role of the state in the economy was only temporary, after the pattern of war-time restrictions, and to be 'of limited duration and confined to specific purposes'. Their aim was to build a more flourishing industrial capitalism. Nehru envisaged an ever-expanding public sector, both absolutely and relative to the private sector, in possession of the commanding heights, fundamentally as a route to a socialist society. Socialism was one of the three pillars of Nehru's ideological system, the other two being nationalism and democracy. Nehru had come to his particular understanding of the role of an expanding public sector, as a mode of transition to socialism, before independence through self-reflection over a considerable period of time on how to adapt socialism to Indian conditions. Nehru had become an admirer of Marxist ideas by the late 1920s after meeting world revolutionaries in Europe and visiting the Soviet Union. Differing with Mahatma Gandhi, he proclaimed in his presidential address to the Congress Party in 1927 that he was a socialist and that India would have to go the socialist way if it meant to remove its poverty and inequality (Norman 1965: 195–210). In the years subsequent to that, he made it his personal mission to convert the youth and intelligentsia to his socialist creed through a whirlwind of speeches, writing and political campaigns. This effort not only earned him the hostility of the capitalist class but also brought him into conflict with Gandhi and other colleagues in the party, who were irked by what they felt to be his divisive activities that diverted attention from the main goal of independence. Gandhi had to rein him in occasionally, but Nehru nonetheless socialized a whole generation of youth into his ideology, and many from this generation subsequently came to occupy strategic positions in the party, government, media and academia after independence.

After he became chairman of the National Planning Committee in 1938, Nehru increasingly turned his attention to the question of adapting socialism to Indian conditions. He came to the conclusion that the mode of *transition to socialism* was to be by way of a 'mixed economy', though it was not yet termed as such, under which all key industries were to be state-owned and state-managed. As the public sector expanded under a regime of planning in the mixed economy, the private sector would be reduced to an economic appendage, and thus a peaceful transition to socialism would take place. At the same time, in contrast to orthodox Marxists who were votaries of revolution, Nehru was committed to democracy as the political route to the socialist society, and for that commitment to socialism by consent he was ridiculed by them. Having arrived at this model before independence, Nehru had to be quiescent about socialism for several years after independence because of the turmoil of partition and the factional divisions within the party and government. Only in 1954, after he had consolidated his power both in the party and government, did Nehru begin to give public expression to the kind of society he eventually envisioned for India. In November, he made it clear that he rejected capitalism, because 'a system which is based purely on the acquisitive instinct is immoral', even as he regarded its days to be numbered. More positively, Nehru (1957: 17) declared:

The picture I have in mind is definitely and absolutely a Socialistic picture of society. I am not using the word in a dogmatic sense at all. I mean largely that the means of production should be socially owned and controlled for the benefit of society as a whole. There is plenty of room for private enterprise there, providing the main aim is kept clear.

A month later, the Lok Sabha passed a resolution supporting Nehru's vision, and in January 1955 the Congress Party in a historic resolution stated that 'planning should take place with a view to the establishment of a socialistic pattern of society, where the principal means of production are under social ownership or control, production is progressively speeded up and there is equitable distribution of the national income'. Significantly, referring to the two resolutions by parliament and party, Mahalanobis (1963: 6) acknowledged in the model document that 'these decisions settled, in principle, the type of economic development of India in future', and in the plan-frame (GOI 1962: 39) he recommended: 'The public sector must be expanded rapidly and relatively faster than the private sector for steady advance to a socialist pattern of economy'.

The Second Five-Year Plan (GOI 1956: 22–23) repeated the theme: 'The basic criterion for determining the lines of advance must not be private profit but social gain.... The public sector has to expand rapidly ... it has to play the dominant role ... the public sector must grow not only absolutely but also relatively to the private sector'. The Industrial Policy Resolution of 1956 then reserved solely for the public sector 'all industries of basic and strategic importance, or in the nature of public utility services'; not only that, 'other industries which are essential and require investment on a scale which only the State, in present circumstances, could provide, have also to be in the public sector. The State has, therefore, to assume direct responsibility for the future development of industries over a wider area'. Even if one supposes that the private sector did not have the capacity to undertake such industries, no purpose other than an ideological one would seem to have been served by this deliberate exclusion of the private sector by fiat. Meanwhile, the private sector was placed under a rigid system of licensing and strict controls over installation and expansion of industrial capacity. The Third Five-Year Plan (GOI 1961: 7, 10, 50) later elevated the role of the public sector to a higher level, both practically and ideologically. It posited an 'even more dominant' role for the public sector in economic development, and projected it 'to grow both absolutely and in comparison and at a faster rate than the private sector'. The end purpose in assigning this role to the public sector was the achievement of a socialist society: 'In an underdeveloped country, a high rate of economic progress and the development of a large public sector and a cooperative sector are among the principal means for effecting the *transition towards socialism*' (emphasis added). Thus, once the principal means of production would come to be publicly owned while the private sector had been drastically reduced to a relatively insignificant position, the transition to socialism would be completed. Indeed, Nehru (1958: 101–03) believed in respect of the future of the private sector that 'gradually and ultimately it will fade away'.

Congress Party, State Power, and Socialism

The question arises as to how Nehru was able to prevail in having his plan in respect of heavy industries and the public sector accepted. For, prior to independence, even though Nehru had succeeded in converting a considerable part of the urban intelligentsia to socialism, the Congress Party as such refused to accept socialism as its ideology or programme. The party did not accept socialism even during the half-dozen years or so after independence. The movement towards such acceptance began only after the death of Sardar Patel at the end of 1950. With Patel removed by the intervention of fate, Nehru then started the process of assuming supreme leadership within the party and government. The major event in the political conflict that followed was the ouster in a 'political coup' of Purshottamdas Tandon from the leadership of the Congress Party. Backed by Patel who had for long controlled the party machine, Tandon had earlier been elected as president by an almost evenly divided party split between the followers of Patel and Nehru. Not all those who supported the nominee of the Nehru group necessarily adhered to Nehru's ideology of socialism. Nehru evoked loyalty among the masses and party members, the basis of which extended beyond ideology, for he was a political hero to them more for his record of sacrifice for the nationalist movement and his personal charisma. The election revealed that there was no consensus over Nehru's socialist model in the Congress Party, as has at times been claimed. The consensus was imposed later by Nehru after he had assumed supreme leadership of the Congress Party and consolidated his power in both party and government. Nehru could impose that 'consensus' because he was critically important to the Congress Party in winning power through elections as a result of his great mass appeal. There was thus an implicit bargain between the party and Nehru, the former exchanging the acceptance of socialism as its ideology for the assurance of power through electoral mobilization in the institutional context of a representative system. In the use of his critical position to such powerful effect, Nehru demonstrated the merit of the 'strategic contingencies theory', which refers to 'the way in which particular participants in an organization can dominate, and influence structure, by their indispensability' (Ham and Hill 1984: ch. 4).

Even conceding Nehru's strategic importance politically, it is still a marvel that one man could move an organization in a direction that it had refused to countenance in the past. What facilitated Nehru's converting the Congress Party to his socialist project was the class configuration within the party. That particular class configuration developed as part of the historical evolution of the nationalist movement. That movement had been launched in the last quarter of the nineteenth century by the new middle class of the urban areas, which grew out of the impact of western education. The new middle class was later joined by much larger numbers from the middle and rich peasantry in several waves in the 1920s and 1930s. This class alliance between the middle class and the peasantry, but under the leadership of the middle class, finally succeeded in replacing the colonial power. Michal Kalecki (1976: ch. 4), the Marxist economist from Poland, conceptualized as *'intermediate regime'* precisely such a situation in the less developed countries, where the intermediate strata of the new middle class and the rich and middle peasantry held state power. It is noteworthy that during the course of the nationalist movement, this primary alliance was supplemented by a subsidiary alliance which encompassed a largely passive capitalist class and a relatively small working class. Nonetheless, the newly-installed intermediate regime in India was able to adopt or accommodate polices largely consistent with the interests of the primary class alliance.

Some have held that the intermediate regime results in the state fostering an active and dominant public sector, referred to as state capitalism (Sobhan and Ahmed 1980: 8–9). Such is not necessarily the case. As seen earlier, the Congress Party after independence was divided equally between the Patel and Nehru factions despite some two decades of strenuous missionary effort on the part of Nehru in behalf of socialism. Only the death of Patel enabled Nehru to use the lever of his mass popularity to implement his ideological platform, that too only in part. The structural factor that enabled him to do so was simply that the capitalist class was not in charge of the state. The Indian state was not a state of the bourgeoisie as has often been proclaimed; rather, as the history of the nationalist movement demonstrates, it was an intermediate state. The historically-based exclusion of the capitalist class from state power, even as the existence of that class was tolerated, allowed Nehru to implement his socialist project in relation to the public ownership of the principal means of production.

By the same token, given the nature of state power, Nehru's attempt at building socialism could not but remain incomplete and therefore eventually non-viable. Just as the exclusion of the capitalist class from state power allowed Nehru to act on his ideological platform against the wishes of the capitalist class, the sharing in state power, and indeed the pressure to achieve a dominant position in the coalition, by the rich and middle peasantry prevented Nehru from acting on the rural counterpart to the industrial strategy in his overall socialist programme—agrarian reform and land cooperatives. It is Nehru's failure on agrarian reform and land cooperatives that often results in questioning the very authenticity of his socialist convictions. However, just because one part of the project is thwarted by the particular configuration of power does not make the execution of the other part any less authentic in terms of its ideological origins.

Summary and Conclusions

Two dominant features of the Indian economic strategy launched with the Second Five-Year Plan in the mid-1950s were the thrust for investment goods industries and their inward orientation in a gigantic ISI programme. In the post-war period, whether in Latin America or in Asia, ISI seemed like a natural policy for the less developed areas, and accordingly a substantial economic literature developed in the 1950s and 1960s endorsing that policy. It is quite understandable, therefore, that economic theorists and planners would detect the influence of economic theory in the Indian economic strategy. The endeavour at discovery of the influence of economic theory seems especially attractive since the economic strategy had its proximate origins in a highly sophisticated theoretical argument developed in the Mahalanobis model. Once the Mahalanobis model had been accepted, the strategy for the Second Plan followed as a matter of course. The Mahalanobis model itself both tempts and facilitates the endeavour to establish the influence of economic theory on it, or at least to find the affinity between it and the economic theory of the time, or at the very least to show the influence of the model as economic theory in its own right on the Second Plan's economic strategy.

Particularly important in the discourse has been the assumed commonality between the prevailing economic theory and the presumed underpinning of Indian economic strategy in respect of export pessimism. However, given that it would have assuredly been a strategic assumption for Mahalanobis in forging a model based on a closed economy, it is surprising that export pessimism does not figure in the model. Rather, that model has its own positive aims of long-term development and economic independence in working out an economic strategy for heavy industries and inward orientation. Thus despite the apparent affinity with ISI programmes elsewhere, the Indian model had its own autonomous origins. Just as there can be several different manufacturing processes for the same product, there can also be different origins for similar economic strategies, and these can be consequential for the economy.

Further investigation reveals, however, that the main features of the Mahalanobis model had all been pre-figured in the pre-independence thinking of Nehru, at whose instance the plan-frame and the Mahalanobis model had been prepared. That only serves to confirm the lack of impact of economic theory on the Indian economic strategy, since such theory was a development only of the 1950s. Rather, in Nehru's thinking the key considerations were sound industrial development, economic independence, and political survival of the nation in a power-driven international system. Mahalanobis can be said to have provided an elegant theoretical structure employing the language of economics for goals which not only Nehru but Mahalanobis himself, as well as most members of the intelligentsia, held in common. These goals had emerged not out of economic theory but nationalism, both economic and political. While historically industrialization has often been driven by economic nationalism (Kitching 1982), India's ISI strategy was rather distinctive in that it emphasized basic and heavy industries instead of consumer goods. The inspiration for that, apart from Nehru's admiration for the Soviet model, originated in his understanding of the logic of power in the international system; in that, Nehru's economic strategy was profoundly in accord with political realism.

The two elements in respect of heavy industries and inward-orientation were joined, in Nehru, with a third one of state ownership in a comprehensive ideology dedicated to the achievement of a socialist society through democratic means. Nehru thus endeavoured through his overall economic strategy to build socialism, and not capitalism as is alleged in Marxist interpretations. The reason he could push through his programme in respect of the heavy industry strategy and the public sector is that, apart from a fairly generalized nationalism, the state was in the control not of the capitalist class but of the intermediate strata consisting of the new middle class and the rich and middle peasantry. However, the class alliance in which the peasantry wielded considerable power also prevented Nehru from enacting agrarian reform and land cooperativization, thus eventually crippling his larger socialist project. In the process, the economic strategy was reduced to building autarky and state hegemony over the economy through a vast far-flung public sector (state capitalism) and a regulatory system of rigid controls over a restricted private sector (state commandism), rather than building socialism which Nehru had aimed for.

Any policy once introduced tends to create structures of support for itself and thus to perpetuate itself. In the case of India, the tendency toward policy inertia was reinforced by the particular origins of policy. India's economic strategy under Nehru issued out of ideology: a widely-supported economic nationalism in respect of heavy industries and their inward-orientation, and a somewhat more narrowly-supported socialism in respect of state ownership. The ideological origins of policy favoured a tendency toward persistence in the policy even if it were shown to be less productive. Only crisis could shake the regime out of it.

Notes

1. The important papers of Mahalanobis are available in a single collection: Mahalanobis (1985). For biographic information on Mahalanobis and his place in the history of Indian economic thought, see Byers (1998: 41–50).
2. Indeed, Mahalanobis (1985: 257) later pointed out that 'a model of exactly this type was developed by Feldman in 1928 in the USSR.... The Indian work, however, was done completely independently of Feldman's findings'. That is correct, for the non-Soviet world did not have access to the Feldman model until the late

1950s when Domar (1957) wrote about it. However, it has to be noted that Mahalanobis could not have been unaware of the material consequences of the Feldman model not only in the provisions of the Soviet Five-Year Plans but also in the concrete performance of the Soviet Union.

3. The discussion of this work in the next few paragraphs relies on pp. 1–19; emphasis in the citations has been added.

4. The discussion in the next few paragraphs relies on Jalan (1991: 13, 22–23, 28–29); emphasis in the citations has been added.

5. See also Manmohan Singh (1964: 153, 338), the burden of whose work was that 'India failed to exploit fully even the available opportunities' and that 'domestic factors operating in India also played a part in the stagnation of India's export earnings during the last decade', particularly 'the rising domestic demand and also ... the stringent import restrictions which have been in force since 1957'.

3

Between Mercantilist Socialism and Liberalism: The Changing Fortunes of the Nehru-Mahalanobis Strategy, 1956–90

With the Second Five-Year Plan, the Indian state launched in 1956 on an economic strategy that was breathtaking in its vision, aiming at nothing short of transforming India ultimately into an industrial and socialist society characterized by national self-reliance. Notwithstanding the later modifications, that strategy largely defined the economic course during the turbulent economic history of the three and a half decades that followed its adoption. The present chapter traces the changing fortunes of the strategy over the subsequent several decades until its formal overthrow in the early 1990s. The discussion is divided into three parts: (1) an analysis of the strategy's consistency with the requirements of the political system and those of the international economic system of which India was an integral part; (2) an inquiry into the pressures for change to move away from, to return to and then again move away from the strategy as revealed in a series of reform episodes during crisis situations; and (3) an examination of the brief attempt at liberalization in the absence of crisis. The second part forms the bulk of the discussion.

Economic Strategy, Political System and World Economy

The two features of the economic strategy of the Second Five-Year Plan (1956–61) in terms of the inward-oriented heavy industry strategy and the 'commanding heights' of the economy in the hands of the state reflected Nehru's deep commitment to nationalism and socialism, which represented two of the three key pillars of his ideological system. The economic strategy itself plus the ambitious scale on which it was undertaken were, however, at odds with the third pillar of Nehru's ideological system—democracy—which, because of him and other stalwarts of the nationalist movement, was embedded in India's institutional structure. Since a democratic system is based on consent rather than coercion, its political and economic goals normally emerge, in the fashion of the market place, out of conflict and bargaining among many groups with different aims; they tend to correspond more closely to the capacity of the system as well as to the demands of the important groups. In such a system, the political leadership must on the one hand assure accumulation, but on the other it must also maintain legitimacy. The leadership has far less tactical flexibility than in authoritarian or totalitarian systems, for it has to take into account the interests of key groups. Economic or other change can proceed only at a rate that is acceptable to such groups. Accordingly, economic policies tend to, and need to, be moderate and realistic, favouring investments in short-term projects with a high rate of return and realizable within the limits of available resources; if not, electoral reprisal can follow for the leadership. In the absence of windfalls, such as oil or gold, capital investment takes place at a lower rate than in non-democratic systems, because of 'one practical limitation inherent in the situation; a high rate of forced savings is politically impossible' (Apter 1966: 398). Economic growth at a rapid rate is not impossible, but it requires 'extensive self-discipline, popular participation, and great civic devotion. These preconditions occur only very rarely in new nations' (Apter 1963: 150). Indeed, the system's survival depends upon its effectiveness in providing adequate gratifications to its members and avoidance of the imposition of deprivations except in the context of crisis or war.

In the perspective of these built-in requirements of economic policy in a democracy, it would seem that there was an *incongruence* between the Second Plan and India's political system of democracy. It was so in the following respects: First, the Plan was an extremely ambitious goal-determined rather than a resource-based plan, imposing 'forced savings' on the community. As the planners stated it: 'The results which the Second Plan promises are impressive, but correspondingly large is the effort that it calls forth by way of mobilization and application of real and financial resources' (GOI 1956: 28). They envisaged relying on heavy deficit financing and doubling of tax mobilization; this implied new burdens on the public, especially in the form of inflation, and by extension considerable political risks for the political leadership. Second, the emphasis on heavy industries meant the postponement of immediate 'pay-offs' or 'gratifications', because of the long gestation associated with such industries. Besides, the high capital intensity of the strategy could hardly have been expected to solve the already difficult unemployment situation. Third, corresponding to the heavy concentration on industry there was reduced emphasis on agriculture. The low priority for agriculture was tantamount to taking risks in the area of basic necessities for the masses, most directly food and agriculture-based consumption goods. Fourth, with the Second Plan the government assumed formidable burdens and tasks in relation to the public sector and cottage industries that were beyond its skills and organizational resources, given the largely 'law and order' orientation of the inherited bureaucracy.

There was thus a basic contradiction between the economic strategy and the political system. The two were strongly in tension. The economic strategy consequently contained the potential for economic crises of one type or another, which could threaten not only to stop the execution of the strategy in its tracks but also to place the democratic framework under severe strain as the crises worked their way through the political system. By the same token, the political consequences could also have the potential to put at risk the prospects for continuing with the strategy. As a result of the economic and political crises, there would likely be pressure to change either the strategy to another strategy more appropriate for the democratic system or to change the democratic system to correspond with the economic strategy.

To indulge thus in referring four and a half decades later to potential crises as being built into the Second Plan is, of course, to take advantage of hindsight, but it is not entirely so. There were critics present at the very formulation of the Second Plan who sharply underlined such consequences. The harshest among them was the economist B.R. Shenoy (1962: 15–26), who in a vigorous note of dissent to the memorandum of the Panel of Economists warned of the risks involved in the economic strategy. Describing the strategy as 'over-ambitious', he strongly opposed deficit-financing in the magnitude that it had been suggested and asked that the Plan should fit the resources available. In a remarkably prescient passage, Shenoy underscored the basic incompatibility between the economic strategy incorporated in the plan-frame and India's political framework and pointed to the possible socially dangerous consequences:

> To force a pace of development in excess of the capacity of the available resources must necessarily involve uncontrolled inflation. In a democratic community where the masses of people live close to the margin of subsistence, uncontrolled inflation may prove to be explosive and might undermine the existing order of society. In such a background one cannot subsidize communism better than through inflationary deficit financing.... Alternatively, if appropriate 'physical measures', familiar to a communist economy, were adopted (in an effort to prevent inflation) we would be writing off, gradually or rapidly, depending upon the exigencies of the Plan, individual liberty and democratic institutions by administrative or legislative action.

Two other economists, C.N. Vakil and P.R. Brahmananda (1962: 114–19), warned of the consequences of the relative neglect of agriculture. Without growth in the agricultural sector, they stressed, investment in industrial expansion will only lead to excess capacity, and cogently argued against following the Soviet model in the entirely different economic conditions of India. The criticisms by Shenoy, Vakil and Brahmananda were picked up by some political leaders, but the votaries of the heavy industry strategy carried the day because the bulk of the economists and political leaders supported it.

If the Second Plan was incongruent with India's democratic structure because of the nature of the industrial strategy adopted and the ambitious scale on which it was envisaged, it was also problematic in its relationship to the international economic system. The heavy industry strategy itself was rationalized as being based on the considerable consensus among economists over export pessimism. The argument had more of a post facto character, since the real aim was economic independence from the world capitalist system. However, it contained an element of self-fulfilling prophecy, for if India assumed that it could not increase exports, because of the limited world demand for its goods, then it necessarily needed to set up its own investment goods industries. In turn, the establishment of these industries required the further throwing up of a mercantilistic wall of protection around India.

But how were the capital goods necessary for establishing the new investment goods industries to be paid for in the first place? Of course, some of the earnings of existing exports could be utilized for the purpose since, with import substitution, some consumer goods would now be produced at home, while additionally some foreign aid would be forthcoming. Still, the ambitious scale of the industrialization effort would surely precipitate a balance of payments crisis once the substantial sterling balances accumulated during the war were exhausted. To avert such a crisis, an expanded effort at exports would be necessary and—unlike Mahalanobis who had neglected the question of balance of payments altogether by assuming a closed economy—the framers of the Second Plan were eager to expand exports by all possible means. Notwithstanding this practical recognition of the necessity of export promotion, the basic economic strategy transformed the problem into a structural one in so far as it, through its mercantilist wall, both oriented producers to the domestic market and impeded exports through the creation of a high-cost economy and thus currency overvaluation, which meant pricing Indian goods out of world markets. The likely resulting balance of payments crisis could pose serious risks because, while the aim of the planners was to create an autarkic economy, the contemporaneous Indian economy was integrated into the world capitalist system, not only for capital goods but also for food and oil, indeed at the time it was simply an appendage of that system. The paradoxical result of such crises could be that, notwithstanding the admirable aim of economic independence, India would be driven into greater dependence on foreign countries for food and aid.

If the Second Five-Year Plan was inconsistent with India's political system and harboured potential risks in relation to both the domestic economy and world economy, how is it that such a strategy came to be adopted in the first place? More importantly, if the strategy was prone to crises, how is it that the strategy in its fundamental aspect of inward orientation was sustained over some three and a half decades? What explains the maintenance of the strategy over such a long period of time? The first question is of more immediate relevance, for policy once adopted has some staying power from sheer inertia and additionally from the creation of pillars of support once it has come into operation.

The adoption of an economic policy or economic strategy as a bundle of such policies is fundamentally a political proposition and not a mere technical undertaking, and reflects the balance of political and social forces in society. At the broadest level, the making of policy can be conceptualized as being a function of three variables: the state, society and international system. A proposition pitched at this level of comprehensiveness has, of course, the shortcoming of being true by definition since almost nothing remains excluded. However, the determination of priority among the three variables alone is an important point for inquiry, at least to begin with. A priori, in so far as policy-making is legally its prerogative, the state is central to the enactment of policy while the other two variables constitute its environment, providing not only the challenges and the targets for policy-making but also the resources for policy-implementation. The three variables do not stand for unitary concepts, however; rather, they are summary terms which encompass many constituent elements even though no consensus exists as to precisely what these elements are. For present purposes, important among the elements of the state are the executive leadership and the governing coalition, particularly their interests and ideological preferences, and the nature and capacity of the institutional structure. While the emphasis on governing coalitions in the social science literature tends to underplay the importance of individual leaders, the latter would seem to have an inherent importance not only in situations of charismatic authority, but also where governing coalitions are equally balanced. In respect of society, interest groups and political culture are of relevance, whether interest groups are understood in terms of production (land, labour, and capital), or economic sectors (industry, trade, and agriculture). At the level of the international system, the important elements are other states, multilateral institutions, business cycles and shocks, but also reigning and contending economic ideologies. This bare outline of a framework for analysis of policy essentially repeats the conventional wisdom on the importance in policy of 'ideas, interests and institutions'.

In the light of this perspective, the brief explanation for the incongruence between India's economic strategy and its democratic system is that India's democracy was in the mid-1950s an unusual one, in the sense that it had just been installed from the top, not one that had been worked for long from the bottom up, and was therefore more formal than substantive in nature. The same political leadership that had installed democracy also instituted the economic strategy from the top. The political leadership had succeeded to power as a result of its long struggle against colonialism under the aegis of the Congress Party. The core value of the anti-colonial struggle unsurprisingly was nationalism, not simply political but also economic. Even though originating with Jawaharlal Nehru, the heavy industry strategy, with its promise of economic independence, was therefore naturally attractive to the political leadership as a whole, by and large.

The additional acceptance by this leadership of socialism was, however, a consequence of a tacit political bargain with Nehru, who emerged as the dominant leader without any significant rival in party and government after the death of the conservative and business-friendly leader, Sardar Patel. Nehru was critical to the electoral prospects of the Congress Party, once democracy with universal franchise had been installed. In the circumstance, the rather conservative Congress Party exchanged the acceptance of Nehru's socialism for the assurance of political power at the polls. The Congress acceptance of socialism as the vision of the future society as well as the present path to development was greatly facilitated by the particular 'intermediate regime' coalition that it had mobilized during the nationalist movement. Ideology, in terms of both nationalism and socialism, was thus crucial to the adoption of the strategy, as was also the structural context in terms of both democracy and political coalition. Additionally, at the beginning, the level of social mobilization was low, understandable because of the poor economic and social infrastructure. The unusual situation of the newness of democracy with a charismatic leader at the top thus provided the state and its leadership with substantial autonomy and allowed it to proceed with the heavy industry strategy even if it was incongruent with the requirements of democracy. However, the interaction between the requirements of economic strategy, on the one hand, and the requirements of democracy and the international system, on the other, would change the balance of social and political forces, and would in turn have an impact on the balance between economic nationalism and economic globalization.

The Crises and Policy Change

The Foreign Exchange Crisis, 1957–58

The Second Five-Year Plan was beset with problems from the very beginning. The key culprit was the lack of resources, not least on the foreign exchange front. Despite new tax measures soon after the plan's inauguration, resources proved insufficient. The planners hurriedly sought to save the plan by restricting investment to a 'core' plan, consisting primarily of its heavy industry component. Even as food shortages developed and inflationary tendencies set in, the increased imports of capital goods in line with the plan's thrust at industrialization rapidly depleted foreign exchange reserves. Six months into the plan, the finance minister warned that 'this rate of drawal cannot be sustained for any length of time' (GOI 1996, I: 252). In response, the government clamped down on imports by strengthening its machinery of import licensing and by limiting imports of capital goods to 'core' projects. It also obtained substantial loans from the IMF. Despite these measures, the balance of payments situation exploded into a crisis as foreign exchange reserves fell precipitously, standing at a mere Rs 1,780 million (Hanson 1966: 161). The situation that faced the planners was therefore grim and the future of the Second Plan was at grave risk.

In this situation of crisis, the World Bank called a special meeting of India's major aid donors in Paris, which pledged additional assistance of $360 million and thus relieved the immediate crisis. Besides, the US signed two agreements to provide foodgrains under PL480 in the value of Rs 1,400 million. The first three years of the Second Plan had been of strain and crisis, but in the final analysis the Plan was rescued by external aid, which over the five-year period added up to Rs 10,900 million, much more than the optimistically assumed sum of Rs 8,000 million. As Barbara Ward remarked, the plan had been 'bailed out from crisis to crisis'. Notwithstanding the additional assistance, there was still a substantial shortfall in investment targets; in real terms, the plan outlay amounted to Rs 37,000 million rather than Rs 48,000 million that had been originally envisaged (Hanson 1966: 162, 170).

The crisis and its management had been an elite affair; it did not involve any mass mobilization, either from above to augment resources or from below to protest the deprivations imposed. The key actors involved in actual fact were foreign states and international agencies. In this instance, they acted to save a plan that had as its aim economic independence from those very actors. But for their help, the planners may have had to do more radical thinking about the very viability of the economic strategy and their approach to economic policy. Although the foreign powers came to the rescue of the plan, the event initiated a psychology of dependence where the Indians came to look to outside agents for help in the solution of their problems. That is ironic since the aim of the plan was to secure the economic independence of India. Nehru, who is justifiably acclaimed as the visionary who launched India on a course to assure economic independence, must surely also share the blame for this turn to dependence. On this occasion, the intervention of the foreign powers was benign in so far as it saved the plan, but in other circumstances it may not fit Indian aims or interests. The Indians were to discover that soon enough.

Partial Liberalization under Domestic and Foreign Pressures, 1964–69

In the mid-1960s, India entered into the throes of a major economic crisis and went through convulsions over economic policy, with the period marked by considerable intervention by foreign actors in its policy-making and by drastic economic retrenchment which generated a long period of industrial stagnation.[1] One stance on a possible explanation for the serious crisis, and the consequent retrenchment and stagnation, was that nothing was inherently wrong with India's basic economic strategy, only that India encountered severe exogenous shocks by way of two wars, two unprecedented droughts, and two political successions that understandably made for considerable political uncertainty. However, others tended to demur and held the basic economic strategy to be at fault. Writing around 1964, when only one war, that with China in 1962, had taken place, Hanson (1966: 220, 231) confidently asserted that the Third Plan was already in trouble. Noting that the assessment of the planners themselves 'shows, beyond all possible doubt, that the plan is in a critical condition', he remarked that, while the defence budget had undoubtedly been doubled, 'the increase in defence expenditure has done no more than intensify certain problems which had already become painfully evident by the summer of 1962'. He concluded that 'the plan is indeed in a critical condition ... the crisis of the Third Plan is deeper than that of the Second'.

At the root of the crisis was the inability of agriculture to deliver sufficient supplies of food for a rapidly growing population as also the inadequacy of resources to fund India's ambitious heavy industry strategy. These two elements now resulted in dependence on foreign powers for food and finance. Notwithstanding the problems that the Second Plan had encountered, the Indian planners had continued with the same economic strategy in the Third Five-Year Plan (1961–66). Still, having been framed in the context of a food crisis, the Third Plan had upgraded agriculture to a higher degree of priority with the aim of achieving food self-sufficiency; agriculture was allocated 14 per cent of the plan outlay as against 11.8 per cent in the Second Plan, so as to double the rate of growth in agriculture. This did not, however, mean any diminution of the priority for industry, for the sector of industry and minerals was allocated 20 per cent of the outlay as against 18.5 per cent in the Second Plan. At the same time, the Third Plan further elevated the role of the public sector, both practically and ideologically. With the public sector now set to play an 'even more dominant' role in economic development, it was expected 'to grow both absolutely and in comparison and at a faster rate than the private sector'. The end purpose of assigning this enhanced role to the public sector was the achievement of a socialist society: 'In an underdeveloped country, a high rate of economic progress and the development of a large public sector and a cooperative sector are among the principal means for effecting the *transition towards socialism*' (GOI 1961: 7, 10, 50; emphasis added). As with the Second Plan, the ambitious nature of the Third Plan resulted in placing considerable reliance on foreign aid for investment resources; indeed, foreign aid constituted the largest single item among the resources required for the plan (Hanson 1966: 212–15).

The Third Plan had promised an annual rate of growth of over 5 per cent; in the event, the economy grew at the rate of only 2.4 per cent, with the result that per capita incomes remained stagnant. However, the greatest failure was on the food front, with agriculture again proving to be the Achilles' heel of the economy. The Third Plan failed to achieve its aim of achieving food self-sufficiency, and as a result India became pathetically dependent on the US for food;

in turn, the US subjected India to what was perceived as national humiliation through its deliberate 'short tether' policy of releasing food supplies in small amounts. In four out of the five years of the Third Plan, foodgrain output was below, and in two of those years substantially below, the level reached at the end of the Second Plan. The fourth year of the Third Plan had seen a big jump to 78.2 million tonnes (MT) in foodgrain production, but more crucially the final year witnessed a disastrous fall to 63.3 MT following an unprecedented drought, a situation which was repeated the next year with production at 65.0 MT (GOI 1997: S-25).

The resulting situation of critical food shortages aggravated the inflationary situation springing from other sources, including deficit financing which was more than twice the amount planned for the five-year period; the consumer price index climbed from 100 in 1960 to 184 in 1966 and 209 in 1967. Food protests and riots broke out, while opposition parties launched massive shutdowns of the economy; in this fashion, the masses became involved in the fate of planning. All this took place despite huge food imports on an escalating scale during the five years of the Third Plan—3.6 MT, 4.5 MT, 6.2 MT, 7.4 MT and 10.3 MT—with imports in the final year reaching an all-time high, while another 8.7 MT was imported the following year. India, particularly its urban population, was simply at the mercy of the US for food and thus survival. That industry, particularly heavy industry, grew at a rapid pace—the index for industrial production having climbed from 100 in 1960 to 153 in 1965—was not of much help in feeding the population. India's economic strategy came under question now, particularly since the 1962 elections had brought into parliamentary prominence opposition parties, especially the free enterprise oriented Swatantra Party, that were opposed to it; earlier, by contrast, the Communist Party of India (CPI), which favoured the heavy industry strategy in an even more aggressive form, had dominated the opposition benches. The agony of the masses, resulting from food shortages and inflation, eroded support for the ruling party. Already reeling under the impact of the reverses in the India-China war in 1962, the Congress Party was further weakened politically by losses in three key by-election contests in 1963.

At the end of the Second Plan, Nehru had believed that its economic strategy was basically sound, and he blamed faulty implementation for the inadequate results. Apparently, he continued to believe the same. Consequently, in the midst of the crisis that dogged the Third Plan, Nehru approved the initial proposals for the Fourth Five-Year Plan (1966–71) that were designed to carry forward the economic strategy embodied in the Second and Third Plans. Further, to protect the economic strategy politically in the future, he responded to the attacks on it by seeking to change the balance of power within the government by forcing the resignation of several key conservative ministers and by obtaining a reaffirmation of his socialist policies from a party that was now divided on the central issues. The reaffirmation came at the annual session of the Congress Party at Bhubhaneshwar in January 1964, five months before Nehru's death; the resolution on 'Democracy and Socialism' constituted Nehru's last political testament. However, the strategy was soon crippled by a combination of forces from both inside and outside the country.

Nehru died in May 1964, and was succeeded by Lal Bahadur Shastri. In the economic turmoil of the mid-1960s, the consensus that Nehru had fostered on India's economic strategy broke down, the economic team underwent change and became divided, and the policy process fragmented into two opposed tendencies. On one side were ranged those who wanted to persist with the earlier economic strategy; to overcome the obstacles it faced, they wanted structural change in the agrarian economy, stricter controls over business and trade, and a greater role for the state in foodgrains procurement and distribution. These supporters were primarily lodged in the left wing of the Congress Party, in the Planning Commission which Nehru had institutionalized as the custodian of his vision of state planning and economic strategy, and in the two communist parties following the split of the CPI in 1964.

On the other side were those who, for practical rather than ideological reasons, thought that in the changed circumstances India should shift to a new set of policies that emphasized: priority for agriculture, economic liberalization through relaxation of licensing and economic controls, employment of economic incentives rather than state controls for advancing food production, and reliance on market forces rather than state ownership in view of the weak capacity of the state. Shastri himself was more a pragmatic leader than a grand visionary in the mould of Nehru. While committed to Nehru's socialism out of loyalty to his political mentor and also sensitive to the importance of heavy industry for self-reliance, Shastri was nonetheless in his understanding of socialism more oriented to the needs of the common man in terms of food and consumer goods. The second group crystallized into a small team of technocratic advisers on whom Shastri relied for advice; the team was, in part, located in the Prime Minister's Office that Shastri had created after becoming prime minister. The views of this team had support, especially in relation to agriculture, among the state chief ministers, who—having assumed greater importance in Indian politics in the post-Nehru era—were wary of schemes that would affect adversely the interests of the rich and middle farmers or make demands on the resources of the states. The team's views were also in accord with the articulated demands of business; the business community had become highly disaffected with the state policy of controls on the private sector and the relentless expansion of the public sector, and it was now quite assertive in its criticism.

Faced with popular protests and agitations over food shortages and fearing a general breakdown of the social order, the government had perforce to rely on concessional food imports from the US over the near-term future notwithstanding the attacks of its radical opponents about dependence on the US. For the long term, Shastri's new and dynamic agriculture minister, C. Subramaniam, decided, with the support of American advisors and the approval of US agencies, on adopting what came to be known as the Green Revolution strategy. That strategy focused on reliance for agricultural growth on the better-off farmers, adoption of modern technology, and market incentives through support prices. As against his vocal critics, Subramaniam claimed that the new strategy was the answer to India's long-term food problem and that it was consistent with India's interests. Even though the policy change in India's agriculture had been firmly made by the end of 1965, President Johnson persisted with his 'short-tether' policy during the mid-1960s. The public rationale for his policy was to force India to undertake effective measures to ensure adequate food production. While perhaps the pressure may have been necessary at the beginning, it continued to be applied, even as the architects of the programme in India who had fought for policy change cautioned US policy-makers that the American stance was counter-productive and only served to threaten the programme's viability by undercutting its legitimacy. As a *New York Times* editorial noted: 'If India were seriously delinquent in self-help measures, there might be an argument for a squeeze at a more propitious time. But an inter-agency memorandum in October 1966, a special task force in November and a Congressional visit in December have all indicated that India's programme is generally satisfactory' (cited in Bowles 1971: 530).

However, high politics, particularly India's critical view of US intervention in Vietnam, was implicated in the US policy on food. That India experienced national humiliation at the treatment to which it was subjected as if it were an American colony should not be seen as an exaggerated reaction of a hypersensitive nation, for the US ambassador to India at the time (Bowles 1971: 534–35) stated in his private diary: 'It is a cruel performance. The Indians must conform; they must be made to fawn; their pride must be cracked'. Subsequently, he noted: 'The United States was more interested in gaining a political advantage or forcing a change in India's foreign policy than in helping fellow beings who were in desperate need of help'. It is in the light of this experience of national humiliation that Indira Gandhi determined at the time never again to be put in that position.

Agricultural policy was not the only one under pressure for change, rather the entire economic strategy was at issue. As witnessed in the approval of the initial proposals for the Fourth Plan and in the Bhuvaneshwar resolution, Nehru and his associates had been committed to carrying out to the end the economic strategy with its focus on heavy industry and public sector, for in their eyes India's prospects of self-sustaining growth towards a socialist and autonomous society were tied up with it. However, the major obstacle to continuing with the strategy was the inadequacy of resources within the constraints of a democratic system. Therefore, it was accepted that reliance had, for a short period of 10 to 15 years, to be placed on aid from foreign powers. As work advanced on formulating the Fourth Plan, Indian planners envisaged an annual aid package of $1.7 billion over the five years of the plan compared to the $1.1 billion during the Third Plan (Frankel 1978: 269, 284). This sum was a lot more than the foreign powers were willing to oblige India with. More importantly, they wanted India to make drastic changes in policy, which they felt necessary for making effective use of the resources.

A World Bank mission, headed by Bernard Bell, visited India in late 1964 to examine the requirements of the Fourth Plan. The Bank had never been enamoured of India's economic strategy, considering it overambitious and overly oriented to the public sector, but it now found the changes in the top leadership and the country's desperate situation in respect of food and resources to be propitious for recommending major shifts in policy, which taken together 'represented a fundamental departure from basic principles of planning laid down by Nehru and followed by the Planning Commission' (Frankel 1978: 271). The World Bank endorsed the new agricultural policy—which it favoured as against agrarian reform or cooperatives—but additionally recommended not only liberalization in respect of discretionary controls and imports as also reliance on private domestic and foreign investment, but also devaluation of the rupee. In return for the adoption of these policies, the Bank promised to support an annual aid package of $1.5 billion during the Fourth Plan (ibid.).

Taking these recommendations to be largely in accord with its own inclinations, Shastri's economic team was receptive to the Bank's advice. However, there was conflict within the administration over the issue of devaluation:

> Some objections grew out of immediate and relatively narrow concerns over the impact of such a step on the Congress party's chances at the forthcoming election. Others reflected more general political resentment at foreign pressure on a matter considered integral to the independence of the nation. There was finally, an emotional resistance to the step, as a confession of failure of the previous ten years of economic policy (Frankel 1978: 272).

More importantly, the confession of failure would relate not just to economic policy but also to ideology with which the policy was invested. That made devaluation harder to accept. Before the issue could be settled, war with Pakistan occurred in the second half of 1965. Even though the war had been initiated by Pakistan, the US suspended aid to both countries. The American action worsened India's already dire economic situation by generating an import compression and forcing down capacity utilization in industry. After the war, resumption of aid therefore became an urgent priority for India. Shastri, who had emerged as a political hero on account of his determined leadership during the war, showed his readiness to proceed with devaluation by first easing out of the cabinet its chief opponent, Finance Minister T.T. Krishnamachari. However, fate intervened; with the death of Shastri in January 1966, the issue was passed on to Indira Gandhi who succeeded him as prime minister.

Inexperienced, rather uncertain about the party's 'old guard' allowing her to continue in office in the future, and inheriting the economic team from the Shastri administration, Mrs Gandhi largely proceeded on the path already charted out in favour of economic liberalization and devaluation. The consideration that loomed large on the horizon as India entered the final stages of formulating a still ambitious Fourth Plan was India's dependence on the US for aid. However, resumption of aid hinged on India's acceptance of devaluation. India's planning chief Asoka Mehta visited the US and laid out the Fourth Plan proposals before President Lyndon Johnson and World Bank President George Woods, revealing a deep dependency on one side and a highly intrusive penetration in India's decision-making process on the other. The US and World Bank provided oral assurances of aid subject to a prior declaration on devaluation. There was last-minute hesitation on India's part, but the compulsions of aid dependency made it finally take the plunge and it announced on 6 June 1966 the devaluation of the Indian rupee by 58 per cent from Rs 4.75 to Rs 7.50 for the US dollar.

Serious political repercussions were to follow from devaluation, but for now it constituted a major policy watershed. Devaluation, however, failed to save the Fourth Plan. For one thing, the summer of devaluation also saw the repetition of the unprecedented drought of the previous year and turned the government's attention to famine prevention rather than planning for the future. Second, the promised foreign aid to the tune of $1.2 billion did not materialize (Frankel 1978: 298); instead only some $900 million was received, a considerable part of which would have to go to debt servicing. What is more, aid fell drastically in the subsequent three years. As a consequence, India could not risk the additional liberalization measures that were necessary as a follow-up to devaluation. Third, short of resources and fearing drought-induced inflation, the government took to a severe dose of fiscal retrenchment, the consequence of which was a long-lasting industrial recession. Fourth, the political uproar over devaluation, which was seen as a surrender to foreign powers, weakened and split the political leadership. Fifth, popular alienation on account of the hardships endured by the people because of food shortages and inflation, as well as dissatisfaction with the turn in economic policy, resulted in heavy losses for the Congress Party in the 1967 elections, particularly in the states. In the midst of these developments, planning was reduced to a shambles; the formulation of the Fourth Plan was not concluded, the plan was in effect simply abandoned, and the thread of long-term planning was not picked up until several years later.

While devaluation was not supplemented by any significant liberalization in sectors other than agriculture, some minor movement took place in that direction. Several committees had during the 1960s underlined the weaknesses of the licensing system in the industrial arena even as they remained reluctant to recommend substantive deregulation. India's licensing system was so strict as to make it a crime to increase capacity beyond that specifically approved by the licensing authorities (Wadhva 1994: 36). In view of the growth-retarding impact of the licensing system, there was some concession to liberalization on the part of the government, but only the most minimal. In mid-1965, the government exempted 42 agriculture-related industries from licensing. In October 1966, it allowed industrial units to increase output by 25 per cent, provided the expansion involved no new expenditure of foreign exchange, no installation of additional plant and machinery, and no competition with industries reserved for the small-scale sector (GOI 1967: 15–17). In this manner, India's industrial licensing regime remained largely unaffected by liberalization during the period of change in economic policy in the mid-1960s.

Devaluation notwithstanding, the drive for liberalization failed to make much impact on India's larger mercantilistic system. The change in agricultural policy—while it made for reliance on the market and incentives, and was therefore unpalatable to those who favoured socialism—could not really be said to have run against the autarkic design of Indian planning. Quite the contrary, with its intention to make India self-sufficient in food it could be considered an essential but neglected counterpart to the mercantilism of the industrial arena. Nonetheless, by strengthening the better-off farmers, the new agricultural policy effectively removed any possibility, if there ever was any, of the socialist transformation of agriculture. That is what made the change in agricultural policy so controversial. However, its underlying inspiration was nationalistic and, because the new agricultural strategy came to successfully serve nationalist purpose, its acceptance was enduring.

However, devaluation failed to generate a larger liberalization process because of its foreign authorship. The questioning of Nehru's economic strategy no doubt existed within India as well, at even the highest levels, and with the entry of the Swatantra Party criticism had become quite vocal. Yet, India could not genuinely claim ownership of the liberalization programme. Instead, western powers were recognized as the authors of the programme in view of their highly intrusive participation in India's economic decision-making. The foreign authorship of the programme had the potential to doom whatever liberalization did take place during the period. It could be argued that western powers had always been hostile to India's economic strategy because of the national autonomy it would foster and make India less vulnerable to outside economic and political pressures. However, on strictly commercial grounds alone it cannot be argued that outside powers should not, when providing loans for India's development, lay down conditionalities—in the fashion of a collateral—to ensure that they will be able to recover their loans, especially since India's strategy was not delivering the goods even according to the Indian government's own assessment. Further, on grounds of realpolitik, it cannot be argued that it is any business of foreign powers to assist India in building up the basis of national autonomy; quite the contrary, one must assume that their purpose would be precisely to make others dependent. Indeed, the Indians cannot be accused of being unaware of this aspect, for their own strategy had as its underlying motivation precisely the intention to escape from the situation of vulnerability and dependence.

This line of argument also suggests a rejoinder, though a somewhat unexpected one, to those critics who would claim that an alternative outward-oriented export-based economic strategy would have been more beneficial to India. To a certain extent, that is true. But, it would be fair to assume, that ultimately, such a strategy would also have run into serious obstacles if it were limited to economics alone. Suppose—in a counterfactual mode of argument—India had adopted all the requirements of an export-oriented industrialization strategy and relied for its exports on the markets of the US and other states within its orbit, would the US have found such a situation tolerable while India continued to stick to its foreign policy of non-alignment? Would not that strategy then have faced serious blocks from the US unless India was willing to change its entire set of state policies? This counterfactual line of inquiry thus takes us to the basic point that economics and politics are fundamentally integrated in the actual world. India's desire to escape from the situation of lack of economic and political autonomy, which it inherited from colonialism, through its economic strategy was thus perfectly matched by the posture of the US, quite becoming of a hegemonic global power, to keep others dependent on it. However, while its economic strategy may have been ideally appropriate from the perspective of its deeper project of advancing national autonomy, India was unrealistic in expecting aid from others to rescue the strategy; true, superpower competition in a bipolar system may yield some foreign aid, but that is based on the calculation of interest by foreign actors, not because of some inherent cooperative instincts.

India was also admittedly constrained by its adopted political framework from taking recourse to more radical measures at home required by the strategy. The domestic constraints had become more salient with the effective entry of the masses into the political arena during the 1960s, as witnessed in the food riots and agitations and in the popular reprisals inflicted on the Congress Party in the elections. Social mobilization had advanced substantially compared to that of the earlier years during which India's distinctive economic strategy was initially formulated. Societal actors—whether in the shape of the farm lobby, business groups, mobs, or even chief ministers—had become more active, reducing the earlier autonomy of the state, not only in relation to society but ultimately also to the international system. The immediate pressures for reform may have originated with the western powers, but the proximate cause was the unacceptability of the contemporaneous economic situation to Indian society. The remote cause, however, was the particular combination of the economic strategy and the political framework, for it brought on in the final analysis both the economic crises in terms of shortages of food and consumer goods and the dependence on foreign powers for resources.

The Radical Revolt Against Liberalization, 1969–73

The practical necessity for the government to cope with the immediate crisis of food shortages and inflation, the tacit recognition that the crisis itself had arisen out of the economic strategy pursued during the Second and Third Plans, and the weak capacity of the state to undertake agrarian reform to spur food production or to mobilize resources for ambitious planning, had made the state dependent on foreign aid. The price for that aid had been a change in economic strategy in the direction of emphasis on agriculture, reorientation of agricultural strategy, currency devaluation, greater openness to the domestic and foreign private sector, and a general reliance on the market rather than the state. However, apart from the change in policy regarding agriculture which became an integral part of the economic scene and the devaluation which had the character of an accomplished fact, other parts of liberalization soon fell victim to a radical shift in policy that not only restored but intensified the economic domination of the state as against the market. This radical shift did not take place through reasoned intellectual debate under the auspices of the Planning Commission, as had been the case with the Second and Third Plans, but in the vortex of politics, electoral reprisals, and political struggles.

The left tendency that supported the Nehru legacy and wanted it pushed further forward had not been overwhelmed by the forces that favoured liberalization, it was only eclipsed for some time. Devaluation was a watershed event and it detonated powerful reactions. As prices rose sharply in the wake of the devaluation, criticism mounted against the government, both within the Congress Party and the country. Demands rose for the resignation of the government, with the communists leading a massive march on Parliament. With the slogans of Bombay Bandh and Bharat Bandh, the communists also organized strikes to shut down India's economy. To mollify the left, Prime Minister Gandhi made some placatory gestures by emphasizing the anti-imperialist aspect of non-alignment and by sticking to an ambitious Fourth Five-Year Plan. In cooperation with the left group, she was able to assure a left-of-centre election manifesto which demanded the securing of 'the commanding heights' of the economy by the public sector and the placing of the banking system under 'social control'.

The Congress Party went into the elections in February 1967, however, in an enormously hostile political environment. The preceding year had been one of particularly acute economic distress as a consequence of the second successive severe drought, the devaluation, and economic recession; besides the physical shortages of food and consumer goods—with the rationing system breaking down—the incessant inflation hit the public hard. The resulting anti-Congress environment made for open divisions within the party, with many groups seceding. In its first elections after the death of Nehru, the Congress Party, even though returning to power at the centre, met with an electoral disaster which put an effective end to the one-party-dominant system characteristic of the Indian polity. Many of the top leaders of the Congress Party were defeated. The party was ousted from power in eight states, while at the centre its majority was reduced from 361 to 283, even as it now faced a more self-confident and increasingly obstreperous opposition. The Congress Party's electoral disaster in 1967 led to an internecine conflict within the party which finally eventuated in a split in 1969, about two and a half years after the elections. The same period saw a radical thrust imparted to government policy, which was manifest in (1) a reversal of the trend of economic liberalization, managed through the adoption of restrictive legislation in relation to the private corporate sector, and (2) a lurch to nationalization, most dramatically in banking. These radical measures were not always the result of calm and deliberate inquiry; rather, they were pushed through in the heat of factional and party conflict, indeed of brinkmanship. However, the radical thrust was a consequence not of any single factor, but of a political conjuncture of several elements.

Foremost among these elements was the insistent pressure on the part of the left group in the Congress Party, which identified itself fulsomely with Nehru's goal of a socialist society for India. Organizationally differentiated as the Congress Forum for Socialist Action, the left group had been strengthened in recent years with the entry into the Congress of former socialists and communists. Some of the latter had entered the Congress Party as part of a deliberate infiltration design to achieve socialism through internal pressure. The left group was deeply disturbed by the implications of the liberalization process for the future of socialism; by downgrading the public sector, liberalization seemed to knock down the earlier comfortable assumption that socialism would be achieved as the public sector expanded inexorably. The group was also angered by the direct participation of business in the 1967 elections and the rise of right-wing political parties to preeminence in the opposition. It consequently was desperate to save the socialist project of Nehru and determined to reverse the course of liberalization. The left group therefore launched an attack on large-scale business in the private sector in order to have restrictions placed on its operation, and pressed for increased nationalization. Given its ideological thrust, the left group was bound to run into collision with the conservative 'old guard' in control of the Congress Party. Ideological polarization proceeded apace within the party, with the left group on one side and the 'old guard' on the other.

Mrs Gandhi had ideological affinity with the socialist goals of the left group, but as head of the government she was initially inclined to stand above factions. However, two factors finally impelled her into an open alliance with the left group. First, Mrs Gandhi read the electoral reverses of the Congress Party as sending the message that the party would have no political future unless it worked out a radical programme and offered a party leadership that appealed to the electorate. Mrs Gandhi's larger design for radical change was thus rooted in a strategic calculation that the political mood of the country demanded change in a leftist direction; her perception of the popular will was decisive in generating political change that put her at odds with the conservative leaders constituting the 'old guard'. Second, since the 'old guard' was hostile to her and she was literally on probation, the threat of removal by it constantly hung over her. As the conservative leaders subjected Nehru's economic strategy to attack, particularly in respect of the role of the public sector, the issue was joined in terms of economic nationalism. Mrs Gandhi rose to the defence of the public sector, proclaiming: 'The public sector was conceived as the base of Indian industry so that the country might have more machines, more steel. It also ensured India's freedom. It catered to defence and agricultural needs. To the extent India depended upon imports, its independence was compromised, encroached upon' (Zaidi 1972: 268).

Mrs Gandhi followed up that stand by assuming the leadership of the left group. As the conflict between the two factions escalated and as the conservative faction manoeuvred to sideline Mrs Gandhi, she nationalized the 14 largest banks, a measure which was greeted with popular acclaim. She then went on to precipitate a split in the party, and all but some 60 Congress MPs remained with her; while this placed her government in a minority position, there was no threat to its existence because of the support offered by the CPI and some regional groups. Bank nationalization was, however, only the starting point of a radical shift in economic policy. Other radical measures soon followed. However, the overturning by the judiciary of one of these, that pertaining to the privy purses of the former princes, provoked the calling of new elections in 1971. In these elections, the Grand Alliance of the conservative forces, including the liberal-oriented Swatantra Party, the Hindu nationalist Jana Sangh, and the 'old guard' leading much of the organizational wing that claimed to be the true Congress Party—with abundant support from an alienated business class—mounted a momentous challenge against Mrs Gandhi and her Congress Party and, by extension, against the existing economic strategy and the new radical turn in economic policy. However, the challenge was decisively defeated by Mrs Gandhi who, running on the populist slogan of 'Remove Poverty', confounded most observers by winning a massive electoral mandate, demonstrating in the process that the electorate endorsed her position on economic policy and rejected the more liberal course favoured by the Grand Alliance. Mrs Gandhi's new government then picked up the thread of the earlier radical path with renewed vigour after the elections. From 1969 to 1974, thus, ideology came to reign; over the period, three types of measures stand out: (1) restrictions on big business; (2) constraints on foreign business; and (3) a spate of acts of nationalization.

Two pieces of legislation imposed new restrictions on big business. Accordingly, all business houses, not simply individual firms, with assets of more than Rs 200 million, or controlling one-third of production or distribution of any goods or services, were barred from expansion or diversification except with the prior and specific approval of the government; these restrictions were over and above the usual licensing requirements. The intent was clearly to curb the growth of large industrial houses, which had become politically vocal in recent years. The state now made it a policy to rely on new entrepreneurs for future economic growth, ignoring the warning by big business that the consequence of these and other similar measures to block its growth would be industrial stagnation.

Big business was also the target of a series of committees inquiring into licensing procedures. The Monopolies Inquiry Commission had recognized in 1965 that 'industrial licensing, however necessary from other points of view, has restricted the freedom of entry into industry and so helped to produce concentration' (GOI 1965: 8). In view of the centrality of industrial licensing, the government also asked R.K. Hazari, already renowned as a resolute critic of industrial concentration and big business, to review its working. Hazari in his report of 1967 concluded that large business houses, more particularly the Birla group, had preempted licensable capacity in many industries even as the system deterred new entrants. His recommendations were directed against the large industrial houses, which were sought to be prohibited from entering or expanding in traditional industrial activities (Hazari 1967: 6–9, 25). A heated and acrimonious debate followed in the upper house of Parliament in May 1967, in which there were blistering attacks on big business, especially the Birla house. The government then set up a larger three-man left-oriented Industrial Licensing Policy Inquiry Committee, which in its report of 1969 recommended a more vigorous and expanded role for the public sector, greater restrictions on large industrial houses, and reservation of certain industries exclusively for the small-scale sector. The government accepted these recommendations, and implemented them through a substantial change in industrial licensing policy on 8 February 1970 (GOI 1969: 183–97).

The basic intent of the new licensing policy, which 'entirely reversed the trend' toward economic liberalization inaugurated in the mid-1960s (Frankel 1978: 437), was to restrict the future growth and economic power of the large industrial houses by strengthening the countervailing power of the public sector and of the medium and small-scale sectors. Henceforth, 20 large industrial houses together with their individual firms were to be restricted to core industries (those that were basic, critical and strategic) and to the heavy 'investment' sector (new projects of over Rs 50 million) where these had not already been reserved for the public sector. In order to provide for further government control in regard to such private investment, the new policy accepted the principle of 'joint sector', combining private and public investment. The medium industries, with investments ranging between Rs 10 million and Rs 50 million, were to be open only to entrepreneurs other than the large industrial houses except where efficiency and exports demanded it. The list of industries reserved for the small-scale sector was also enlarged. The new policy, in addition, envisaged a substantial expansion of the scope of the public sector over and above the fields already allocated to it in the Industrial Policy Resolution of 1956 Furthermore, the new policy raised the threat of backdoor nationalization of private industries through empowering the government's finance-lending institutions to convert their loans into equity in the future. A government announcement in July 1970 made the inclusion of a 'convertibility clause' in loan agreements mandatory for loans of over Rs 5 million from public financial institutions and discretionary for loans of less than Rs 5 million. One consequence of this measure was to inhibit the growth of existing industrial enterprises for fear that reliance on assistance from public financial institutions may lead to control passing out of the hands of owners.

The most noteworthy aspect of the radical period from 1969 to 1973 was the thrust for nationalization. Indeed, the period itself had been ushered in by the dramatic act of the nationalization of the 14 largest banks. However, other acts of nationalization soon followed, making the period the grand era of nationalization: (1) general insurance in May 1971; (2) coking coal mines in October 1971; (3) non-coking coal mines in January 1973; (4) Indian Iron and Steel Company in July 1972; (5) the copper industry and refractories in 1972; (6) 46 textile mills in 1972; and (7) the wholesale wheat trade in April 1973. Although Mrs Gandhi and her chosen leftist advisors are often blamed for these ideologically-motivated actions in respect of big business and nationalization, it seems fair to acknowledge that, even though Nehru may not have pushed these particular measures and indeed may have urged caution against hasty action, he and his socialist associates had laid the ideological and political basis for them.

Not all actions in economic policy were aimed against the capitalist class, however. Others were more generally inspired by nationalism. The initiation of the period of radicalism coincided with the inauguration of the Nixon administration. The relationship with the US over PL480 foodgrain releases, devaluation and pressures for liberalization had already left behind a lot of scarred sentiment in India. There followed a burst of nationalism in India directed against the US as the US further began to befriend China in addition to siding with Pakistan when its military dictatorship violently crushed the autonomy movement in East Pakistan, sending ten million refugees into India. In response to the growing US-China-Pakistan relationship, India reached an agreement with the USSR on security ties, which proved useful when war erupted between India and Pakistan in 1971. The war resulted in the suspension of American economic aid, which in effect put an end to the bilateral aid relationship. Further, in a nationalist response to American hostility towards India during the crisis, India barred receiving concessional food imports from the US. More generally, the government became restrictive in relation to foreign investors in India. For some time the government put pressure informally on foreign corporations in India to dilute their foreign equity. Some corporations responded to such pressure, but the government was not satisfied. Accordingly, it eventually gave statutory form, through the Foreign Exchange Regulation Act (FERA) of 1973, to its aim that foreign equity should normally be 40 per cent or below unless foreign companies were engaged in priority, sophisticated technology-based or substantially export-oriented industries; however, all foreign companies were required to bring foreign equity down to 74 per cent.

Ideology reigned during the 1969–73 period. Socialism was ascendant and found expression in the many cases of nationalization and in the placing of restrictions on the corporate sector. Nationalism was not manifest in as dramatic a form. Its major evidence was the renunciation of PL480 food aid, the enactment of FERA, and the pledge of the economic planners, even if unrealistic, to phase out foreign aid. Yet, fundamentally nationalism underlay developments during the entire period, in the sense that policy actions throughout were inspired reactively against all that the foreign powers had coerced India into doing in the preceding period. There was seething rage at American interventionism not only in India's economic affairs during the mid-1960s but also in Vietnam. This rage intensified as the US aligned de facto with China and sided with Pakistan in the military crackdown in East Pakistan and war with India. However, during this period, external actors had little role in India's economic policy; basically, the Indians were masters of their own economic house.

Within the domestic system, the state at first sight seems powerful, given that it had faced little resistance to the many acts of nationalization and mandatory restrictions on private enterprise. However, state actions were fundamentally inspired by the experience of the electoral reprisals of 1967 and the powerful perception that society wanted the state to shift leftward in economic policy. State and society thus cannot be taken to be separate entities, as the statist approach tends to do, but rather are interacting forces. State actions also revealed the real power of different groups in society. Notwithstanding its alleged economic power, the capitalist class could not prevent actions inimical to its interests. On the other hand, the new agricultural strategy inherited from the previous period was not touched, evidencing the power of the farming lobby. The nationalization of the wholesale wheat trade in April 1973 was in an immediate sense directed at the numerous trading community, but it had implications for the farming community as well. The eventual fate of this particular nationalization nonetheless showed that the government had erred in taking on these powerful sections. For, the measure failed in its aim of mobilizing the food surplus. Within nine months, in January 1974, the government was compelled to withdraw it.

Indeed, the rescinding of the nationalization of the wholesale wheat trade, rather than its planned extension to rice, was a turning point. The failure of the experiment in socialization of the wheat trade was significant for the change it sparked in economic policy as it had evolved since the 1967 general elections. The perceived failure of a rightward or market-oriented solution in the form of devaluation in 1966 had led to a leftward swing in economic policy. Similarly, now, the results of the leftward course—particularly the failure of the socialization of the wheat trade but more generally an economic crisis resulting from the hostile attitude to business and the expansionary state interventionism—brought the government to call a halt to that course, and instead to initiate a policy of economic restraint and greater reliance on the market mechanism and a favourable attitude toward the private sector. The year 1974 thus heralded, as it were, an end to the reign of ideology that had prevailed since 1969.

The Retreat from Radicalism, 1974–84: Inducting Liberalization by Stealth

By late 1973 and through 1974, India was in the throes of another grave economic crisis. This crisis was of momentous consequence in engineering a shift in overall economic policy. Several factors went into the building up of the economic crisis. First, there was the international crisis in 1971 relating to Bangladesh, which diverted national energies from economic and social advance to face the serious threat to national security from Pakistan, in turn backed by China and the US. The influx of 10 million refugees constituted an enormous economic drain not only on its financial resources but also on its foodstocks. In addition, preparation for the impending outbreak of hostilities, the actual war, and then looking after 100,000 POWs for almost a year, added immensely to India's defence burden.

Second, but relatedly, compounding the economic burden was the suspension by the US of economic aid and its effective discontinuance. Moreover, India's renunciation of concessional food imports from the US made more difficult the management of the country's food economy. Again, spending scarce foreign exchange on food imports, in a period of high food prices on the international market, placed a great strain on the country's budget and balance of payments.

Third, very critically, the economy was in a state of persistent stagnation during the early 1970s, with the result that per capita income remained below the 1970–71 level for the subsequent four years. This overall economic stagnation was reflective of a production crisis where, similarly, agricultural production for the same four years remained below the 1970–71 level while industrial production grew at a rate of only 3.5 per cent. Fourth, the economic crisis was further fed by the sharp jump in oil prices in October 1973, dictated by OPEC. The oil price increase fuelled inflation, added to the pressure on the country's balance of payments and, with its cascading effect on fertilizer prices, affected the consumption of fertilizer in agriculture and thus agricultural production.

Fifth, importantly, state policies and the public sector's poor performance aggravated the economic crisis. This was most vividly manifest in the area of foodgrains, where the takeover of the wholesale wheat trade worsened food shortages and price increases. Nor was that all. Production in many industries was crippled by shortages in power, coal and transport, with all three fields being largely in the public sector. Furthermore, the restrictive measures enacted against big business and the various nationalization actions did not inspire much confidence in the business community about government intentions. That community held government policy responsible for the industrial stagnation. Moreover, neglecting economic discipline, the government resorted to deficit financing in the implementation of populist policies to satisfy different sectors of the population. Sixth, the cumulative impact of the preceding factors was to fuel inflation enormously and thus to intensify public discontent. By April 1974, prices were 58 per cent higher than three years earlier, having increased at the rate of 10, 12, and 30 per cent successively over three years. The agony of the public in the face of inflation of this intensity and widespread shortages of essential goods, including food, burst forth into riots and violence. Most social classes in the rural and urban areas became alienated from the government, which thus lost its legitimacy despite the massive majority in Parliament. The inflation and shortages ravaged the poor everywhere and the working class and middle classes in the urban areas. Industrial unrest was widespread. The acute economic crisis and the resulting social disorder were soon transformed into a political crisis as the opposition naturally moved in to exploit the public discontent to mount a major offensive against the government.

Late 1973 marked a turning point. In the face of the economic crisis, the government was now determined to jettison its earlier radical and populist posture of restrictions on the private sector and relentless expansion of the public sector, and to replace it with a growth-oriented strategy. Mrs Gandhi had apparently become disillusioned by the results of the earlier radical measures, especially after the fiasco in the wake of the takeover of the wholesale wheat trade. Prem Shankar Jha (1980: 171) underlines: 'It was part of a process of disenchantment, which can be traced back to the oil crisis, and the suspicion that grew in Mrs Gandhi that she had been made use of by the communists and their fellow-travellers in the Congress to pass legislation whose effect was to disrupt production, without making society significantly more egalitarian'. The new growth-oriented course was signalled by stern actions on the labour front. First, the government in May 1974 ruthlessly crushed the railway strike, which indicated its determination not to concede workers' demands for higher wages since that would, in the government's view, compound the economic crisis by intensifying inflation and depleting resources for public investment. This action came on top of the government's earlier crushing of strikes by employees of Indian Airlines and the Life Insurance Corporation—both vast far-flung public sector units. Then the government instituted a deflationary policy package. In July 1974 the government issued three presidential ordinances that shifted the focus of economic policy from the pursuit of social justice and socialism to discipline in the management of the economy through the adoption of orthodox measures. Toward the end of controlling inflation, which the government considered to be the single-most important threat to economic stability, two of the ordinances placed limits on the distribution of dividends, on the one hand, and on the other impounded any increase in wages and half of any additional inflation-indexed allowances, which were now to be compulsorily deposited with the government. Besides, the government applied restraint to its own expenditures and a squeeze on credit to

the private sector. Even earlier, in 1973, the government had relaxed somewhat its licensing guidelines—though such relaxation
continued to be hedged by restrictions against the large industrial
houses—to assure expanded production in 54 industries.

There can be no doubt that the severe economic crisis had induced
recourse to economic orthodoxy and resort to the liberalization
cure. The government technically had the choice of persisting with
the same path that it had adopted earlier and, indeed, intensifying its
application on the calculation that India's economic situation
required a more radical, deeper, and more comprehensive approach.
That course was recommended by many, especially the CPI and the
radical economists, on the ground that a mixed economy in which
the private sector continued to operate could not effectively cope
with the country's economic problems; rather, what the situation
required, within their intellectual framework, was the elimination
altogether of the corporate private sector, described as consisting of
'monopolies'. However, the government instead decided to take the
alternative route of changing course.

Critical to the government's decision was its conclusion about its
earlier series of policies. Given the immensity of the crisis and the
perception that its roots lay in the previous complex of policies, the
government resorted to a set of more orthodox policies which constituted a radical departure from reliance on the earlier policies,
without overthrowing the physical consequences of those earlier
policies. Importantly, in making this shift, the leadership was influenced by its perception that the public mood was no longer hospitable to the earlier path, for the public had come to associate its own
agony with precisely the socialist measures undertaken earlier. This
was certainly the case with the takeover of the wholesale wheat
trade and the nationalization of the coal industry, both of which had
resulted in a deterioration of the existing situation through higher
prices and shortages; that deterioration was experienced directly by
the public. Besides, the informed sections of the urban middle
classes and the leaders of the prosperous peasantry had become
alienated from the public sector because of its failure to perform and
the huge losses it incurred, the burden of which was then transformed into higher taxes on the population. Just as Mrs Gandhi's
turn to a radical path had been influenced by her perception of what
the public mood wanted, so similarly her turning away from continuing on that path was influenced by a changed political mood. The

change in the public mood was thus critical to the policy change in 1974. Although the IMF and World Bank may have also offered advice to the government on an orthodox stabilization package, not much need be made of it. The real source of the policy package was the economic crisis itself. Indian economists themselves were in the forefront of advocating harsh measures; 140 of them recommended a deflationary package that amounted to 'a major surgical operation', compared to which the government's measures 'were rather moderate'.[2]

The harsh economic measures of the government had a dramatic impact on inflation by the end of September 1974, when prices began to decline; they were to assure price stability for the next year and a half. What is more, in retrospect that year also marked the end of the economic stagnation that had dominated the economic scene since the mid-1960s. The left economists had characterized the phenomenon as structural retrogression, and had argued that the stagnation was likely to be persistent in the absence of structural change. Others had concluded that India was fated not to perform better than the alleged Hindu rate of growth of 3.5 per cent. However, the subsequent record showed the critical role of policy as against Hindu predestination. The policy change related not only to the growth-oriented package but also to linking the rupee with a weak sterling and thus stealthily devaluating it. The credit for the policy break-through, it would seem in all fairness, belongs to Mrs Gandhi. Apart from the change in the pattern of growth, Mrs Gandhi at the end of her term in 1977 left behind an economic legacy of an unparalleled food buffer stock in India's history of some 18 million tonnes; an unprecedented pile of foreign exchange reserves of the order of nearly $3 billion; relative price stability compared to the hyper-inflation of the early 1970s; and a toned-up public sector. No earlier regime in India had been able to establish such a record of economic performance.

In the meantime, however, the political crisis that was associated with the economic crisis had acquired its own momentum and it deepened as a result of Mrs Gandhi's entanglement with the courts on the issue of electoral improprieties. Perceiving a political up-heaval generated by the opposition forces, Mrs Gandhi imposed an emergency regime on the country in June 1975. In the 1977 elections following the end of the emergency, Mrs Gandhi and her party were defeated and the hastily-assembled, and therefore divided,

Janata Party took over power. The Janata was in office for too short a period to make much of an impact on policy, but among its important actions were: the spectacular enlargement of the list of industrial products reserved for the small-scale sector, from 180 to 504; the ouster of IBM and Coca-Cola from India for their unwillingness to comply with the requirements of FERA on shareholding; a substantial shift of resources to agriculture and rural development, indicative of the newly-achieved political power of the rich and middle peasantry at the centre; and the consequent neglect of critical sectors such as power, coal and transport.

As the Janata government first collapsed, because of its internal divisions, and then lost in the elections, Mrs Gandhi and her Congress Party returned to power at the beginning of 1980 with a massive mandate and they now carried further the logic of the economic policies that were initiated in 1974. The hallmark of these policies was pragmatism and the shedding of ideology. The ideological orientation of the party's parliamentary delegation and party organization had undergone fundamental change, as few ardent leftists remained with Mrs Gandhi; her cabinet was bereft of any committed socialists. Beyond the change in the party's ideological orientation, however, what underlay the pragmatism and the erosion of ideology in the posture of the new government was the economic situation that it inherited from the Janata Party. Outstanding among its features was inflation over the preceding year of some 20 per cent. But inflation was, in turn, a manifestation of serious deterioration in the economy; there were serious shortages of essential commodities such as coal, steel and cement. There was also grave impairment, or even breakdown, of the infrastructure in respect of power and transport. Besides, after the drastic price hikes in oil by OPEC in 1979, the country was confronted with an enormous crisis in its balance of payments, with the oil import bill as a proportion of export earnings jumping from 30.4 per cent for 1978–79 to 53.7 and 90.0 per cent for 1979–80 and 1980–81 (GOI 1983).

The imperative of expanded production, both to relieve domestic shortages and to increase exports, resulted in new policy initiatives. However, if the old formula had been that the public sector was both an instrument of socialism and of faster economic development, that sector was no longer perceived as the engine of growth. Most striking for the leadership was the inability of the public sector to generate economic surpluses for new investment, which was attributed to its inefficiency, even as the public sector represented half the entire capital investment in the organized industrial sector. The leadership's perception of the performance of the public sector was critical to the change in economic policy. To the extent that that perception coincided with reality, it confirmed the observation of the Scandinavian scholar Knud Erik Svendsen in another context that 'the worst enemy of a socialist policy in any ... country is bad economic performance' (cited in Tordoff and Mazrui 1972: 439). In the circumstance, the leadership perforce had to turn to the corporate private sector. But in doing so, it undertook no overthrow of the existing framework of the economy; no denationalization of the public sector was contemplated. Rather, it made changes at the margin to accommodate itself to its new compulsions. There were several areas in which policies underwent modification, or indeed reversal. Such modification was manifest in respect of (1) some liberalization of the economy, which earlier had been marked by pervasive controls and restrictions; and (2) a tougher attitude toward performance in the public sector and resistance to taking over of sick firms in the private sector.

Deregulation and competition were the new watchwords of the government in order to expand production. No doubt, the IMF—which provided India a massive loan of over $5 billion to cope with its impending balance of payments crisis—also favoured this course. But the impact of the IMF was to influence marginally the balance of opinion within the government in that direction, for the regime was oriented that way in any case. There was a time when government leaders had threatened penalties for enterprises that exceeded their licensed capacity. But now the regime adopted a more positive attitude, though still within the framework of bureaucratic control and monitoring, toward increased production in the private sector. In 1975, similarly compelled by the need to expand production, the government had already allowed automatic expansion of capacity by 5 per cent annually or 25 per cent over a five-year period in respect of 12 engineering industries out of a list of some 40 core industries; this expansion was over and above the normal 25 per cent expansion allowed. In 1980, the government made this facility available to the other remaining industries included in the list of core industries, such as chemicals, drugs, ceramics and cement. A more dramatic shift in industrial policy followed Mrs Gandhi's declaration to make 1982 'the year of productivity'. This declaration in itself reflected the dominant new-found pragmatic thrust in the government's economic policy. As *India Today* (15 February 1982: 62–71) expressed it, 'right now, the mood of the Government is not to be unduly bothered about theoretical issues—about distributive justice and socialism and such other relics from the bygone eras'.

The new industrial policy, which was announced in April 1982, was immediately hailed by the industry-controlled press as 'economic pragmatism' and 'dilution of dogma'. It incorporated two new measures. One, it accepted the principle of automatic expansion of licensed capacity by one-third over the best production level in the preceding five years rather than just one-fourth as before. Two, it enlarged the list of core industries that would be open to large industrial houses and FERA companies. The second measure was considered to mark a significant departure from the earlier posture of the government which had sought to bar the expansion of big business. Again, the government opened to the private sector areas of industrial activity, such as power and oil exploration, that were earlier closed to it. Still again, to help manufacturers generate resources for modernization and expansion by preemption of what was being cornered by middlemen into the black economy, the government abolished administered prices in respect of pig iron; similarly, it decreed partial decontrol in relation to cement. All these measures reflected a realization on the part of government that it could not impose restrictions that inhibited the functioning of the private sector and at the same time expect industrial growth; they also reflected the realization of the futility of negatively identifying socialism with the imposition of controls on the private sector.

Furthermore, the government sought to create a more favourable climate for investment by business through its annual budgets, which sought to provide incentives to encourage savings and direct them to productive investment. In addition, the government adopted a more liberal policy on the import of raw materials, spare parts and technology. The greater openness to technology import was reflected in the increased number of technical collaboration proposals approved; this new posture reflected the government's fear of increasing technological obsolescence that hampered the country in competing in world markets. The literal overthrow of past economic orthodoxy in respect of restrictions on import of technology and the size of undertakings became especially manifest in respect of electronics and telecommunications, where earlier positions were reversed in 1983 to favour liberal import of technology, economic size units, and participation by big business. Needless to say, the new trends in policy were welcomed by big business.

Liberalization in the 1980s has often been considered to be a worldwide trend, inaugurated among the industrial democracies by Ronald Reagan in the US and Margaret Thatcher in the UK and, among the communist countries, by Deng Xiaoping in China and Mikhail Gorbachev in the Soviet Union, with the rest of the world following in imitation. The evidence presented here demonstrates that the origins of liberalization in India lay in its own specific experience in the early 1970s, even though later it may have felt encouraged in that path by the worldwide trend. However, Mrs Gandhi's policy changes were not proclaimed as heralding liberalization as such. With her shrewd political sense, she sought to avoid—unsuccessfully—attacks by the left, through proclaiming that these gradual and pragmatic measures within the traditional socialist framework were necessary either because of a crisis situation or because India had achieved self-reliance through the policy regime fostered by Nehru and her. Mrs Gandhi's approach was essentially one of introducing liberalization in small instalments by stealth.

Liberalization in the Absence of Crisis: Its Acceleration and Abandonment, 1985–90

Following the death of Mrs Gandhi in October 1984, her son and political successor, Rajiv Gandhi, made liberalization the centre-piece of his political programme, holding it forth as an essential requirement of the modernization thrust to carry India into the 21st century as an advanced industrial power. Fortunately for him, he also received the most powerful electoral mandate in India's history, largely out of sympathy for his mother's martyrdom and the fear of national disintegration. His position was truly path-breaking, for he was the first prime minister, indeed anybody in high office, to openly espouse liberalization, at least at the beginning of his tenure. In a series of highly visible and salient actions, the Rajiv Gandhi administration seemed to launch India on a new economic course, which not only marked an acceleration of the liberalization policies adopted by Mrs Gandhi earlier but also aimed for the first time to take the country out of the inherited socialist framework altogether.

Ambitious as his vision was, however, Rajiv Gandhi did not as yet envisage a paradigm shift and an overthrow of the old system, rather he aimed for incremental revisionist change within the overall framework of that system.

It is instructive to note that Rajiv Gandhi took to the new course when India faced no immediate economic crisis. The absence of an economic crisis is, indeed, the most distinctive aspect of his liberalization effort compared to all other earlier policy shifts. This was in large measure the result of Mrs Gandhi's legacy; she had left behind an enormous food buffer stock, a comfortable foreign exchange reserves position, a functioning public distribution network for basic commodities for large segments of the population, and a break with the Hindu rate of growth through sustaining a growth rate of over 5 per cent for a decade. At the same time, the absence of an economic crisis perhaps also explains why, notwithstanding the apparently dramatic measures undertaken, the liberalization effort undertaken soon stalled.

Rajiv Gandhi's liberalization was, in considerable part, a reflection of his personal orientation; he was fascinated by modern technology and computers. But he was also inspired by the seeming success of the earlier liberalization policies and coincidentally by the realization that, despite it, India's growth rate had been insufficient to make a dent on domestic poverty even as the country was becoming increasingly marginalized internationally. We have it on the authority of his closest economic advisor at that time, L.K. Jha (1987: 26), that

the state of the economy gave him considerable cause for concern. India's ranking as an industrialized nation had slipped from the 10th to the 26th position in the world. Our share in world trade had gone down from 2.4 per cent in 1950 to around 0.5 per cent. If the same trends continued, then by the turn of the century, the gap between India and the developed countries of the world would be far wider, while he was anxious to see it disappear.

The situation of marginalization had become increasingly unacceptable to the new leadership, and Rajiv Gandhi sought to reinterpret the concept of self-reliance, which as India's overall national aim in the past had, in the main, been interpreted to mean that the country ought to produce domestically whatever it could, regardless of considerations of cost. As paraphrased by L.K. Jha (1987: 26), the new prime minister thought: 'Self-reliance for a country like India cannot have the limited meaning of the country not being influenced one way or another by external economic forces. It should instead be measured in terms of India's contribution to the shaping of the international economic forces'. In his own words, Rajiv Gandhi stated in the Seventh Plan: 'Self-reliance does not mean autarky. It means the development of a strong, independent national economy dealing extensively with the world, but dealing with it on equal terms' (GOI 1985: v).

The root cause for India's existing marginalization was, quite correctly, ascribed to economic inefficiency; that, in turn, was laid at the door of the poor functioning of the mammoth public sector, which dominated the organized economy, and of the complex regulatory framework. As a consequence, the government decided to rely on the private sector as the growth mechanism of the future, while reorienting the public sector to facilitate expansion of the private sector. To allow the private sector to function adequately as a growth mechanism, it then moved to reduce the plethora of regulatory controls except those that were necessary for strategic purposes—in other words, to go in for further liberalization, domestically for now, externally only later.

The new policies represented a continuity with the process of change that had been under way for a decade. But they represented a marked shift as well. First, there was an accentuation of the pace of change. Moreover, such change was proclaimed boldly and forthrightly, and its irreversible nature was underlined; as L.K. Jha (1985: 97–98) pointed out, important as the changes under Mrs Gandhi were, 'liberalization was still being looked upon more as an exception than a ruling principle', while 'Rajiv Gandhi and his government have shown a much deeper commitment to liberalization'. Second, the changes took place along a considerable front in several areas of economic life, they followed several serious inquiries and studies, and they occurred within a finite period of time. As a consequence, they added in the aggregate to a broad package, constituting as it were a distinctive economic model or strategic economic design with its own coherent underlying philosophy, even though one was not explicitly articulated. Third, the policy changes were presented without being masked by any pretence or rhetoric about socialism, as had been the pattern in the past.

The key feature of the changes was reliance on the private sector—instead of the public sector—as the mechanism for economic growth in the future and the provision of the required resources and appropriate environment to facilitate its performance. The public sector would be expected to play a complementary but subsidiary role to the private sector, concentrating on the core sector, primarily infrastructure. Designed to influence both the supply side and demand side, the changes were particularly manifest in three areas: taxation, industrial licensing, and trade policy.

In respect of taxation, the noteworthy event was the budget presented in March 1985 which, rather than raising additional resources through increased direct taxation, reduced such taxation substantially. It lowered corporate taxes so as to bring them more in line with other capitalist economies, with the nominal tax rate being lowered by 5 percentage points from 57.7 per cent to 52.5 per cent; estate duty was totally abolished while wealth tax was severely cut. Again, the budget raised the exemption limit for personal taxation from Rs 15,000 to Rs 18,000 and reduced personal taxation by 20 to 30 per cent (so that the marginal tax rate—which at one time had stood at 97.7 per cent—came down from 62 per cent to 50 per cent).

In relation to licensing, the basic intent was to remove barriers to entry and to achieve economies of scale by expanding capacity levels. The more significant changes—which centred on redefining big business, delicensing, broadbanding and automatic capacity expansion—were: (1) raising the level of assets that had brought firms under the purview of MRTP from Rs 200 million to Rs 1,000 million, thus drastically reducing the number of firms under MRTP restrictions and giving more freedom to many large business houses; (2) delicensing of 25 broad categories of industries over a wide area plus another 82 bulk drugs and related drug formulations; (3) permitting MRTP companies to obtain licences for 27 industries without being subjected to MRTP restrictions; (4) delicensing of 22 industries for MRTP and FERA companies when located in backward areas; (5) broadbanding of product-mix for 28 industry groups that continued to remain under the licensing regime, in order to provide greater flexibility to entrepreneurs with licences; (6) automatic permission to expand capacity by one-third per year; and (7) removal of virtually any upper limits on capacity in non-consumer electronics, and permission for liberal import of technology and foreign collaboration in electronics.

In regard to trade policy, with its major aim the thoroughgoing technological modernization of industry in order to expand exports, the new administration relaxed the restrictive trade regime in the first half of 1985, and adopted a more liberal policy toward imports of capital goods, technology and raw material inputs. Many categories of industrial machinery were simply put on Open General Licence, thus no more requiring specific licences for import, even as customs duties were lowered sharply. In the case of capital goods for projects, customs duties were drastically slashed from 105 per cent ad valorem to 45 per cent, but the cuts were even severer in the case of particular industries, such as fertilizer projects (0 per cent) and power projects (25 per cent). In regard to technology and computer systems, the government raised the upper limit for each case of import from $0.5 million to $10 million. In respect of electronics, the government declared, in a reversal of its past posture, a literally open door policy in relation to foreign investment. It is noteworthy that liberalization at this stage was essentially limited to internal competition rather than exposing the economy to external competition and to reliance on domestic entrepreneurs rather than foreign direct investment.

Although liberalization was welcome to the upper and middle classes, by the same token it made the government politically vulnerable as it came to be identified with the rich. The trade unions and the communist parties were especially opposed to liberalization, holding it to constitute the overthrow of established national policies and a surrender to imperialism. Surprisingly, the first serious challenge to the government came from key segments within the Congress Party, where concern mounted at the handicap of being labelled 'a party for the rich and no longer for the poor' (*India Today*, 31 May 1985: 5). In the face of a virtual party revolt in May 1985, the government beat a hasty retreat, proclaiming once again 'unequivocally its commitment to socialism'. However, the government's concession was merely rhetorical and it remained steadfast in its determined course. A more forceful challenge to the government came in early 1986 from the urban middle class, which raised a storm of protest in reaction to the raising of prices of public sector goods to mobilize resources. The experience chastened the government even as enthusiasm for Rajiv Gandhi dimmed among the middle class. The government then began to moderate its policy posture in order to have it correspond with its political compulsions to maintain support among key groups. The emphatic liberalization policy that was proclaimed in the first budget thus soon became moderated and attenuated, indeed arrested. Instead of new initiatives, the government now only fine-tuned its policies and modified them to cope with the objections of particular groups.

Particularly striking was the failure of the Rajiv Gandhi government to reform the public sector (Nayar 1992). It promised a white paper on reforming the public sector, but failed to bring it out. It tried to privatize a single chronically loss-making commercial enterprise, Scooters India Limited, but was unsuccessful. The public sector seemed politically unassailable because of its association with the ideological legacy of Nehru. More importantly, there were key massive and powerful veto groups with concrete material interests, lodged inside the state in the form of bureaucracy and public sector labour, that opposed privatization or reform of the public sector. Besides, Rajiv Gandhi became politically preoccupied with fending off charges of corruption, especially in regard to defence purchases. In the final analysis, his liberalization effort amounted to only tinkering with the existing system.

Despite his failure on the public sector and on a deeper liberalization, however, Rajiv Gandhi changed the nature of the debate on the economy where, as against the earlier ideological hegemony of socialism and mercantilism, it now became legitimate to regard liberalization as an appropriate alternative economic strategy. Even though he lost the 1989 elections, perhaps for causes unrelated to the economy, he was to leave behind the legacy of his 1991 election manifesto, which the Congress Party posthumously took to be a mandate for a paradigm shift to liberalization. Meanwhile, the National Front that came to power in 1989 was, as a coalition government, unstable and divided over issues of economic policy; however, it contained a strong impulse for further liberalization of industrial policy, which proved abortive because of the Front's break-up.

The economy saw a slight acceleration in the annual growth rate, from 5.4 per cent during the Sixth Plan (1980–85) under Mrs Gandhi to 5.8 per cent during the Seventh Plan (1985–90) under Rajiv Gandhi. No doubt, some improvement in productivity as a result of the several doses of liberalization since 1974 played a part in the better economic performance during the 1980s. However, a major factor in the higher growth rate was that the state followed an imprudent expansionary policy, relying for investment and populist subsidies—in a shift from its traditional fiscal and monetary conservatism—on successive large fiscal deficits and external commercial borrowings in the absence of adequate concessional aid. Thus, while Latin America was coming to terms with its devastating debt problem in the 1980s, India was in the process of quickly buying its way into it, banking on its good credit rating at the time. A future crisis was thus being quietly put in place through fiscal profligacy. The higher growth rate on the back of fiscal deficits was in the long term unsustainable. The gathering crisis can, however, be rationalized in more positive terms by the argument that it was better to have deliberately introduced dynamism, even if risky, into the economy than to have accepted a low-level equilibrium, which was not necessarily risk-free. The argument is strengthened by the consideration that crisis, whether induced or otherwise, seems to have been essential for economic policy reform in India. Nonetheless, the gathering crisis finally exploded when the Gulf War in 1991 aggravated the already serious balance of payments problem that was developing in 1990. That crisis led to a paradigm shift to a market model under a new government, marking a break with the earlier model of self-reliance launched with the Second Plan.

Summary and Conclusions

The policy of economic liberalization launched in 1991 often appears as a dramatic act that suddenly catapulted India in a paradigm shift from the mercantilist-socialist path, which had been sustained for some three and a half decades since 1956, to a liberal market-oriented course that integrated India into the global economy. The reality, however, is that the mercantilist-socialist model was in trouble from the very beginning. Indeed, the history of that path is marked by a series of recurrent crises, the resolution of which was attempted initially through oscillation between economic liberalization and economic radicalism and then through progressive increases in economic liberalization.

When India started out with its ISI strategy—focused on heavy industry and its ownership by the state—in the context of a democratic political system, there was no existing model of such a mixed economy to follow. India thus did not have the advance benefit of the experience of an existing model to draw on in determining the ambition and scale of the industrialization effort that would be consistent with the requirements, on the one hand, of legitimacy within a democracy in which the bulk of the population lived at subsistence level and, on the other, of advancing national autonomy and welfare in the shortest possible time. Necessarily, therefore, there were imbalances between the economic strategy and the political system. It is instructive nonetheless that, viewed from a long-range perspective, the Indian leadership attempted, not always successfully or in timely fashion, to react to perceived shortcomings in the economic strategy. There was thus a learning process involved for the leadership as it experimented with different policies, discovering on the way their respective costs and benefits and evaluating their acceptability or not to key groups in society as well as assessing the capacity of the state to implement them.

As the leadership attempted to arrive at an accommodation between economic strategy and political system, it encountered intrusive foreign intervention in its policy-making process during the mid-1960s. This was a period in which India was subjected to tremendous pressures by the US. These pressures did not have to do with economic policy reform alone; rather, India's foreign policy of non-alignment, particularly in respect of Vietnam, was implicated as well. Therefore, it seems that those who facilely suggest that India should have moved to an export-oriented strategy fail to appreciate that, first, it would not have been easy to give up the inward-oriented heavy strategy because it was invested with ideology and, second, that India would also have had to give up its foreign policy independence in order to have access to the markets of the West, particularly the US. The export-oriented policies of the Asian tigers did not simply stand in isolation as economic policies but were part of a larger integration of these states into the foreign policy orbit of the US.

The economic policy reform that was generated in the mid-1960s in the cause of economic liberalization could not be sustained (except in agriculture), primarily because its foreign sponsorship proved unacceptable to nationalist and leftist forces within the country. Indeed, the consequence of foreign sponsorship was a rejection of the reform and a swing to the radical left. Only when this radical course had been exhausted and had proven patently counter-productive that the leadership picked up the thread of liberalization again in the mid-1970s, this time on the basis of its own assessment.

It is fair to acknowledge that when the national interest demanded change, Mrs Indira Gandhi broke with the radical course and started India, even if hesitantly, on the trajectory of economic liberalization. This break with the course of the past was later carried forward incrementally by her and her son and successor, Rajiv Gandhi.

In general, it is manifest that the process of economic policy reform in India, even when its need has become apparent, has been stretched over a long period of time. That has patently to do with the difficulty of enacting reform in a democracy. The state under democracy, as in India, has less *policy flexibility* (Nayar 1992) than do authoritarian regimes, such as those in East Asia. However, democracy does not altogether preclude reform, but it often requires a crisis to push it through, and even then there are limits to it, as is made evident by the liberalization undertaken in 1991.

Notes

1. The account of economic policy under Lal Bahadur Shastri, Mrs Indira Gandhi and Rajiv Gandhi draws on Nayar (1989: chs 6–8; 1990: chs 2–3; and 1992).
2. Vakil et al. (1974: 98); and Vakil and Brahmananda (1977: 4). The eminent economist V.K.R.V. Rao and his associates also advocated an orthodox anti-inflationary policy package; see Rao et al. (1973). See also Jha (1980: 144–53), who effectively demolishes the case for the influence of international financial institutions.

4

Changing the Balance, 1991–96: Political Structure and Economic Reforms

The economic policy reforms launched in 1991 constitute a watershed in India's economic history. Until then, despite the liberalization during the 1980s under prime ministers Indira Gandhi and Rajiv Gandhi, India remained a comprehensively and stringently controlled economy, both internally and externally. Indeed, Joshi and Little (1996: 63) maintain that 'In June 1991 India was the most autarkic non-communist country in the world', while the IMF (Chopra 1995: 57) notes that India was 'one of the most heavily regulated economies in the world'. India thus represented a strong case of economic nationalism, combining high levels of external protection and internal regulation, as illustrated by A1 in Figure 4.1, which conceptualizes different possible balances between economic globalization and economic nationalism.

It is into this scene that reforms were dramatically introduced in 1991. There was, no doubt, continuity with the reforms of the 1980s, but there was also a marked acceleration, indeed a clear break with the pattern of what had been done until then. With little evident embarrassment, the top leadership now made a *paradigm shift*—what critics called a U-turn—from the state to the market, openly and enthusiastically embracing globalization and integration of the Indian economy into the world economy and initiating the dismantlement of physical controls along a broad front of the Indian economy. Although not all that was intended was achieved, a substantial movement took place in the direction of globalization and

Figure 4.1
Types of Balance Between Economic Globalization and Economic Nationalism

			Internal Regulation		
			High 1	Medium 2	Low 3
External Protection	High	A :	A1 :	A2 :	A3
	Medium	B :	B1 :	B2 :	B3
	Low	C :	C1 :	C2 :	C3

Notes: This figure is intended to be only suggestive; it is not intended to offer precise indices of measurement. The purpose is merely to illustrate graphically, if only broadly and tentatively, the discussion in the text on the nature and direction of the shift in economic policy, the limits of the shift, and the possible trajectories of policy change in the future. *External Protection* refers essentially to the degree of protection accorded to national firms from foreign competition through tariff and non-tariff measures, while *Internal Regulation* concerns the degree of regulation of the market and firms in the domestic economy by the state. The differentiation between *high*, *medium* and *low* within these two dimensions follows rule of thumb categorization; high and low are polar categories, while medium implies selectivity in terms of sectors, duration and extent.

liberalization; as Raja Chelliah (1996: 9) noted: 'These reforms taken together constitute a comprehensive and thoroughgoing overhaul of the economic policy regime'. Similarly, the World Bank (1996: xvii, 31) declared that 'India has fundamentally altered its development paradigm' and that the reforms 'have ended four decades of planning and have initiated a quiet economic revolution'.

The reforms undertaken over the period 1991–96 covered both the internal and external dimensions of the economy,[1] and effectively altered the balance between globalization and nationalism. Externally, the rupee was sharply devalued by about 20 per cent and, through a series of calibrated steps, made fully convertible on the current (though not capital) account; licensing was virtually abolished for imports, and tariff levels were drastically cut; and direct foreign investment was allowed to the extent of 51 per cent automatically in a wide range of industries even as portfolio investment was now welcome. Internally, the entire edifice of industrial licensing was abolished except in the case of 15 industries of strategic or environmental importance; anti-trust legislation was amended to facilitate expansion and diversification of capacity by large firms; the number of industries reserved for the public sector was drastically reduced to only six; the taxation system was rationalized, while tax rates were slashed; and major reforms were introduced to put the banking system on a sounder footing.

The reforms made for a spectacular change in the inherited structure of economic policy. Their comprehensive and far-reaching nature, their obviously irreversible character and, significantly, their intellectual grounding in an alternative set of philosophical assumptions about economic behaviour than that which had guided India's earlier economic policy, add up to a persuasive, indeed compelling, case for a shift from type A1 to type B2 in Figure 4.1 in the nature of the balance between globalization and nationalism. True, a lot that was on the agenda remained undone. The rupee was not made convertible on the capital account, the import of consumer goods was still largely subject to quantitative restrictions, the public sector was neither restructured to assure genuine autonomy to the enterprises nor authentically privatized, the reservation of industries for the small-scale sector remained unchanged, the labour market was untouched by reform, the insurance sector was still closed to competition from the private sector, and subsidies were far from being reduced, let alone abolished. Still, in several of these areas considerable groundwork had been done by way of serious studies and recommendations by high-powered committees. More importantly, if all that remained undone had actually been accomplished, assuming its desirability, then the designation of type B2 in Figure 4.1 would no longer have been sufficient to describe the change but rather that of type C3; and, if only partially accomplished, then, depending on the sectors, type B3 or C2 would have been more appropriate. All aspects considered, therefore, type B2 seems the most reasonable characterization of the new balance, given the striking amount of change that had occurred.

The more important question—which serves as the organizing framework for the next two sections—however, concerns the reasons for (1) the substantial degree of change that had been brought about and, equally, for (2) the change remaining limited to that level. In regard to the first aspect, one side in the general debate on economic policy reforms favours an international explanation, in which the important elements are (a) external shocks; (b) the political power of international financial institutions or IFIs and international bankers as also of the countries that support them; and (c) ascendant or reigning ideas or ideologies, whether on their own inherent merits or because they are imposed by external agencies. On the other side of the debate are those who see only limited utility in the international explanation, and instead find greater value in a domestic explanation, where the key variables generally are: (i) the state, with its institutions and elites and their policy preferences; and (ii) society, with its economic and social groups and their interests (Haggard and Kaufman 1992a: 3–37). The basic proposition that informs the discussion below is that it is domestic forces, rather than the international system, that were fundamental to reform; those forces comprised the pressures of an economic crisis, which was generated by the changing dynamics of state-society relations within a democratic framework, and altered experience-based elite preferences about economic policy. Again, the democratic nature of the Indian state explains the limited nature of change, for the requirements of legitimacy of such a state place limits on reform that imposes sacrifices on key societal groups, particularly in the absence of a crisis.[2]

Explaining The New Balance: Why The Change?

The larger project of economic policy reform usually consists of two phases, economic stabilization and structural adjustment. Stabilization is a short-term programme, of 18 months to two years' duration, designed to rectify the immediate problem of macroeconomic imbalances, such as high fiscal deficits, high inflation and severe balance of payments problems; the key prescriptions are currency devaluation externally and contractionary policies domestically. Structural adjustment, however, stretches over a longer period of three to five years and aims to advance economic efficiency by attacking the more fundamental or structural features of the economy that are, in the ultimate analysis, seen as lying at the root of the macroeconomic imbalances, such as the relationship between the state and market and between the national economy and world economy. In the Indian case, the two phases were initiated relatively simultaneously, but the discussion that follows treats the two phases separately for clarity of presentation.

Economic Stabilization

The immediate occasion for the initiation of the economic policy reforms in 1991 was the economic crisis, primarily in the area of balance of payments, that had built up over the previous year and had reached a stage where India would have been forced to default on its external obligations. Such balance of payments crises can have their origins in external shocks—such as the OPEC oil price hikes and collapse of commodity prices—or in the earlier economic policies of the state (Haggard and Kaufman 1992a: 3–37). There is, no doubt, a school of thought that holds external shocks, largely the Gulf crisis, to be the primary cause of India's economic crisis.[3] This view seems, however, to be limited in its perspective. While external elements were undoubtedly present as immediate precipitants, the proximate causes of the crisis lay principally at home, fundamentally in the persistent fiscal deficits budgeted by the state year after year for more than a decade. The crisis was thus basically the consequence of earlier economic policies, not of external shocks. India's economic decision-makers had traditionally been reputed to be prudent in matters of public finance, but in the 1980s they became less conservative, indeed reckless, in their attitude toward balancing the books. Increasingly, current expenditures outstripped current revenues, and fiscal deficits at high levels persisted year after year in the 1980s. Whereas the average fiscal deficit of the centre was 6.3 per cent of GDP in the first half of the decade of the 1980s (Parikh 1997: statistical tables) it was 8.2 per cent in the second half and 8.4 per cent in 1990–91 (see Table 4.1); contrast all this with the average of 3.9 per cent for the 1970s. Apart from resorting to the printing press to meet the deficits, the state took recourse to increased borrowings from the market. Borrowing rapidly expanded the national debt and, in turn, made for increased interest payments in subsequent years, which then constrained the government financially even more and, in a vicious cycle, forced it to resort further to the printing press and borrowing.

Although the fiscal deficit in a particular year may or may not affect the economy adversely, large fiscal deficits sustained over a whole decade could not leave the economy and its balance of payments situation unaffected. Persistent fiscal deficits led to persistent inflation (see Table 4.1). In turn, the persistent inflation affected the balance of payments situation; it made exports increasingly uncompetitive, which then had to be supported with higher export subsidies from the state. At the same time, increased demand within the country, which was fuelled by the fiscal deficits and was reflected in the inflation, pulled in larger imports, such as of oil and petroleum

Table 4.1
Selected Macroeconomic Indicators

Year	GDPfc (1980–81 Prices) Rs Bill.	GDP Growth Rate	Fiscal Deficit % GDP	Inflation: Index Nos	WPI Annual Rate	Current Account Deficit % GDP	Outstanding Debt	
							External US$ Mill.	Central Rs Bill.
1980–81	1,224.27	–	6.2	91.5	18.2	1.7	22,397*	597.49
1985–86	1,565.66	4.1	8.3	125.4	4.4	2.8	40,960	1,374.84
1986–87	1,632.71	4.3	9.0	132.7	5.8	2.6	48,257	1,665.46
1987–88	1,703.22	4.3	8.1	143.6	8.2	2.5	55,702	1,955.61
1988–89	1,844.61	8.3	7.8	154.3	7.5	3.1	60,627	2,297.71
1989–90	2,014.53	9.2	7.9	165.7	7.4	2.8	75,557	2,681.93
1990–91	2,122.53	5.4	8.4	182.7	10.3	3.4	83,862	3,145.58
1991–92	2,139.83	0.8	5.9	207.8	13.7	0.7	85,516	3,546.62
1992–93	2,252.68	5.3	5.7	228.7	10.1	1.7	90,120	4,019.24
1993–94	2,388.64	6.0	7.4	247.8	8.4	0.7	93,968	4,778.68
1994–95	2,560.95	7.2	6.1	274.7	10.9	0.9	101,501	5,386.11
1995–96	2,742.09	7.1	5.5	294.8	7.3	1.8	93,766	NA

* Figure is for 1981–82.

Source: World Bank (1995 and 1997). Fiscal deficit figures for the years 1980–81 to 1989–90 are from Parikh (1997: statistical tables). GDPfc means GDP at factor cost. Central debt is at current prices and includes external debt.

products, to satisfy it. The balance of payments had been critical even before the onset of the Gulf crisis. Whereas the current account deficit in 1980–81 was 1.7 per cent of GDP, it was 2.8 per cent in the second half of the decade of the 1980s and 3.4 per cent in 1990–91 (see Table 4.1). Finance Minister Madhu Dandavate had located the cause for it in the fiscal profligacy of the state, remarking in his 1990–91 budget speech, 'The fiscal imbalance is the root cause of the twin problems of inflation and the difficult balance of payments position' (GOI 1996, II: 1253). The trade and current account deficits in the second half of the decade of the 1980s had been financed through drawing down the foreign exchange reserves and resorting to commercial borrowing abroad. Banks abroad were only too eager to lend, given the country's good credit rating at the time. Between 1985–86 and 1990–91, India's foreign debt more than doubled. India had, no doubt, accelerated its growth path in the 1980s and in the process broken the barrier of what the late Raj Krishna termed 'the Hindu rate of growth', but the growth was, in part, based on unsustainable fiscal profligacy. The situation could not last, there was bound to be a reckoning at some point.

What was the source of such fiscal profligacy? Long time ago, Adam Smith had called attention to the tendency of the state to waste capital, for its officials are given to extravagance. However, society cannot be so easily absolved of blame, for state and society in India are linked together through the institutional structure of parliamentary democracy. Not surprisingly, this state structure compelled securing legitimacy through offering economic incentives to the electorate, and was no doubt implicated in the high incidence of fiscal deficits. Yet this natural tendency of democratic systems toward providing such incentives had been restrained during the first two decades of the post-colonial state in India. The crucial element that differentiated the earlier period from the subsequent years was the extraordinarily high degree of state power[4] for an underdeveloped country. In that period, the Congress Party was literally the natural party of governance within a single dominant party system, and was, therefore, not compelled to engage in competitive outbidding with other parties. This high degree of state power up to the mid-1960s rested on a tripod of factors—the personal charisma of India's first prime minister, Jawaharlal Nehru, who served in that office for 17 years; the institutional charisma of the ruling Congress Party, acquired through the struggle for national liberation from colonial rule over two-thirds of a century; and the administrative 'steel frame', manned by a group of rather incorruptible generalists. Whatever the origins of the earlier fiscal conservatism, it had been sustained by a situation of high state power.

In the late 1960s, a serious deterioration of state power followed the unleashing of social forces in the wake of the wars with China and Pakistan, the death of Nehru, and the enormous economic crisis of the mid-1960s and the consequent rise in social mobilization. In the 1967 elections, the Congress Party's institutional charisma was shattered as it lost power in about half of the states while its majority at the centre was drastically reduced. Factional struggles broke out within the Congress Party, and finally the party split in 1969. The subsequent decade saw enormous political turmoil and deterioration in state autonomy and state capacity. The politics of consensus through a single party dominant system was replaced by the politics of bitter confrontation. In 1977, the Congress Party was defeated at the centre by the hastily arranged Janata coalition, which, however, could not sustain itself in power beyond two and a half years. Even though the Congress Party returned to power in 1980, it now operated on new political terrain where, with the other parties having tasted power, accession to political office was highly contested, where time-horizons had shortened, and where competitive outbidding for support—through subsidies and costly welfare programmes—from powerful groups, especially the rising upper and middle peasantry, became central to winning elections. Therein lay the real cause of the fiscal deficits—and thus of inflation—rather than some mysterious decline in fiscal conservatism.

As the distinguished economic adviser, I.G. Patel (1993: 113–33), once explained:

> Inflation is essentially the result of a struggle between different sections of the community for a large share in the national cake than what others are prepared to surrender; and its outward manifestation generally is an excessive supply of money. Too much attention to the medium—that is money supply—can divert attention from the underlying forces.

However, neglecting the larger constraint that India's political framework imposed, Patel himself was particularly harsh on the leadership in stating that 'successive governments chose to abdicate their responsibility to the nation for the sake of short-term partisan political gains and indeed out of sheer political cynicism'. He failed to recognize sufficiently the role played in the imprudent fiscal policies by the imperative, springing from the political framework, to gain support from powerful lobbies through subsidies. It was, indeed, this imperative that lay behind the decision by Mrs Indira Gandhi not to draw the third instalment of the generous IMF loan in 1981 of 5 billion SDRs after the second OPEC oil price shock. Behind the vaunted claims of self-reliance lay the real reason—the intent (in Patel's words) 'to escape from the discipline of the IMF' which would have accompanied that instalment. The piling up of fiscal deficits continued over the whole decade of the 1980s as if, according to Patel, 'money did not matter'. While neglecting to rectify the macroeconomic imbalances, the government at the same time liberalized imports. The country was heading for an internal and external debt trap, but clearly the political framework was implicated in the failure to make timely adjustment: 'nothing was done to take corrective action or to buy time for such action and create confidence, for example, by going to the IMF. This was obviously politically inconvenient in 1988 and 1989 when winning elections was the only concern' (Patel 1993: 120).

The decline and decay of the Congress Party had another consequence which weakened state power. India is a continental polity of immense size, comparable to Europe if the latter were a single political system, and it contains an awesome degree of social diversity. The Congress Party had risen as a single reasonably cohesive organization in this situation of immense diversity because of historical reasons. However, it has been awfully difficult to construct an alternative coalition with any degree of cohesion and stability. The internal divisions within any coalition government so far have made decisive governance, let alone reform, an arduous undertaking. Of course, even the Congress Party as a broad encompassing coalition was handicapped in the area of reform by the system's overall tendency toward policy immobilization. Often, crisis has been essential to policy change in this situation.

The developing economic crisis at the end of the decade of the 1980s coincided with the electoral cycle in 1989 in which the Indian electorate chose to express its dissatisfaction by opting for political weakness and instability at the centre by electing a parliament with no party in majority. The largest group, the Congress Party, refused to form the government, feeling that it had been rejected by the electorate. A small minority group therefore took over power, backed opportunistically by two ideologically contradictory and opposed political formations—the Bharatiya Janata Party and the Communist Party of India (Marxist)—in order to hold the Congress Party at bay. Rather than taking action on the developing economic crisis, this group in power soon launched populist policies, both economically and socially, worsening the economic situation. The waiver of repayments on all loans of up to Rs 10,000 from public sector and regional rural banks to farmers, promised during the elections, impaired confidence among foreign investors and creditors about the fiscal responsibility of the new leadership in government. The additional policy of caste-based affirmative action, designed to permanently co-opt the ascendant middle castes of the rural areas (officially, 'other backward classes') as a support base, also had the same effect. By provoking political turmoil and violence across north India, the policy raised questions about political stability in the near future.

The economic crisis was thus of India's own making, and in the face of it India withdrew $660 million from the reserve tranche with the IMF in July 1990. But then occurred the Gulf crisis as a coup de grace that gravely aggravated the country's plight. For one thing, India had to incur large expenditures to evacuate some 112,000 expatriate workers from the Middle East at the state's expense in the largest civilian airlift in history. Importantly, the ballooning of the oil prices worsened the balance of payments situation. Joshi and Little (1996: 14) decidedly understate the significance of the Gulf crisis when they note: 'External shocks played only a minor role in the crisis. Oil prices increased following the Iraqi invasion of Kuwait in August 1990 but only for a few months'. More broadly, the Gulf crisis seriously affected inward remittances from Indian expatriate workers even as it resulted in the loss of a large market, perhaps the largest market in the Gulf area, for Indian exports. The Gulf crisis was thus a critical element in exacerbating India's economic crisis even though it was clearly not the primary cause. It was time for action. The IMF warned India of the developing situation, but the minority government's energies were focused on sustaining itself in office. In the end, the government fell as a faction broke off and took over power with the backing of the Congress Party, which still insisted on staying out of the government. The whole episode disturbed I.G. Patel (1993: 120): 'You do not inspire confidence abroad when the largest party in Parliament abdicates its responsibility to rule or demand new elections but adopts the cynical course of riding on the shoulders of a small minority which commands little support and even less respect'.

The weakness of the new government and its dependence on the Congress Party for support worsened the economic situation. In January 1991, the government obtained US $789 million from the first credit tranche and $1,025 million from the contingency compensatory finance facility of IMF. But all this proved insufficient to staunch the crisis. Nor did the hurried compression of imports help much. Meanwhile, India had now reached the end of easy finance from the IMF. Surprisingly, despite its weak position, the government was ready to negotiate loans with tougher conditionalities. But, as Patel (1993: 120–21) notes in dismay at the behaviour of the Congress leadership,

> the rug was pulled from under its feet when it was not allowed to present a budget which ... was discussed with the Fund and contained at least some features of sensible adjustment. It is no secret that IMF assistance was widely assumed to [be] forthcoming as soon as the budget was passed.... But our political masters willed otherwise.

With the government thus paralyzed while the economic crisis persisted, India's credit rating fell. Foreign bankers proved unwilling to lend while Non-Resident Indians (NRIs) hastened to withdraw their bank deposits and route their remittances through illegal channels. In this situation of capital flight, India's foreign exchange reserves plummeted. As a desperate measure, the government sold 20 tonnes of its gold holdings for $200 million. However, that action proved insufficient to boost reserves. Meanwhile, the reserves were driven so low that they could cover only two weeks of imports. Finally, the government, only a few months in office, called for new elections, which then had to be delayed because of the assassination of former prime minister Rajiv Gandhi during the election campaign. India teetered on the brink of default externally, while domestically the population groaned under inflation at double-digit levels, reaching 17 per cent by August.

It is in the midst of this dismal economic situation of massive macroeconomic imbalances that the Congress Party took over power as a minority government, some two dozen votes shy of a majority, under the leadership of its newly-chosen leader, Prime Minister P.V. Narasimha Rao. Rao's most important task was choosing a Finance Minister, and for that he went outside politics and made the surprise appointment of Manmohan Singh, a well-known economist and technocrat, with a Ph.D. from Cambridge and a long and varied record of service in the government, most recently as deputy chairman of the Planning Commission and earlier as the governor of the Reserve Bank of India. The new government, faced as it was with an economic crisis of enormous proportions, saw little alternative to economic stabilization. The new Finance Minister described the situation thus while presenting his first budget in the middle of fiscal year 1991–92:

> The new Government, which assumed office barely a month ago, inherited an economy in deep crisis. The balance of payments situation is precarious.... Due to the combined impact of political instability ... the accentuation of fiscal imbalances and the Gulf crisis, there was a great weakening of international confidence. There has been a sharp decline in capital inflows through commercial borrowing and non-resident deposits. As a result, despite large borrowings, from the International Monetary Fund in July 1990 and January 1991, there was a sharp reduction in our foreign exchange reserves. We have been at the edge of a precipice since December 1990 and more so since April 1991. The foreign exchange crisis constitutes a serious threat to the sustainability of growth processes and orderly implementation of our development programmes. Due to the combination of unfavourable internal and external factors, the inflationary pressures on the price level have increased very substantially since mid-1990. The people of India have to face double digit inflation which hurts most the poorer sections of our society. In sum, the crisis in the economy is both acute and deep. We have not experienced anything similar in the history of independent India.... The balance of payments has lurched from one liquidity crisis to another since December 1990. The current level of foreign exchange reserves, in the range of Rs 2,000 crore, would suffice to finance imports for a mere fortnight (GOI 1996, II: 1291–93).

The Finance Minister was to reiterate in subsequent years that 'we inherited an economy on the verge of collapse' and that 'the country was on the verge of bankruptcy' (ibid.: 1333, 1400). In the light of the situation, economic stabilization and seeking help from the IMF followed as a matter of course. The Finance Minister dismissed the various suggestions for resource mobilization proffered as an alternative to going to the IMF: some such as unearthing black money suffered from 'romantic illusions'; others about raising taxes would only lead to increased tax evasion; and still others, such as the one mooted by West Bengal Chief Minister Jyoti Basu, about approaching NRIs for help, were themselves dependent on a prior backing by the IFIs of a credible stabilization programme (Das 1993, II: 243–55).

The economic stabilization programme had as its immediate objective the restoration of macroeconomic stability and international confidence in the economy (Singh 1997: 16–42). At the beginning of July the government devalued the rupee. Then it set out its commitments to the IMF in a letter of intent at the end of August while asking for a standby arrangement of SDR 1,656 million.[5] With devaluation already out of the way, the most important commitment in so far as stabilization was concerned was to bring down the central government's fiscal deficit from 8.4 per cent of GDP in fiscal year 1990–91 to 6.5 per cent in 1991–92 and further to 5.0 per cent in 1992–93. The 1991–92 budget, presented in the middle of the fiscal year, had necessarily to drastically cut expenditures and the axe fell heavily on the social sectors and capital expenditures. India used the IMF loan to build up its foreign exchange reserves rather than let up on import compression and facilitate easier imports. The government's obvious determination to tackle the economic situation soon restored confidence among investors. As the foreign exchange reserves started building up, there was public acclaim of the decisive action to meet the crisis.

In the situation of dire economic crisis, where there was public recognition that hard-headed decisions needed to be taken by the leadership, the new government's bold effort at stabilization was tacitly accepted by Parliament, for no party was ready to go back to the electorate so soon after the election. However, the government was subjected to savage criticism by the parties of the left for its alleged surrender to imperialism. The stabilization programme was regarded as having been dictated by the IMF as a price for the loan to bail India out. Much was made of the use of American spelling for some words in the letter of intent to IMF, as an indication of its having been drafted by the IMF. Later, some critics accused the Finance

Minister of being a quisling. One author (Swamy 1994: 254) concluded, after examining this reform episode, that 'the history of liberalization and globalization in India is a chronology of external pressures'.

The government held its ground, however, maintaining that India was a founding member of the IMF and had every right to claim loans from it at a time of need, and that it would not be averse to taking advice when it was in consonance with India's interests, no matter if it originated with the IFIs. In truth, there was nothing extraordinary about the 'conditionalities' for the IMF loan; they followed the conventional menu for an economy under stress. Having had a permanent director on the IMF board, India was not unfamiliar with them; it had taken part in endorsing the application of such conditionalities to scores of other countries. However, if the conditionality on the fiscal deficit was, indeed, dictated by the IMF then the latter cannot be considered to have been especially successful, for India persistently failed to meet the target for several successive years and there was little that the IMF could do about it. Once the crisis passed, and India's foreign exchange reserves built up, the IMF lost whatever leverage it had. Also, the conditionalities could hardly be labelled dictation, for in some other respects India soon went beyond those requirements, because of its own perception that that was what was necessary in its situation.

In brief, the causes of the economic policy reform by way of economic stabilization lay fundamentally not in the pressures from the IFIs but, more realistically, in the pressures from the economic crisis that India faced in an immediate sense and in the cumulative pressures from the economic profligacy over the preceding decade in a more proximate sense.

Economic Restructuring

As is evident, the policy response to the economic crisis in 1991 was not limited to stabilization. Indeed, the immediate turn to economic restructuring was the most remarkable aspect of the leadership's effort in facing the challenge. Of course, it can be argued that the elaborate package of reforms was 'really not necessary' to meet what was only a liquidity crisis (Sengupta 1995: 39–44). However, there seem to have been powerful reasons for the apparently 'novel' effort.

There was a time when balance of payments crises provoked the attention only of the IMF, while its cure for economic stabilization focused on devaluation and demand-contraction. The radical 'structuralist' school of Prebisch's persuasion was critical of the IMF's monetarist approach for its being essentially superficial since it focused exclusively on economic factors and failed to go beyond demand side considerations to attend to the rigidities on the supply side where deep-rooted structures of economy and society, such as class and drastic economic disparities, were implicated. By the 1980s, however, both the IMF and the World Bank had, in shifting to a revived economic orthodoxy, ironically bought the structuralist argument—in a transformed version that turned its radicalism on its head—that the fire-fighting measures of devaluation and deflation were not sufficient to assure the long-term viability of economic stabilization. Under the new economic orthodoxy, they had concluded that economies in crisis needed to attack the more deep-seated structures of the relationship between market and state through 'structural adjustment'. They now required that developing countries go beyond economic stabilization and break down the structures of regulation within and of trade barriers without, that is, shrink the state in favour of the market, both internally and externally (Kahler 1990).

Since India decided in 1991 to go in for structural adjustment beyond measures of economic stabilization, for which it was dependent on the IMF and other IFIs for help, it may be logical to assume that it was either independently persuaded of the merits of the new economic orthodoxy, with its advocacy of liberalization and globalization, or it was coerced into structural adjustment by the IFIs. Although the whole complex of ideas of inward orientation, tight state regulation, and public ownership had earlier exercised ideological hegemony in the country over several decades, there had grown since the early 1980s a significant minority among the elites that shared the assumptions of the new economic orthodoxy. This minority was strongly represented on the economic team that presided over India's structural adjustment, and several of its members had been socialized into it through training or work at the IFIs, such as Montek Singh Ahluwalia, Raja Chelliah, and Shankar Acharya. The impact of the new economic orthodoxy from the outside cannot therefore be excluded. At the same time, neither can coercion at the hands of the IFIs be ruled out, given that India appeared as a suppli-cant and also in view of their past experience with India trying to evade economic conditionalities. In either case, whether it is the 'ideas' model or the 'power' model, the source of the impulses for reform in India would, in this view, be regarded as external. However, the applicability of either model in its blunt form is questionable.

It would seem that the resort to the wider economic policy reforms by the new government was fundamentally rooted in the belief that macroeconomic stabilization by itself was not sustainable unless it was simultaneously accompanied by restructuring of the economy. The Finance Minister stated in his first budget speech, as if echoing Dandavate, that the origins of the economic crisis lay in 'large and persistent macroeconomic imbalances and', he added significantly, 'the low productivity of investment'. At the same time, he acknowledged that: 'Macroeconomic stabilization and fiscal adjustment alone cannot suffice. They must be supported by essential reforms in economic policy and economic management as an integral part of the adjustment process'. Outlining the reforms summarily, he implicitly suggested what was wrong with the economic structure in existence:

> The thrust of the reform process would be to increase the efficiency and international competitiveness of industrial production, to utilize for this purpose foreign investment and foreign technology to a much greater degree than we have done in the past to increase the productivity of investment, to ensure that India's financial sector is rapidly modernized, and to improve the performance of the public sector, so that the key sectors of our economy are enabled to attain an adequate technological and competitive edge in a fast changing global economy (GOI 1996, II: 1294).

At the base of the new government's seizing the opportunity of the crisis to initiate economic restructuring was a prior diagnosis that economic policies pre-dating the fiscal profligacy of the 1980s were to blame for leaving India behind in respect of the two key goals of the republic's founding fathers: (1) making India a major economic player in the world, and (2) raising the standards of living of the population. Instead, India had over the preceding four decades become marginalized on the international economic scene while one-third or more of the population was mired in poverty. The contemporary leadership was no less nationalist in its aims than the founding fathers; however, the world in which it functioned had meanwhile changed and required a different approach. In its view, there was nothing wrong with the earlier goals, which therefore required no change.

Quoting Victor Hugo on how 'no power on earth can stop an idea whose time has come', the Finance Minister resoundingly declared that 'the emergence of India as a major economic power in the world happens to be one such idea' even as he reiterated the determination to remove 'the stigma of abject poverty, ignorance and disease'.[6] In the leadership's view, the basic reason for the inability to achieve these goals, however, lay in the failure to push through rapid economic growth as a result of India's earlier economic policies. Other countries in Asia, such as Indonesia and Malaysia, had removed poverty and become major economic players through rapid growth; he poignantly noted that over the years all these countries have 'passed us by' (Singh 1993: 13–24). The leadership attributed the failure to achieve rapid growth in India to earlier policy choices, which had resulted in the country's isolation from the world economy and in an overly regulated national economy. If so, India now needed to integrate itself into the world economy and to dismantle the structures of overregulation. Hence, the drive for globalization and liberalization.

The alternative to policy change was seen as the increased marginalization of India in the world; as the Finance Minister (Singh 1992: 108–14) forthrightly and cogently stated:

> Structural change is inevitable in any society where there is rapid technical change and we live in a world where science and technology have emerged as the major determinants of power and wealth of nations. And, therefore, if our economy is not equipped to absorb, to assimilate, and to adopt this technical change which is taking place, all over the world, I think we will be marginalized. Many developing economies are already being marginalized in the new global economic system that has emerged. And it is only by successfully absorbing, assimilating, and adapting modern technological change that developing countries can acquire a minimum amount of bargaining power and influence in the management of the global interdependence. And, therefore, preparedness for handling problems of structural change is essential. This is the broad justification for economic policy initiatives taken by our government in recent months.

Indeed, it is this basic line of reasoning—holding failure to absorb modern technology as leading to marginalization—that makes intelligible the new government's alacrity for economic restructuring simultaneously with economic stabilization.

If ideas are important in the Indian stance, they are important, however, not for some inherent power of their own but only in the light of India's past economic performance. Through a process of 'social learning' key leaders had come to the understanding that earlier policies had failed to meet India's own goals, and there was hardly any merit in persisting with them. The same conclusion was, of course, self-evident to the IFIs, but the line of causality was different in India's experience. That line of causality embodying disenchantment with the earlier policy regime stretched back to Mrs Gandhi's change of economic course in 1974 and the liberalization measures adopted by her government in the first half of the 1980s. That line continued through Rajiv Gandhi with his ambitious, though stalled, liberalization programme. His thrust for liberalization is particularly important since it was inaugurated without the presence of any economic crisis and without any involvement of the IFIs. It is not only Mrs Gandhi and Rajiv Gandhi that are important but also their economic advisors, most preeminently L.K. Jha, who sought to educate the intellectual elites about the perverse effects of earlier economic policies. Besides, a series of high-powered committees had since the late 1970s made recommendations for deregulation in specific areas of the economy. An important segment, albeit small, of India's political and bureaucratic elites had thus become convinced of the need for change in direction, without needing to be convinced at the behest of the IFIs. If the IFIs applied pressure at all, they were pressing against an already opened door. A crucial piece of evidence to this effect lies in the election manifesto of the Congress Party for the 1991 elections, prepared personally by Rajiv Gandhi.

As the most important political party in the election, the Indian National Congress (1991: 22, 35–38) declared in its manifesto, without using the word 'liberalization' for fear of being attacked, its intent nonetheless to pursue the content of liberalization through 'a sound policy framework: encouragement of entrepreneurship, development of capital markets, simplification of the regulatory system, bringing in new technology and increasing competitiveness for the benefit of the common man'. Again, it asserted that 'foreign investment and technology collaboration will be permitted to obtain higher technology, to increase exports and to expand the production base'. More significantly, it acknowledged that 'some public sector companies have become lethargic, inefficient and expensive' and pointedly underlined that specific spheres could no longer be the assured preserve of the public sector by declaring that it would 'abolish the monopoly of any sector or any individual enterprise in any field of manufacture, except on strategic or military considerations, and open all manufacturing activity to competition'.

Finance Minister Manmohan Singh was, therefore, not wrong when he asserted that 'the bulk of the reform programme is based on the election manifesto of our Party' (GOI 1996, II: 1335). What the manifesto said was, of course, consistent with what Rajiv Gandhi had endeavoured to push through during his tenure as prime minister. Incidentally, the need for policy change on the basis of the poor economic performance of the past was not confined to the Congress Party. The rising Bharatiya Janata Party was even more emphatic about dismantling the regulatory apparatus, though its position on globalization was moderated by its economic nationalism. Thus, over a substantial period of time there had built up a cumulative discontent with the earlier economic paradigm, and since the mid-1970s successive governments had attempted to shift policies, though on a piecemeal basis. It is in the light of this background that it becomes intelligible why the Finance Minister saw 'no reason to be defensive about our agenda', holding 'this programme is for a self-reliant India'. He repudiated any inference about having surrendered India's sovereignty 'when we are implementing our own agenda' (Singh 1993: 23–24).

Although the new leadership did not come to office with a predetermined design for the economic policy reforms, there had been considerable preparation about the general direction that it should follow. Indeed, in launching the restructuring programme, the leadership was encouraged by the confidence gained from the experience of the several doses of liberalization during the decade of the 1980s. That decade evidenced a remarkable break in the earlier pattern of slow growth. Even though there is room for serious argument over whether it was fiscal profligacy or the partial liberalization that was responsible for the decade-long growth rate of over 5 per cent, a strong belief prevailed that liberalization accounted for it. Meanwhile, developments in the international system reinforced the new leadership in its conviction that the course it had chosen on the basis of domestic factors was correct. The collapse of the Soviet bloc as a result of failure on the economic front, while China marched forward triumphantly as it integrated with the global economy and took to the path of the market, held little future for the socialist model that India had thus far followed. The combination of the domestic economic crisis and the external collapse of the command economy model served 'to change the mindset' in India (Singh 1997: 26).

To be sure, the circle that was convinced of the need for globalization and liberalization and was enthusiastic about reform was narrow, and constituted perhaps a rather lonely group; it consisted primarily of the Prime Minister, the Finance Minister, and Commerce Minister P. Chidambaram, and their team of bureaucratic and technocratic advisors, principally Finance Secretary Montek Singh Ahluwalia, Reserve Bank Governor C. Rangarajan, public finance specialist Raja Chelliah, and chief economic adviser Shankar Acharya. Most of the cabinet was indifferent to the reforms and concerned only that they should not affect their support groups adversely. There were opponents as well, such as N.D. Tiwari and Arjun Singh. Despite the narrowness of the circle of reformers, the reforms nonetheless had a wider basis of support in society beyond the commonplace notion of the immediate necessity to overcome the crisis through stabilization measures; seasoned economist Vyasulu (1996: 4–5), not unsympathetic to the left, underlined the nature of this support:

> it is undeniable that across the country, articulate people, especially those in the middle class, are responding positively to newly emerging opportunities.... it is interesting that most seem to recognize the need for reform, although there are fierce disagreements about the content and pace of the reforms....
>
> One reason could lie in the fact that the liberalization and deregulation of the economy and society that has begun is appreciated by an articulate section of Indian society whose support is sought by all parties.... People are in the mood for change; the old ways, it is felt, do not offer us an adequate solution any more; and so people are ready for new ways of doing things. There are high hopes and expectations.... Most people accept that the process of change has just begun; much more needs to be done, even if it is

not very clear exactly what is needed. This is a major, and significant, change in the Indian economy in the 1990s. Its importance must not be underestimated.

The optimism that one sees in the articulate middle classes is in stark contrast to the depression and gloom that characterized the same groups in the economy in much of 1991. This transformation, at least in the mind of the so called middle class has not been clearly understood yet.

Once the economic policy reforms were implemented, even if only partially, they themselves had a profound impact by way of changing the mindset of the country. One manifestation of this was the more immediate effect on the debate among the political parties. As Vyasulu (1996: 3) observed when the initial reform process was under way:

> Whatever the issues in the debate, the fact remains that now, four years after the NEP was launched, it is, for all practical purposes, irreversible in many essential ways. In its inevitably political responses to the fiscal crisis of 1991, the government has begun a process of economic and social change that now has a logic of its own. No one wants a return to the Raj of Regulation and Control in which decisions were taken by the bureaucracy on a case by case basis; that, it is hoped, has gone for ever. The opposition parties too are struggling to redefine and differentiate their positions on the matter of economic reforms, with some brazenly jumping on to the reform bandwagon; interesting cases of such change (noted in passing without rendering any judgement), are the Marxist government of West Bengal; the Janata Dal government of Karnataka which has also accepted the reforms as they are; and also the BJP government in Gujarat. Today, all political parties are committed to some kind of reform, even though they are reacting to initiative of the Congress Party and have no clearly articulated economic or political logic of their own: with the Bharatiya Janata Party and its slogan of 'swadeshi' as a possible exception.

The nature of the economic debate in the country had thus visibly changed.

The economic policy reforms had, therefore, less to do with the pressures of the IFIs or simply the intellectual power of new economic ideas, but more with the experience-based realization that earlier economic policies had failed to achieve the national goals to which the leadership was committed and that reforms were there-fore necessary to achieve those goals.[7]

Explaining the New Balance: Why the Change was Limited

In launching the process of economic policy reform, reformers theoretically have a choice between two approaches to the pace of reform: (1) big bang or shock therapy, and (2) gradualism or incrementalism. Mainstream economists often favour and recommend— as do the IFIs—the course of shock therapy. They hold it as delivering better results since it sweeps away the debris of the previous system with all its accumulated irrationalities; the pain that goes with its austerity is taken to be the necessary cost for the subsequent gain of better economic performance. Against this, the gradualist approach is less well regarded, for it is considered to retard the process of economic policy reforms after the first flush of enthusiasm as lobby groups mobilize to defeat change that would affect their narrow interests even if it is beneficial for the country as a whole. Countries often cited in support of the case for the advantages of shock therapy are Chile and Poland, and their performance is contrasted with the poor record of some of the other East European countries that took the gradualist path.

Even though the preference for the shock therapy approach may, when expressed in strictly economic terms, seem technically neutral, it hides a powerful political prescription, for it requires an authoritarian regime, as is obvious in the case of Chile, to suppress the protests of those who are hurt by the reform measures. The shock therapy approach thus implicitly requires not simply a change in economic policy but also a change in the political system. Moreover, the choice of shock therapy is not open to all regimes; typically it has occurred in states where the earlier regime has been discredited or overthrown (as in Chile) or has collapsed (as in the Soviet bloc). This was not the case in India, and consequently the course of shock therapy was not available to Indian decision-makers even if the leadership had been so inclined. There was, therefore, no immediate and wholesale overthrow of the previous set of economic policies, notwithstanding the implicit rejection of them by the new leadership.

Instead, though it may not have all been blueprinted in advance, a deliberate phased or sequenced transition was adopted by the leadership towards the goal of a more deregulated and globalized economy. There was no automatic following of a generalized menu from the IFIs or other sources; rather, policies had to be filtered through the leadership's own assessment of what was in the overall national interest, of what amount of reform would be a feasible basis for building a political consensus, and what would be acceptable to the populace at a given time. Thus, for example, India refused to follow IMF advice on the immediate convertibility of the rupee, even on the current account, but phased it over a considerable period of time. Similarly, despite the rhetoric, there was little attempt at privatization of the public sector, or at formulating an exit policy, or at a sustained attack on subsidies.

The fundamental reason for this cautious and gradualist course was India's political system of democracy, which required balancing the concerns of both accumulation and legitimacy and therefore dictated policy-making on the basis of consensus. Finance Minister Manmohan Singh himself gave expression to the need for consensus in India's political system: 'In a large democratic setup such as ours, the dilemma of a reformer is compounded in as much as he has to balance economic logic with political and social acceptability and carry out the tasks laid out' (Singh 1995: 17–22). At the initiation of the reforms, the government had the additional handicap of being a minority government, and had to carry the other political parties with it to enact policy; in some cases, the opposition parties were able to block action, as in the case of patents policy. But even if the government had a majority, it would have had to be sensitive to the larger concerns of legitimacy.

The reforms were sequenced over a period of time, from one budget to the next. Before they were enacted, high-powered committees were set up to make recommendations; thus, the Tax Reform Committee, the Committee on the Financial System, and the Insurance Reform Committee. The recommendations were made a part of public discussion with key groups with a view to building a consensus on reform policies and gaining legitimacy for them. All along, the government was mindful of the concerns of crucial groups, such as the middle classes, who could riot, or organized labour, which could strike. It is as if the leadership was acting on the basis of lessons from the experience of Rajiv Gandhi's encounter with these groups that had blocked his reform programme. Indeed, the salient characteristic of the reforms was that they were rather painless; they could, in fact, be called 'adjustment without pain'. In essence, the leadership counted on the private sector, particularly foreign investors, to resolve its problem of economic growth while it provided a hospitable economic environment for it through partially dismantling controls and widening the market through the bonanza of reductions in corporate and personal taxes. It would seem that no group was particularly hurt by the reforms. India enacted the 'soft' reforms, but stopped at the door of the 'hard' reforms, illustrating in the process the limits of the consensus on reform. If there was pain inflicted, it was as a result of the initial stabilization with its expenditure-cutting which affected investment in development, the social sectors and, especially, defence. However, that was more a consequence of the original economic crisis rather than the reactive policy, for the pain would have been more severe if the crisis had been allowed to continue. Even the initial cut in expenditures on the social sectors in the first two budgets was followed by large increases in investment in these sectors, including new initiatives in job creation and poverty alleviation, in subsequent budgets.

Of particular concern for the leadership in the reform process were impending elections, not only at the centre of a vast continental polity but also in more than two dozen states. The frequency and scheduling of these elections was not within its control. It faced major state elections in 1994 and 1995. The dread of these elections put the leadership on the defensive. It is not important for the analysis here whether the leadership was correct in its fear of electoral reprisal from key groups in reaction to imposition of sacrifice for purposes of reform. What is important is that this calculus has been at the heart of the electoral strategy of all governments since the end of single-party dominance; the fervour for reform evaporates with the approach of elections. As much was publicly acknowledged by Manmohan Singh.[8] Consequently, once the crisis passed—as it did in about 20 months—there was a return to normal politics and the dramatic reform process essentially came to a halt. The commitment to reducing the fiscal deficit weakened in the face of new elections while the propensity to provide subsidies intensified. As the Finance Minister admitted, the crisis passed too quickly and, since politics is the art of the possible, not all that the government wanted to do could be achieved. In the end, caution did not save the government;

it lost the general elections in 1996 and gave way to another coalition government.

It is evident nonetheless that policy did not necessarily follow what reform-minded economists, whether in India or the IFIs, recommended except only in so far as it fit in with the leadership's reading of what was economically necessary and politically feasible. However, this posture of the leadership was fundamentally dictated by the nature of the state which was so structured as to compel taking the interests of key groups into account in its policy-making.

Summary and Conclusions

Economic globalization and economic nationalism are interactive forces and are constantly undergoing change. The type of balance that exists between them varies from country to country; no single type can be said to prevail everywhere. In the Indian case, the earlier balance which incorporated high levels of both external protection and internal regulation (type A1 in Figure 4.1) came to be replaced after the economic policy reforms of the early and mid-1990s by another balance which combined medium levels of protection and regulation (type B2). Much was achieved by way of reform, but equally much remained unaccomplished, whether viewed in terms of the overall design of the reformers or the agenda of the IFIs. The fundamental reason for that lay not in ignorance about what was required technically in terms of new policies, but in the very nature of the state where the democratic framework of politics placed limits on what could be achieved.

The economic policy reforms that were accomplished have, no doubt, by virtue simply of their having taken place, created a slow momentum for piecemeal reform in one sector or another, but a concerted attack on a broad front seems unlikely in the absence of an economic crisis. Even the reforms that had been pushed through took place because of the contingent circumstance of an economic crisis; the triggering mechanism for the reforms was the economic crisis. Key economic and political leaders had been aware for some time of the need for reform, as was evident under Rajiv Gandhi in the mid-1980s, but only a crisis could propel them to bold decisions. Initially, even the crisis did not lead to action during the period between the Gulf crisis and the new elections in mid-1991, because the minority government in power was paralyzed by the lack of support in Parliament. Only when the electoral cycle assured a reasonably stable government, though not yet in absolute majority, could swift and bold action take place, demonstrating in the process the capacity of a democracy to act in a situation of crisis. The crisis provided the state with sufficient autonomy to push through reforms, while ongoing responsibility to an elected Parliament imposed restraint against actions that would have imposed—in line with the prescriptions of shock therapy—unacceptable burdens on key groups. At the same time, a cohesive economic team managed the transition from a situation of macroeconomic imbalances to economic stability relatively smoothly and painlessly. The measures undertaken were dictated by the existential fact of the economic crisis—itself a result of earlier fiscally imprudent state policies—rather than the IFIs, even if formally the targets were decided in negotiations with the IFIs.

Almost simultaneously with the stabilization measures, the state took on with alacrity the task of economic restructuring, thus going beyond any IMF conditionalities that may have been required. The incentive for this course was the fundamental realization on the part of strategically-placed state elites that previous policies had failed to achieve India's goals of poverty elimination and acquisition of a major role in international economic affairs. Although the reform measures came piecemeal and were stretched over a half-decade, they were part of a larger design to decisively shift the economy from a highly insulated and controlled regime to one that was integrated with the world economy and relied primarily on the market. One may not agree with this vision, but it is not the case—as critics charged—that there was no vision behind the reform measures. However, the design could not be fully implemented as the crisis dissipated relatively quickly. In the absence of a crisis, further reform became difficult because the state's institutional structure required the support of key groups, especially labour, which would be hurt by reform. Where reform would hurt any substantial and powerful group, the state generally refrained from it. What had been pushed through by way of reform, however, seemed to have become institutionalized into the system, in view of the evident consensus on it. Significantly, fundamental to the entire process—the generation of the crisis, the initiative for policy change, the limits to reform, and the consolidation of policy—was the nature of the Indian state, predominantly its democratic character and its institutional complexity.

Notes

1. On the content of the reforms, see Chelliah (1996); Gupta (1993); GOI (1996, II: 1251–1477); Joshi and Little (1996); Vyasulu (1996). For a critique of the reforms from a left perspective, see Bhaduri and Nayyar (1996); Kurien (1994); and Nayyar (1996).
2. The distinction between crisis and non-crisis contexts forms one of the distinctive themes of Grindle and Thomas (1991).
3. See, for example, Nagaraj (1997: 2869–79), who holds: 'A sudden drying up of inward remittances and the west Asian markets because of the Gulf War, and the collapse of the Soviet economy—then India's largest trading partner—were the proximate economic causes of the crisis'. See also Basu (1993: 2599–2605).
4. On the concept of state power, see McFaul (1995: 211–43); it consists of two analytically distinct elements: (1) state autonomy, which involves the ability of the state to define goals or preferences, where 'the degree of consensus within the state is the key determinant of its ability to define preferences independently of leading economic interest groups'; and (2) state capacity, which involves the ability of the state to implement goals on which a consensus has been reached, where the key determinants are 'the effectiveness and cohesiveness of government institutions'.
5. For the text, see *Business and Political Observer* (New Delhi), 18 December 1991; see also Das (1993, I: 296–322).
6. GOI (1996, II: 1300, 1331–32). In his 1995–96 budget speech, the Finance Minister declared: 'It is this vision, of a resurgent India, taking her rightful place as an economic power house in Asia, which has inspired our economic policies' (ibid.: 1401). Note also the comment in Chelliah (1996: 9): 'Indeed, the overall objective of the reform programme is to accelerate the rate of growth of the economy as a means of making India strong and to eradicate poverty'.
7. A strong case has been made by two authors from the left, Patnaik and Chandrasekhar (1998: 67–91), on the pressures of the IFIs as the source for India's economic restructuring. However, it remained for another progressive, albeit non-Indian, scholar to dismiss their stance as an implausible 'conspiracy theory' and to attribute the change in economic policy to India's past mediocre economic performance: 'The reforms in India, I suggest, reflect not tutoring and arm twisting by the Bank and Fund but the lessons of bitter experience in India itself' (Keith Griffin, in Baker et al. 1998: 92–94). It is curious that nowhere in their long article do Patnaik and Chandrasekhar refer to the collapse of the command economies of the Soviet bloc, let alone discuss its impact on the thinking of India's decision-makers; the same is the case with Ghosh (1998: 295–334).
8. 'We have slipped into a system where we have elections somewhere or the other every year. When elections are round the corner, the politicians' minds get diverted to short-term electoral gains and sometimes the longer-term gains of restructuring the economy get second place' (*Economic Times*, 19 March 1996).

5
Business and Economic Reforms

The paradigm shift in India's economic policy through the reforms during the first half of the decade of the 1990s effectively changed the balance between globalization and nationalism in the policy. The country moved from a situation of high regulation internally and high protection externally to a situation of moderate regulation and moderate protection. An interesting question that arises relates to the responses of different social and political groups to the reforms. Apart from its inherent importance in respect of the stance of particular groups, the question has an essential bearing on the future of the reforms. For, groups in India can influence the course of policy since state and society are joined through a set of institutions in the making of policy under the country's political system of representative democracy.

Given India's immense social diversity and its democratic framework, it is to be expected that there would be a plethora of social groups oriented toward the state for the satisfaction of their demands. However, it would be an arduous undertaking to deal with all of them. Here, the analysis will focus on business, which—as the owner of economic enterprises and the employer of managers and labour—is a key group. In discussing the response of business to the reforms, this chapter is divided into three parts: (1) a general overview of the changing business response after the launching of the reforms; (2) an analytical exploration into the factors underlying the particular pattern of business response; and (3) a discussion of the overall strategy of business to cope with the challenge presented by the reforms.

The Changing Response of Business

Even when the discussion is focused on the single group of business, it is obvious that this social category is overly broad, covering in function both trade and industry and in size from the small-scale traders and industrialists through the medium enterprises to the large industrial houses. These constituent elements diverge in their interests at times and they have their own organizational expressions. The treatment here is largely focused on the corporate sector, which carries the greatest economic power and gets the most attention in the media.

At the apex, this corporate sector is represented by three separate business associations. The most eminent among them has been the Federation of Indian Chambers of Commerce and Industry (FICCI) which—arising in 1927 as a counterforce to the lobby for foreign business in order to protect the interests of Indian business and industry—had allied itself with the nationalist movement; while it was the most influential business association for much of the half-century after independence, it was over most of that period alienated from the Indian state because of the latter's ideological penchant for socialism and for possession of the 'commanding heights' of the economy; more nationalist and outspoken than the other two associations, its well thought out positions on policy carry considerable weight. The second association, the Associated Chambers of Commerce and Industry, or more commonly Assocham, was founded in 1920 and is the oldest but weakest of the three; before independence, it was the bastion of foreign business interests, primarily British, but it now includes Indian business as well, giving the organization somewhat of a split personality; foreign MNCs continue to have a major presence and its pronouncements are coloured by the intent to protect the interests of that lobby. By the 1990s, these two organizations had become overshadowed by the more powerful CII (Confederation of Indian Industry) because of its larger resources—1996 budget Rs 393 million compared to FICCI's Rs 53 million and Assocham's Rs 35 million—its action-oriented approach, and its greater influence; founded in 1974 as the Association of Indian Engineering

Industry, and recycled in 1986 as the Confederation of Engineering Industry, CII represents the more modern, younger and professional face of Indian industry.

When the economic policy reforms were launched in 1991, they were greeted with great enthusiasm by the business community. In key respects, the reforms met the longstanding demands of the community. For years, business had been critical of the ubiquitous licensing system requiring government permission for establishing and expanding capacity, of the excessively high rates of corporate and personal taxation, of the severe restrictions on imports of goods and technology, and of the tight controls on foreign investment and foreign exchange transactions. Suddenly, in 1991 much of the licensing and control structure was dismantled because of the exigencies of the state's economic crisis. Meanwhile, taxes were cut drastically and customs duties were slashed. Big business was delighted at this unexpected turn of events. Though there may have been grumbling on the part of the small-scale industrial sector about the threat to its existence from greater competition, it was eclipsed by the welcome accorded by big business. As one observer noted: 'Ask any industrialist to go on record with what he thinks the sweeping economic reforms in 1991 mean for business and industry and chances are he will gush about how these are bold and historic changes, how they could change the future of the Indian economy, how industry will now be on the fast track and, of course, how Indian business had been rooting for all these reforms all along' (Narayan 1992). Indeed, FICCI president-elect V.I. Dutt declared: 'Most of the government's policies that have been announced originated in FICCI. Others just rephrased the suggestions' (*Economic Times*, 7 September 1991).

If there was some scepticism expressed in private about the reforms, it related more to the suspicion that the turn in the government's orientation was too good to be true, because: 'For too long, the private sector has been suffering what, to its mind, were the whims of government and a recalcitrant bureaucracy whose sole objective too often seemed to be to make things as difficult as possible for business'. In the circumstance, 'industry feels like a prisoner who is suddenly paroled.... But the prisoner isn't convinced. Years of confinement have taken its toll and he's sure there's a catch somewhere' (Narayan 1992). Despite the scepticism, there was welcome for the change, but it applied fundamentally to only one side of the reforms—that which pertained to liberalization, or more accurately 'internal liberalization'—since it apparently pushed the government off the backs of business. There was another side to the reforms, however, that of globalization or 'external liberalization', which opened the Indian economy to competition from abroad through allowing more and cheaper imports as also foreign investment. At the beginning, the reaction to this aspect was muted, because its impact was not immediately obvious, but it was not altogether absent. Not surprisingly, that reaction came from FICCI, which was unhappy with the red carpet treatment accorded to foreign companies and NRIs; its president K.K. Birla let it be known publicly, which did not endear him to the authorities, that the reforms were not in the best interests of the country or industry; more particularly, he objected to the automatic raising of the level of permitted foreign equity to 51 per cent, rendering local companies into second class citizens since restrictions continued on Indian promoters (founding shareholders) from expanding their share of the equity (*Times of India*, 1 August 1991).

As recognition of the depth of policy change dawned on Indian business and as the latter realized the consequences of the pulling down of the barriers of an earlier protectionist regime against imports and as well of the state's new embrace of foreign investment through concessions, misgivings became more widespread among Indian industry over the sudden and hasty exposure of the domestic economy to the stormy gales of foreign competition. Misgivings soon turned into apprehension. The first serious omens of discontent appeared with the news of a private meeting among several prominent industrialists in Bombay in 1993—chief among them Rahul Bajaj, the owner of the scooter manufacturing giant Bajaj Auto—to share their concerns and plan strategy. This particular group of businessmen, who were sceptical of the proffered wisdom on economic liberalization, was soon dubbed as the Bombay Club, though there was hardly any organizational reality to it.

Even though these businessmen were, in the atmosphere of the apparently state-endorsed, if not state-induced, xenophilia of the time, put on the defensive for being allegedly anti-reform and anti-foreign, business discontent mounted and it gradually found more public and authoritative expression. Even the CII, normally bending over backwards to be friendly to MNCs, now felt uneasy at the threat that foreign capital posed to Indian industry. In March 1996, in an unexpected broadside, CII Director-General Tarun Das sharply attacked the behaviour of foreign multinationals in India, pointedly referring to their 'cowboy' approach toward their local partners.[1] Most opposition parties, especially the Bharatiya Janata Party (BJP) and the Communist Party of India (Marxist), saw a vindication of their position in this attack, even as the Congress Party regarded it as a political gimmick on the eve of national elections, indeed a sinister move on the part of the CII to ingratiate itself with the BJP. CII insisted that it welcomed foreign investment, but that MNC behaviour was a legitimate issue. 'The debate ... generated by the CII changing its attitude to multinationals, from being an ardent supporter to becoming a staunch critic' (Pani 1996) marked a significant stage in the developing posture of business towards MNCs.

In the subsequent months, the debate over the issue intensified. Assocham president H. Somany made known his own distaste for what he regarded as the government's pro-MNC policies (*Economic Times*, 19 October 1996). Then in early 1997, there was considerable sensation caused by the report of an Assocham committee chaired by prominent industrialist Lalit Mohan Thapar. That report asked the government to limit foreign equity in joint industrial ventures to 40 per cent outside the case of some 50 industrial sectors where foreign investors had already been allowed majority ownership, to require disinvestment on the part of 100 per cent foreign subsidiaries through a time-bound programme to levels that were normally operative at the time of their exceptional approval, and to bar 100 per cent subsidiaries in the future.[2] However, there was an uproar within Assocham, given the strong presence of MNCs within it, and it was averred that Thapar's position was merely an expression of his personal opinion and not the official policy of the association. Interestingly, earlier in 1996, even CII had discussed a paper on regulating access for foreign investment, but the furore it aroused among its MNC members similarly resulted in CII's softening of its position (*Business Standard*, 4 February 1997).

It was abundantly evident, however, that Indian industry was unhappy with the impact that state policy was having on it. Behind the increase in stridency of the business community over foreign competition lay the worsening of the economic environment, what with the liquidity crunch given the very high interest rates, the weakening of the capital market, and the deepening perception that the government was indifferent to the problems of domestic entrepreneurs in contrast to its alleged fondness for foreign MNCs. The rising business discontent provided the BJP the opportunity to exploit the issue effectively and to highlight, consistent with its established ideological posture, the importance of its economic programme of *swadeshi* (economic nationalism). In turn, business came to see economic virtue in a political party that so far had been treated as an outcast by the business leadership, enhancing in the process, the BJP's legitimacy within the political system.

The Underlying Causes for Business Disenchantment

Business discontent could not all be attributed to some peculiar economic xenophobia. In the new economic situation resulting from the reforms, Indian business had some genuine grievances. In the absence of redress or even a sympathetic hearing for them, business felt its future to be in serious peril. Several factors lay behind this perception of threat, chief among them: the nature of the business world in India as conditioned by its past, state policy and the resulting unfavourable economic situation as it unfolded with liberalization, and the behaviour of foreign business towards its Indian partners and competitors.

The Legacy of the Past

In its contemporary situation of having to face economic competition from the global capitalist economy both in terms of imports and foreign MNCs located in the national economy, the Indian business community started out with certain disabilities or handicaps that it inherited from the past. The modern Indian business class had struggled to come into existence and develop against a state under British colonial rule that was apathetic, indeed hostile, to Indian aspirations for industrialization while it was protective of metropolitan (British) economic interests. This class had grown out of the traditional trading communities of the pre-colonial era, and accordingly bore the imprint of the ethos of the trader, eager to make a quick profit out of an existing economic situation, rather than carrying the orientation of the capitalist entrepreneur intent on creating new profit opportunities through transformation of the means of production. Business firms typically remained tightly-controlled family operations (Datta 1997: 3–24), with the façade of the joint stock company, rather than become transformed into modern professionally-managed corpora-tions with widely-held public ownership. This tendency was rein-forced by the dominant British practice of operating business in India through the managing agency system, under which a variety of firms were managed through a holding financial company, the main interest of which was to siphon off funds to its controllers from the various economic enterprises. Because of its trading origins and its development within the constraints of British imperialism, the busi-ness class as it entered the post-war period did not bear the marks of a mature or developed capitalist class, even though it was not a com-prador class since it had developed in opposition to imperialism and was allied with the nationalist movement.

The half-century after independence could have made for the cre-ation out of this business class, as in Japan, of a number of business giants with a reasonable chance of not only adequately meeting the competition from foreign MNCs when the economy was finally thrown open, but also with the potential of becoming global players themselves. However, that possibility was effectively scotched by the high policy of the state to prevent the development of business giants in the private sector in the name of avoiding private monopo-lies. Instead, ideologically convinced of the superiority of the socialist path, the leadership at the helm of the state preempted the creation of business giants for the public sector. Note, for example, that all of the first 9 of the top 10 and that 20 of the top 25 economic enter-prises in India in 1986–87, ranked according to sales income, were from the public sector (*Quarterly Economic Report*, Nos. 124–25, July–December 1988). However, these public sector enterprises, barring a few cases, had their own infirmities—flowing out of state ownership and control—in meeting global competition. What is more, they were largely commodity-producing enterprises rather than firms with branded consumer goods, precisely the area in which foreign MNCs posed the threat of economic domination. Also, the private corporate sector was barred from large segments of the con-sumer goods sector, which were reserved for small-scale industry.

The private sector in post-liberalization India thus started out with this important strike on the basis of size against it in the compe-tition with foreign MNCs. Its enterprises are today largely pygmies compared to the foreign players. Interestingly, it is not well known that Mahatma Gandhi had dealt with the question of competition between local and foreign economic players under colonial rule, more specifically in the case of shipping. In a series of articles on the subject in his periodical *Young India*, he declared himself to be an 'out and out protectionist' while he castigated the British for building their prosperity 'upon the ruin of India's commerce and industry'. He remarked: 'The cottage industry of India had to perish in order that Lancashire might flourish. The Indian shipping had to perish so that British shipping might flourish'. He disputed the British logic in opposing any coastal reservation for Indian shipping as flag discrimination, pointedly asking: 'What is equality of rights between a giant and a dwarf?' (Jog 1969: 67, 84). The same issue has arisen with even greater poignancy for Indian business in the contemporary era, where state policy seems to have forced local dwarfs to face competition with foreign giants. As an MP from West Bengal once expressed it, the globalization of the Indian economy is like integrating a mouse into a herd of elephants (*Business India*, 22 June–5 July 1992: 118). However, it is noteworthy that the absence of local giants in the private sector is related directly to the earlier economic policy of the state which made the public sector the chosen site for local giants.

Even in the limited arena that was left over to the private sector, the state further fostered for almost half a century, both positively through incentives and negatively through licensing and controls, an economic environment which essentially precluded the private sector from acquiring genuine experience of competition or the structural capacity for it. On the one hand, the state provided important incentives to the private sector for growth. It made available cheap and ample finance to private firms through development-oriented public financial institutions (PFIs). Indeed, only a small, even nominal, equity stake was required of the promoter of an enterprise; the rest was provided by the PFIs such as ICICI and IDBI, either in the form of equity or loan finance. Such was the massive presence of PFIs in the financial structure of private sector firms that observers seriously asked as to what was private at all about the private sector. The easy availability of public finance enabled promoters to create and expand firms in the private sector in areas that were not reserved for the state. In changed circumstances, however, this state-fostered growth could not but become a source of serious vulnerability for private firms. Given the small equity stake of the promoter, the fate of the firm depended on the PFIs. At the same time, the small stake of the promoter encouraged unethical business practices to siphon out finance from the firm, resulting in large-scale industrial sickness in the economy, particularly in the small-scale sector which was the special beneficiary of state-sponsored largesse. It was this kind of private sector, with the shaky and uncertain hold of promoters, that was asked to face competition from the global economy.

Beyond public finance, the greatest incentive that the state provided for growth and expansion of firms in the private sector was by way of making available a captive market, thus assuring economic success for literally any and every enterprise. Externally, this was done through quantitative restrictions and steep customs duties under the state's inward-oriented economic strategy. With little fear of competition and therefore failure, Indian firms became accustomed to producing goods of poor quality, since anything was bound to sell, and offering poor service to customers, for they had nowhere else to go. The firms were thus in no shape to face competition from the global economy under a more liberalized regime. Internally, the state provided a guaranteed market through the licensing system, under which installation or expansion of capacity was sanctioned largely to correspond to known demand.

On the other hand, in its desire to prevent the possible growth of private monopolies, the state issued licences for such capacity, not on the basis of economic-scale units of production, but by fragmenting capacity among many producers. The licensing policy encouraged business houses with the necessary resources to capture licences in order to corner the market, but capacity fragmentation by the state led them at the same time to attempt diversification through extensively branching out into all kinds of unrelated fields rather than expand through intensively developing select industries. The result was an inefficient and flabby industrial structure of agglomerative firms under family control, with fragmented capacities and without economies of scale, largely stagnant technologically, dependent on the state for finance and protected market, hemmed in by the straitjacket of controls in literally every aspect of the economy, with little experience of real competition, and with a vested interest in an economy of scarcity and shortages which the system of controls had provided. It was this state-dependent and non-dynamic mutant of a private sector—which Manmohan Singh once characterized as 'functionless capitalism'—that liberalization forced to face competition, not just among its internal constituents, but from the global economy at that.

Most commentators in India's financial press, in their latter-day conversion to liberalism, are quick to decry, even condemn, the Indian industrial class for its weaknesses and its past neglect of the consumer, as if they are somehow congenital characteristics. They are further ready to allow it to receive its just deserts at the hands of foreign players in the name of competition, the natural working of the market, and the interests of the consumer. They tend to forget, however, that the acquisition by the Indian business class of its alleged features was but a rational response to the overarching framework that was installed by an ideologically-committed leadership and entrenched by a political class that found it to be an eminently useful arrangement for itself.

State Policy and the New Economic Situation

Even though businessmen operating under the licensing system may have privately worked out profitable arrangements with political leaders—no doubt for a price which the latter could extract because of their control of political power—the business class under that system was excessively dependent on the state; it appeared as a supplicant at the doors of the state, and it was treated with disdain and contempt by a mostly arrogant political leadership and bureaucracy. Its pleas over the years for liberalization and deregulation had been simply brushed aside. When the state finally undertook liberalization, it was not in response to the entreaties of business but to its own compulsions in an economic crisis.

Given the economic legacy of the past, it would seem that, from the perspective of Indian industry, this liberalization was introduced too suddenly and too quickly, without local business having been prepared adequately for competition over a period of time through a gradual, carefully modulated and selectively applied process of liberalization. In retrospect, some saw merit in a sequential priority for 'internal liberalization' as against 'external liberalization' over a significant period, which choice would have—by weaning the Indian business class away from the deep-rooted regime of controls—aided in socializing that class into competition and in developing domestic giants with the potential capacity to meet foreign competition. While such an option may seem ideally preferable, it is doubtful that the Indian political system would have had the capacity to generate a process of such gradual structural change, on its own. In any case, the die had already been cast in the context of economic crisis in favour of liberalization simultaneously on the internal and external fronts, which suddenly exposed Indian firms to what was regarded as ruthless, indeed predatory, competition from foreign giants. In this situation of fait accompli, Indian business continued to swear by competition, but more and more it found merit in the argument of 'an even playing field' in the competition between local and foreign players. There was some justification for this stance, for the new economic situation after liberalization confronted Indian business with unequal competition, in which the cards were stacked against it in several respects.

First, as already pointed out, Indian business suffered in comparison with foreign MNCs from the smaller size of its enterprises and as well from a certain structural deformation through having operated for four decades under a regime of controls. Second, the cost of capital for Indian business has been significantly higher as compared to that for MNCs. Real interest rates have been much lower in the world economy outside India—to which much of Indian business does not have access—than within the country. For example, in India the prime lending bank rate in 1997 was 13.5 per cent compared to 10.10 per cent in Malaysia, 9.50 per cent in Hong Kong, 8.5 per cent in the US and South Korea; even though the Indian prime lending was lower than before yet the real interest rates were around 16 per cent (*Hindu*, 8 January 1998). Meanwhile, long gone are the days of easy finance that was available to Indian industry before liberalization. In contrast, foreign MNCs have huge financial resources at their disposal, not only to set up industry but to buy out existing Indian enterprises. The financial strength of MNCs also enables them to bear losses for sustained periods and thus to muscle out Indian partners from joint ventures, grabbing control of their companies in the process, and to oust Indian competitors from the market. Third, Indian firms still continued to suffer from handicaps developed under the earlier regime of controls. For example, structural adjustment at the macroeconomic level necessitated restructuring at the level of firms as well, but such restructuring encountered problems because labour legislation basically bars retrenchment of excess manpower inherited from the pre-reform era. Thus, downsizing had been rendered difficult for Indian companies except at the cost of expensive voluntary retirement packages. As against this,

MNCs start their new enterprises with modern technology and reduced requirements for labour.

Fourth, in several respects Indian firms have been at a disadvantage in relation to the global economy, if not always in relation to foreign MNCs located in India. For one thing, even though direct taxes on both corporate and personal income have in recent years been brought down, making them comparable to world levels, the indirect tax structure continues to be unreformed so that high, multiple and cascading taxes—especially at the local level, where they are not applicable to foreign imports—result in making Indian goods uncompetitive. FICCI president K.K. Modi called this aspect the 'subsidization of imports' (*Economic Times*, 3 February 1998). In addition, the tariff structure has at times contained some serious anomalies, such as when finished goods attract lower tariffs than raw materials and components. Thus, one representative of the electronics industry pointed out how tariff distortions—with the burden of import duties on raw materials at 40–50 per cent as against 25 per cent on finished products and components—had a ruinous impact on indigenous industry: 'the electronics industry is losing its strengths in manufacturing and is changing into an agency which merely markets imported goods. Previously active manufacturing organizations have now become trading posts' (ibid., 20 June 1996). Again, as Rahul Bajaj pointed out, the state has allowed imports from MNCs in areas that are reserved for the small-scale industry whereas Indian business is not allowed to produce in those areas (*Hindu*, 8 December 1997). From the perspective of domestic manufacturers, the state has thus not been sufficiently vigilant about their interests, for it has allowed profit margins of domestic firms to be squeezed by cheaper imports. Furthermore, with India's infrastructure in poor shape, the costs for Indian manufacturers, particularly in respect of power, have been very high.

Fifth, in some areas the state has pursued policies that have discriminated in favour of MNCs. Thus, in the power sector the state has offered counter-guarantees only to MNCs for fast-track projects without making available similar concessions to Indian firms. Again, the taxation of capital gains have favoured foreign firms with far lower rates, which could further be avoided altogether by such firms coming through Mauritius. Still again, while MNCs are allowed 100 per cent subsidiaries, Indian promoters are not so allowed because of the lack of share buy-back provisions. The new takeover code allows only a creeping acquisition of 2 per cent a year, which is too low and slow (*Economic Times*, 24 April 1998). The attempt to acquire a higher percentage triggers public bidding for takeover.

In all these respects, Indian business was placed at a disadvantage in relation to foreign competition, and there was considerable force to its grievance about unequal competition.

The Behaviour of Foreign Multinationals

Nothing has antagonized the Indian corporate sector more than the prospect of subordination or eventual takeover at the hands of foreign MNCs, or the threat of being squeezed out of business by them. While recognizing India's need to attract foreign investment for faster growth, particularly in infrastructure, the corporate sector has come to the definite conclusion that its interests diverge significantly from those of foreign MNCs.

There was already sufficient awareness of long standing within India, particularly among the left, of the general case against foreign investment as an instrument for draining out a country's economic surplus while supplying only obsolete technology. However, that case aroused little concern earlier outside narrow circles, for the magnitude of foreign investment in India had been small, in fact minuscule in comparison to the large capital flows into East and Southeast Asia. Indeed, Indian business had in the pre-liberalization era seen collaboration with foreign investors, whether financial or technical, as an important resource for growth and expansion. At the same time, government restrictions on the extent of foreign equity in Indian ventures provided it with considerable security against foreign domination, control or takeover.

The reforms of 1991, however, created a new world. Not only was there now an acceleration in the flow of foreign investment but, with the removal of restrictions on majority foreign ownership in a wide swathe of industry, the domestic corporate sector for the first time saw itself as the target rather than the beneficiary of the heightened activity of foreign investors. The swiftness, vigour and aggressiveness with which foreign investors sought to penetrate and capture the domestic market along a broad front, and more crucially to sideline or oust earlier local partners in joint ventures, surprised the Indian corporate sector and spread consternation among its members. Particularly, in respect of joint ventures, it appeared as if the MNCs were alarmingly eager to reduce or eliminate Indian participation and to assume complete control. The rush on the part of MNCs to shove aside their Indian partners became a source of nightmare for the Indian business class even as it was indicative of a certain contempt for that class. MNC activity raised the spectre of the Indian corporate sector being eventually swallowed up by the multinationals, and it fuelled a revival of 'the East India Company syndrome'.[3] If it has been a matter of pride for many Indians that, unlike most countries in Asia, they had produced a genuinely domestic capitalist class, then that achievement seemed now to be grievously threatened.

The reaction to the prospect of marginalization of the Indian business class was not long in coming. One part of it was a public airing of the appraisal by the Indian business class of MNC behaviour. In early 1996, the Das-authored CII memorandum entitled 'MNCs: Indian Strategy Needs Rethink' forthrightly declared on behalf of Indian business that 'there is discomfort with dominance and control, there is discomfort with a one way street approach and there is clear discomfort with outdated or obsolete technology and products' (Das 1996: 5). But individual businessmen were more outspoken about what they saw as a new menace. Addressing a CII national conference, EID Parry's managing director M.V. Subbiah complained: 'The multinationals have a strong financial power. They are buying Indian brands and gradually killing them. There should be some sort of regulatory mechanism to prevent this. The idea of inviting multinationals into India is to promote competition and not to build up monopolies by killing the Indian brands'. Another important industrialist, S.K. Birla of the VXL Group, affirmed:

> Multinationals should not be allowed unfettered freedom in India. If the multinationals are allowed to hold a majority stake in the Indian joint ventures in an unfettered way, Indians would be second class citizens in their own country. The Indian entrepreneur has been exploited in the name of socialism earlier and continues to be exploited in the name of freedom and liberalization now (*Economic Times*, 24 March and 18 April 1996).

Assocham president H. Somany stated, 'We would like to caution [against] the predatory nature of foreign capital, sometimes manifesting in the form of hostile takeovers' (ibid., 30 October 1997).

The most consistent and vociferous critic of the MNCs has been Rahul Bajaj, regarded as the architect of the Bombay Club. Bajaj is insistent on deregulation and privatization as essential for the Indian economy, but he dismisses the notion that ownership of industry in a country does not matter, holding instead: 'Capital does have colour; ownership is important. We have moved from one extreme of not allowing foreign companies at all to an absolutely opposite extreme'. Bajaj has opposed foreign companies holding a majority or even 50 per cent equity stake in several industries, such as paints, automobiles, cement, steel, textiles and others where India already has a major presence. While believing that globalization is inevitable and that Indian industry cannot be shielded from competition for ever, he nonetheless wants time for local industry to prepare itself for it: 'It is a matter of time, but after all time is everything. Let more Tiscos, Telcos, Reliances and Bajaj Autos be formed and then Indian industry will be ready to compete with every one'. Nor is he squeamish about being called an economic nationalist, and pointedly reminds others of the nationalism prevalent in the developed countries:

> Indian industry would like to ensure that, like in most countries, conditions are created in India for the emergence of a large number of truly Indian MNCs. Indian industry welcomes foreign technology and capital. However, it would like foreign capital to supplement rather than replace Indian capital.... I believe every Indian and not only every Indian industrialist should be a nationalist.... Being a nationalist means a recognition of the fact that India and Indian industry will and should be built by Indians. To this extent, in my view, capital does have colour even in this era of globalization. I can give enough examples from the US, Europe and Japan to prove this fact (*Economic Times*, 22 August 1997; *Times of India*, 9 January 1998).

Indirectly, Bajaj raised here a pertinent question which is often neglected in discussions of the tension between globalization and nationalism. Columnists in the financial press, particularly the *Economic Times*, often mock at *swadeshi* and the Bombay Club, but they fail to ask why is it that, if some dose of economic nationalism is so bad for India, the major economic powers engage in it behind the facade of liberalism. Bajaj is not against interaction with the global economy but wants it on India's terms: 'We need foreign technology without giving up ownership and control. We want technology, growth and employment, but without sacrificing on ownership and control.' He also sees the argument on consumer interests differently: 'We should not unduly favour foreign companies by waving the red flag of consumer interest. We do not need old-fashioned protection, but we should keep the interest of the nation in mind' (*Economic Times*, 17 August 1997).

Fundamentally, Indian business has not been opposed to foreign investment as such. It is in the forefront of advocating foreign investment in the country's infrastructure, for the development of which the country does not have sufficient means. But other areas, where Indian business has already developed a significant role for itself, are a different matter. Here, even though the issue is often framed in terms of MNCs getting away with 100 per cent equity stake in local enterprises, the real concern for Indian partners in joint ventures is the passing of majority ownership to the foreign partner. As a consequence, 51 per cent equity stake in the hands of the foreign partner is the crucial point. But the Indian partner encounters severe problems here, for 'given that the foreign partner holds the whiphand in regard to the supply of technology and components, he can often dictate terms, and in an increasing number of cases is doing so' (*Economic Times*, editorial, 8 May 1996). The real crux of the issue thus is one of control; just as Humpty Dumpty tells Alice in *Through the Looking Glass*, 'the question is which shall be master—that's all'. The Indian bourgeoisie has not been, by and large, a comprador bourgeoisie; it is not without significance that the founder of the house of Bajaj was a friend and disciple of Mahatma Gandhi and treasurer of the Congress Party from 1920 until his death in 1942. Not surprisingly, members of this bourgeoisie 'would like to be senior partners in consumer goods and much else. That is the unspoken agenda' (ibid.).

The ownership of individual enterprises in their own country is important to individual entrepreneurs, but there are still larger issues related to foreign control of industry. Often, economists take a limited, indeed one-dimensional, view of matters relating to economic development and foreign investment. But there are other observers who explicitly connect control of industry to matters of high politics; in their view, the consequences can be serious for national security if there are no checks on foreign investment: 'Minus checks, we might find one day that the top 100 Indian companies are all foreign owned. Even if it smacks of paranoid nationalism, it is worth wondering if in that event India would be able to take the kind of stand it is currently taking on CTBT [Comprehensive Test Ban Treaty] or NPT [Nuclear Non-Proliferation Treaty]' (Sen Gupta 1996). On the other hand, it is also important for reasons of high politics to create a stake by the developed countries in India's economy and polity through foreign investment.

Even as business perceived itself to be under economic siege from the MNCs, it was aggrieved by what it believed to be the inimical posture of the Indian state. To business it seemed that the state had delivered a traumatic shock by way of exposing it to global competition without providing support to cope with the shock. Former RBI governor S. Venkitaramanan (1997) saw deep distress and a sense of alienation among businessmen, noting: 'They feel ... they are treated with disdain by the real rulers of India. Foreign investment is all that matters to New Delhi.... They look with pained anger at fast pace of takeover of some of India's enterprises by foreign multinationals'. Business was distressed by the apparent glamourization of foreign investors by decision-makers and media personnel in their new-found fervour for the market, by the easy access of foreign fund managers to the bureaucracy, and by the fiscal concessions to foreign companies so much so· that business came to regard government budgets as largely MNC budgets.

The question arises as to whether the perception of threat by business has a basis in fact. Or, is it that, as one of India's respected financial editors, T.N. Ninan, suggested, 'no great damage has been done to Indian industry or to Indian companies, and the great fear of foreign control is misconceived' (*Business Standard*, 3 January 1998)? The problem with this view is that perception is not necessarily based on reality and, as Ninan himself further acknowledged, 'Indians have been so scarred by 200 years of the colonial experience that the facts of the case seem irrelevant'. Again, others have remarked that foreign investment forms about 2 per cent or so of India's total investment and therefore could not constitute a significant threat. But this view tends to underestimate the impact of foreign investment by referring to total investment in the economy. A more appropriate perspective would require looking at the areas of impact more narrowly where foreign investment has been concentrated, such as consumer goods or the capital markets. Thus, in the area of 'fast-moving consumer goods', it is noteworthy that the top 10 most popular companies are foreign MNCs: Hindustan Lever, Procter & Gamble, Cadbury, Nestle, Pepsi, Colgate-Palmolive, Lakme Lever, Pond's, Coca-Cola, and Britannia.[4] Similarly, the capital markets have come to be dominated by foreign brokerage firms. Looked at from another perspective, MNCs already dominate several important areas of consumer goods, such as soft drinks, soaps and detergents, toothpaste, chocolates, confectionery, cosmetics, sanitary napkins and breakfast cereals. Granted, such domination is not always the result of hostile takeovers. And Ninan's assessment is, in part, based on discounting acquisitions that are a result of negotiation. However, that only underlines the tremendous financial power of the MNCs and in no way serves to diminish the perception of threat by Indian business.

Three strategies seem evident in the activities of MNCs to penetrate the Indian economy through FDI.[5] One, some foreign investors have bought off existing local enterprises along with their branded products with the aim of replacing such products with their own internationally-known brands, eliminating in the process the possibility of competition from the local products. The salient case here is that of Coca-Cola which purchased outright Parle Exports with its popular brands of Thums Up and Limca, and thus gained instant market dominance by capturing 60 per cent of the soft drinks market. Two, other foreign investors, while establishing new business ventures, initially took on local partners on an equal basis but, after having acclimatized themselves to the local economic and political situation, reduced their partners to a subordinate position or ousted them entirely. There has been understandable rage in Indian business that MNCs use Indian partners as a doormat to gain entry and spread risk at the beginning and then dump them later. MNCs have used the tactic of proclaiming the intent to vastly expand the enterprise, for which the Indian partner is unable to bring matching finances and is therefore either discarded or reduced in role. The underlying problem is that the Indian partner has few bargaining strengths, since it lacks technology and finance, and is able to only facilitate contacts with government and provide local knowledge; after a while that asset has little value. As RPG Enterprises CEO Harsh Goenka points out, 'A lot of JVs find that the value provided by the Indian partner is not enough since what value it could add has already come in' (*India Today*, 15 August 1996: 68). There are several important cases of this pattern in the automotive sector. Three, some foreign investors, even as they started out with local partners in a joint venture, then went on to set up parallel 100 per cent subsidiaries of their own in the same field, which were then favoured with greater resources and more modern technology, rendering the joint venture uncompetitive or useless. The outstanding case here is the ill-fated joint venture in the soap business in 1992 between Godrej Soaps and Procter & Gamble.

Coping with the Challenge

Given its perception of the threat from foreign MNCs, the business community has adopted, it would seem, a two-pronged strategy. One part of the strategy is, as is evident from the earlier discussion, carried out at the level of the political system and involves the articulation of the interests of business, and the putting of pressure on the state to accommodate those interests. The other part of the strategy is entrepreneurial, operates at the level of one or more firms, and involves restructuring of business in order to survive and flourish in the new economic environment.

Interest Articulation

The three business associations, that is, FICCI, Assocham, and CII—at their annual meetings and at the various meetings of their executive committees, as also through the statements and declarations of their officials, in the public sphere or in private meetings with state officials—report on the current condition of business and maintain a constant barrage of demands on the government of the day for new policy or policy changes to ameliorate that condition. On the threat that business perceives from international competition, whether through imports or domestically-located foreign MNCs, it is as if business feels that unless it screams, and does so repeatedly and continuously, the government is not likely to pay heed to its situation. In part, this apprehension arises, notwithstanding Marxist analyses about the power of business in a capitalist state, from a feeling that the state is biased against business. It sees this bias in the past in the command economy with its preference for the public sector and the regime of controls, and in the current phase in its supposedly preferential treatment of foreign investors. It is significant that the state has been, in the liberalization phase, extremely wary of policies that would adversely affect the interests of other vocal or organized groups, such as the middle classes or labour in the formal sector, or the intermediate castes of the rural areas. However, business cannot be said to have suffered particularly as a result of liberalization, for industrial growth during the four years from 1993–94 to 1996–97, especially 1994–95 and 1995–96, was considerable. Individual business firms have, nonetheless, been affected by cheaper imports and foreign takeovers.

The overall business demand is for *a level playing field*. More specifically, business would like the government to call a halt to any further reduction in import duties and, while it does not perceive a general increase in tariffs to be necessary, nonetheless it wants current import policy modified so that additional duty is imposed on specific items to compensate for the extra taxes that local business has to bear. Further, business wants the government to strengthen the anti-dumping machinery. There is a sense that India should follow the example of the developed countries and erect similar 'barriers' to protect local industry. While its president K.K. Modi called India's accession to the WTO agreement a blunder, FICCI pointed out that developed countries like Japan, France and South Korea have created such barriers, specifically pointing out how South Korea protected its car industry by placing restrictions on imports and that France put up a facility 130 km from the port with only one official for the clearance of electronics imports from Japan (*Hindu*, 8 January 1998). At home, business would like the government to make available capital at lower interest rates so as to even the playing field with foreign competition. FICCI officials have asked that interest rates should not be more than 3 per cent above the rate of inflation (*Economic Times*, 6 January 1998). There seems to be a general consensus on these aspects of the issue among the three apex associations.

On the issue of foreign direct investment, all three associations endorse greater FDI to accelerate industrial and economic growth, but at the same time they want protection for local industry. However, there are subtle differences among the associations in that Assocham is likely, barring an aberration from time to time, to remain silent or articulate reservations about swadeshi or economic nationalism; CII is likely to express its concerns over the FDI threat but in diplomatic language; and FICCI with the largest proportion of family-owned business among its membership is likely to offer a more comprehensive and explicit position. Overall, FICCI's position is that FDI should play a dominant role in the infrastructure, a leadership role in the export sector, and a supportive role in other sectors (*Economic Times*, 6 January 1998). It supports FDI for the creation of new assets within this three-fold division of roles, but wants the transfer of existing assets to MNCs to be discouraged. It endorses the employment of a 'multiplicity of instruments' for the protection of domestic firms against hostile takeovers, and requires that takeover bids by foreign MNCs should have the prior approval of the government. Believing that there is nothing extraordinary about its position, it points out that many governments intervene in corporate mergers and takeovers, specifically:

> The most significant example for India is the law in UK where under the Industry Act, 1975, read with the Fair Trading Act, 1973, the government is empowered to prohibit any takeover which is against public interest or where any important manufacturing undertaking would pass on to a person resident outside the United Kingdom and the transfer would be contrary to the national interest.... The Japanese law, like the laws in UK, France and elsewhere, does allow takeover of Japanese companies by foreign companies. Yet not a single Japanese company of significance has been taken over by a foreign company. The reason for this lies in a variety of permissions including social pressures which have successfully prevented such takeovers.

FICCI called attention to how France had recently barred a South Korean company from acquiring a major French company. In similar fashion, it wants the government to put in place an adequate mechanism for local companies to protect themselves against hostile takeovers (*Business Standard*, 7 February 1997). Indeed, FICCI president K.K. Modi has asked that foreign MNCs should be barred from establishing 100 per cent subsidiaries if they already have a joint venture in India (*Hindu*, 8 January 1998). Earlier, his predecessor Deepak Bunker had suggested that MNCs should be mandatorily required to disinvest after a pre-determined period (*Economic Times*, 11 October 1996). Other businessmen want adequate safeguards against Indian partners being forced to sell out to MNCs and demand restrictions on MNC entry. Thus, Hero Honda chairman B.M.L. Munjal stated: 'We should stipulate a percentage upto which the foreign companies can go in an industry'. Similar views have been expressed by Escorts group chairman Rajan Nanda (ibid., 3 March and 24 April 1998).

Of course, such demands from industry have met with a divided reception. Some have opposed them in the name of the consumer, the larger nation, and the removal of poverty:

> the nation is far more important than a clutch of large business families. The welfare of the people of the country should get priority over the prosperity of a group of rich influential industrialists. The consumer ... is more important than the producer, whether Indian or foreign. In short, the prime minister should put the nation before the Bombay Club.... The therapy is competition. We need to increase competition from both Indian and foreign companies. We are a country where 37 per cent of the population [is] living in poverty. The only quick way to lift them above poverty is high growth. The colour of capital does not matter, so long as it creates more jobs and riches for the people (*Economic Times*, editorial, 1 November 1997).

One question that remains unanswered in this wholehearted endorsement of competition is why, if competition is so beneficial, developed nations that are so strong economically to begin with erect barriers to competition from outside. Another question that is also relevant pertains to the situation where local industry is overwhelmed by imports; in that case, where will the consumers come from if there is no local industry to provide employment.

Other commentators have taken a position different from those who support competition at all cost, maintaining instead that 'no government can give MNCs a mandate for decimation of domestic enterprise' and that 'when Indian corporates are under mounting pressure, worry about the former's future is quite a rational response. There is no politics in this. Obviously, MNCs cannot set the nation's agenda and liberalization cannot also be for the corporates from overseas' (*Financial Express*, editorial, 24 January 1997). Indeed, there are much sharper critics; one of them (Sen Gupta 1996) underlined: 'The laws here allow unrestricted entry to MNCs, that is, they can fully own companies here, not only greenfield ventures, but also the companies they buy up here. Now, this is something which none of the so-called Tigers ... allow'. Questioning the wisdom of not being restrictive, he asked: 'So, is it that we are crawling when we had only to bend?' Making a case for policies that foster balanced well thought-out growth, he stated:

> What is the point of letting foreign companies buy out well-run Indian companies and gain market share here? The law should instead be so devised that it ensures entry of hi-tech and creates fresh capacity. If this means controls, so be it. Firstly, India will not be unique in this. Secondly, there is no guarantee that there will not be more Ramesh Chauhans who will sell at the first instance and usher in a process of foreign monopoly rather than healthy competition.

Business reservations on customs duties and foreign takeovers should not be taken to mean that it is not in favour of liberalization. Quite the contrary, it is liberalization's greatest supporter and favours more rapid advance along a broad front. It would like the government to move forward on exit policy so as to facilitate restructuring in order to enable business to meet foreign competition, on removal of restrictive legislation on urban land and rent control, and on reform of tax laws, on the opening of the insurance sector, on privatization of the public sector, and on radical improvement of infrastructure.

Despite the impression that may have developed during the period immediately after the launching of liberalization in 1991 that business was delighted at the dismantlement of licensing and controls and at the greater role accorded to the market, business has since the economic slowdown that began in 1996 become enamoured of the activist state. Much like the left, it has come to recognize the virtues of an expansionary public investment policy as a spur to higher investment in the private sector. Business advocates an especially activist role for the state in the infrastructure sector.

If industry had been anxious under the Congress government (1991–96) about its future against what it considered an onslaught from the global economy, whether in terms of imports or foreign takeovers, it was no less disenchanted by the continuation and intensification of external liberalization under the United Front government that came into power in 1996 after the defeat of the Congress Party. However, the persistent protests and demands on the part of business evoked assurances of protection from the new United Front government (1996–98). True, business does not have the numbers that the middle classes and organized labour have, but it is nonetheless a highly organized group and its financial muscle is a powerful resource. Besides, business is a 'privileged' group everywhere in the modern world. The source of that privileged status is not a result of some capitalist conspiracy but, as Lindblom (1977) has explained, modern governments everywhere must for reasons of assuring their own legitimacy have constant economic growth and, accordingly, must provide rewards to business to help foster that growth. Therefore, the Indian government, like governments elsewhere, has to listen to the legitimate demands of business for the instrumental reason that it needs business to assure growth.

It is understandable, then, that industry minister Murasoli Maran of the United Front government, usually known for his openness to foreign investment, promised business that 'We can't allow domestic industry to suffer. Every country takes care of its own industry. Look at the US and their protection to the domestic automobile industry'. He stated: 'Competition is okay—and foreign investment continues to be welcome—but we can't allow domestic industry to be killed' (*Economic Times*, 8 October and 7 November 1996). Surprisingly, even the Congress Party seemed to recognize the force of the business argument in an economic resolution, moved by Manmohan Singh, which seemed to bring it close to the BJP position on the Bombay Club: 'Domestic policies should not encourage a flow of foreign investment to the consumers sectors, unless it is accompanied by high technology.... All reasonable measures should be adopted to help Indian industry to compete effectively with foreign investors both in domestic and international markets' (ibid., 9 August 1997). The most emphatic statement of support on behalf of the United Front government came from its prime minister, I.K. Gujral; at a CII conference, he declared in reference to the Bombay Club and its demand for an even playing field:

I share your discomfort. The country must strike a golden mean between opening up the economy to foreign investors and providing level playing field for the domestic entrepreneur. We will not allow 16th century capitalism where any outsider can come and overwhelm you. We will look after you and give you the benefits of paternity. Outsiders are welcome but not to take over, not to drown you. Foreign investment will be welcomed only in sectors where we want investment. Our policies will not make you non-competitive. We will not protect you but it won't be that anybody can come and throw you out (*Economic Times*, 17 August 1997).

He repeated the theme at an Assocham meeting, promising 'protection against foreign capital invasion' and declaring, 'We can't go on thinking that everybody can come in and swamp our industry' (*Economic Times*, 30 October 1997). Despite all these brave words, nothing concrete emerged in terms of specific policies or policy changes, perhaps in part due to the early collapse of the government. The BJP-led coalition government that came to power in 1998 was more forthcoming with special customs duties to protect Indian industry besides taking a more vocal supportive position on the industry's demand for an even playing field.

Business Restructuring

Interest articulation, support mobilization and pressuring the state in defence of local industry is not the only activity visible on the part of business in its interaction with intensified globalization. All across the industrial scene there has been a churning underway as business attempts to cope with the challenge of globalization. This activity is on a more decentralized scale and affects individual business firms. The hallmarks of this activity are downsizing, focusing on core competencies, and expansion (or dissolution) through mergers and acquisitions (M&As). Therefore, while there is pressure on the state to change or modify policy to protect industry, there is a simultaneous effort on the part of business to confront competition through setting its own house in order. If liberalization had as its key intent to pressurize business to become more efficient through competition from the global economy, then it is seemingly having an enormous impact.

The process of restructuring did not commence immediately after liberalization. Perhaps that was a consequence of the considerable devaluation which provided protection even as tariffs were reduced. The tariff reductions were modest at first, but as their incidence increased in successive years they began to tell on local industry.

Furthermore, immediately after liberalization, business had added capacities in the euphoria of expectations of a rapidly expanding market with a burgeoning middle class. Again, the relatively high GDP growth at the average rate of over 6.5 per cent in the five years after 1991–92 provided a sufficient market to accommodate both increased production and imports. However, as the economy proceeded to slow down in 1996, the cumulative pressures—stemming from the successive slashing of tariffs on imports, the comparative overvaluation of the rupee after 1993, and the building of surplus capacities—squeezed the profit margins of local firms and induced them to undertake measures to survive.

Restructuring followed, with the sequence taking the form, though not necessarily always, of downsizing, shedding non-core activities in favour of core competencies, and expansion through M&As. Downsizing to forge leaner and meaner enterprises was necessitated by the more competitive regime in the context of the deployment of excess manpower inherited from the earlier protectionist regime. However, business had a heavy price to pay for it through voluntary retirement packages because labour legislation barred retrenchment of labour. Focusing on core competencies was dictated by the heightened competition, both from domestic and global sources, in the context of the earlier legacy of agglomerative enterprises from the days of extensive licensing. This policy resulted in the reduction of size of enterprises. However, there also developed the realization that the increased competition required not only focusing on core competencies but also bigger size in facing the multinationals, hence the trend toward mergers and acquisitions.

The process of restructuring can be illustrated by a brief reference to a few cases. Take, for instance, the Thapar group headed by Lalit Mohan Thapar, who chaired the controversial Assocham committee on foreign investment. Like other industrial houses, it has been a diversified group. Following liberalization, as its projects in shrimps and publishing suffered, the group encountered liquidity problems, and it responded by withdrawing from its prestigious joint ventures with Du Pont for the manufacture of nylon and with Owens Brockway for making glass containers, by selling off its edible oils business, by hiving off some businesses, by shutting down the Mumbai edition of the newspaper *Pioneer*, and by reorganizing the core activities of the flagship Ballarpur Industries relating to paper and chemicals (*Times of India*, 22 February, 31 March and 19 April 1998).

An illustration of expansion through acquisition is the public bid by India Cements Limited (located in Chennai, Tamil Nadu) in early 1998 to acquire a controlling stake in Raasi Cement Limited (of Andhra Pradesh) with a view to an eventual merger. India Cements was successful in buying out the share of the promoter of Raasi and his associates, in the process laying the foundation for the rise of a cement conglomerate comparable to the present market leader ACC and for the control of 30–35 per cent of the market in the four southern states (*Economic Times*, 27 February, 29 March and 7 April 1998). For sheer audacity there is the noteworthy attempt in early 1998, even though it met with resistance, by an upstart company, Sterlite, which had turned around a sick aluminium company, to acquire through a public bid a substantial stake in Alcan's Indian subsidiary, Indal, with the objective of obtaining a strategic partnership. The pace of M&As quickened during 1997, and the accompanying chart lists the important cases (see Table 5.1). As is evident, much of M&A activity has been at the instance of foreign MNCs, but it also indicates by the same token the selling of non-core activities (such as Lakme and Tomco of the Tatas) by Indian entrepreneurs. At the same time, the process is catching on with Indian business houses as well.

It is the hope of many that, through restructuring, Indian business can not only meet the foreign competition, but that it can lay the groundwork for the rise of a substantial number of MNCs, with Rahul Bajaj wishing for a '100 Indian MNCs' in 20 years (*Economic Times*, 17 August 1997). At first blush, this seems a vain hope, and in any case speculative. However, the case need not be dismissed lightly, for the Indian business class has emerged out of the traditional trading communities which have had a long history, stretching over centuries, of adaptation to changing circumstances with their many challenges, of which globalization is the latest one. Besides, there are already several enterprises which have a multinational extension outside India. Significant among them is the A.V. Birla group, led for many years by the late MIT-trained Aditya Vikram Birla (d. 1995), referred to as 'the first Indian globalizer'; even under the constraints of the earlier regime of controls, he established a multinational empire with 15 major corporations overseas in competition with foreign MNCs. He supported liberalization and kept his distance from the Bombay Club, proclaiming 'We are not afraid of global competition. Let it be afraid of us'. The group is the largest producer of

Table 5.1
Mergers and Acquisitions: 1995–97

Date	Acquirer	Target	Status
Apr. 1995	Brooke Bond Lipton	Milkfood Ice-Cream	Acquisition
Mar. 1996	Asea Brown Boveri	Birla Kent-Taylor	Acquisition
Apr. 1996	Brooke Bond Lipton	Kissan	Acquisition
Apr. 1996	Hindustan Lever	Brooke Bond Lipton	Merger
1996	ICICI	SCICI	Merger
1996	Sandoz	Ciba Giegy	Merger
Jan. 1997	DCM Shriram Consolidated	Ghaghara Sugar	Acquisition
Jan. 1997	Vickers	Vickers System Inter.	Acquisition
Feb. 1997	Cherry Fashions	Unity Agro Industries	Acquisition
Feb. 1997	Priya Holdings	Volvo Steels	Acquisition
Feb. 1997	Zuari Agro	Indian Furniture Co.	Acquisition
Mar. 1997	Cummins Engine	Kirloskar Cummins	Acquisition
Mar. 1997	Polysindo	Best & Crompton	Acquisition
Mar. 1997	Sun Pharmaceuticals	Gujarat Lyka Organics	Acquisition
May 1997	Bagri Family	Hindustan Sanforiser	Bid
May 1997	Bridgestone Corporation	Bridgestone Corp. Ltd.	Acquisition
May 1997	Wartsila Diesel	NSD India	Acquisition
May 1997	GE-Caps	SRF Finance	Acquisition
Jun. 1997	Assam Timber Products	Chipboards	Acquisition
Jun. 1997	Daimler-Benz	Mercedes-Benz India	Bid
Jun. 1997	Phillips Carbon Black	Carbon And Chemicals	Acquisition
Jul. 1997	British Gas	Gujarat Gas	Bid
Jul. 1997	Nicholas Piramal	Boehringer Mannheim	Acquisition
Aug. 1997	Crompton Greaves	Goa Electricals	Acquisition
Aug. 1997	Merind	Tata Pharma	Bid
Aug. 1997	Nirma	Gujarat Heavy Chemicals	Acquisition
Sep. 1997	Cheminova	Lupin Agro	Acquisition
Sep. 1997	Polysindo	JCT Synthetic Division	Acquisition
Sep. 1997	Polysindo	SPIC Petrochemicals Corp.	Bid
Oct. 1997	Escorts Finance Ltd.	Span Financial Services	Merger
Dec. 1997	ICICI	ITC Classic	Merger
Dec. 1997	Swiss Banking Corp.	United Bank of Switzerland	Merger
1997	Escorts Ltd.	Escorts Tractors	Acquisition
1997	Gujarat Ambuja	Modi Cement	Merger
1997	Hindustan Lever	Tasty Bite	Merger

Source: *Economic Times*, 22 February 1998.

viscose staple fibre (VSF) in the world. Under the leadership of his son, Kumaramangalam Birla, the group made a major acquisition abroad of a wood pulp unit in Canada to supply chemical grade wood pulp to three of its companies for VSF manufacture. Besides, the son has set in motion plans to bring greater focus to the still much diversified group (*India Today*, 15 September 1994: 86; *Economic Times*, 3 October 1995, 25 February 1998). Be it noted, however, in order to be fair to other business houses, that this group is not in the consumer goods business.

Similarly, in the pharmaceutical field there are several players that are in the global league, such as Torrent, Lupin, Reddy's Lab, and particularly Ranbaxy which specializes in generic drugs and has subsidiaries in Europe and China. More broadly, a chemical engineer underlines India's strengths in the sector:

> In pharma, in sulfamethoxazole and trimethyl phosphite, we lead the world. We have about 40 per cent of the world Ibuprofen market and are largely integrated, being well-off in the intermediate IBB with Herdillia and Vinati as producers. In fact, Boots, the innovator, couldn't compete cost-wise and stopped manufacture (*Economic Times*, 21 February 1997).

Beyond drugs, there are market leaders in other fields, too. Arvind Mills, focusing on denim and discarding other products, became the third largest denim manufacturer in the world, and its owner Sanjay Lalbhai aspires to making Arvind the 'Sony of textiles'. Then there is Reliance Industries, the top firm in the private sector, which is dedicated to building world class and world size plants; focusing on its core competency in polymers, it is set to compete with world leader Du Pont in the field. In paints, there is Asian Paints Limited (*India Today*, 7 July 1997: 46). A sector that ought not to go unmentioned is that of information technology, where several firms have emerged as important players in software exports.

Summary and Conclusions

After the first flush of enthusiasm about liberalization, business turned to a more realistic appreciation of the challenges that liberalization provided through foreign competition. It came to the conclusion that liberalization had been too sudden, too hasty and too far-reaching. Business developed a perception of threat to its continued survival in the face of cheaper imports and foreign takeovers of domestic companies. Its overall demand now is for *a level playing field*.

It is ironic that business is perhaps the only organized group which has lived under a sustained threat as a result of liberalization.

The government has been unable to do anything comparably hurtful for the sake of economic policy reform to any other major group, such as labour or the middle classes, or even the poor. This perhaps is because of the small numbers that business commands compared to the vastly larger numbers of the other groups. Earlier, perhaps for the same reason, the state could impose a command economy against the wishes of business. But business, too, cannot be left to its own fate in the face of global competition, for government needs business to assure growth; besides, business demands are aligned with the larger forces of economic nationalism in the polity. Perhaps more effective than any promises on the part of government for support, if not protection, will be the restructuring that liberalization has provoked among business firms. Indian business has greater resilience than is suspected, because of its history of adaptation to challenges over the centuries.

Notes

1. *Economic Times*, 20 March 1996. For a more elaborate presentation, see Das (1996).
2. Associated Chambers of Commerce and Industry of India (1997: 6); see also *Business India*, 27 January–9 February 1997: 45; and *Business Standard*, 8 February 1997.
3. The East India Company syndrome refers to the fear that foreigners are likely, if given an opening, to take over control of a company, the economy or the country. The essentials of the original process on which the syndrome has been erected are clear: a foreign multinational from the developed world arrives at the shores of an underdeveloped country to trade but, with the backing of the power of the home country (economic, political and military), is able to extract extra-territorial privileges, sets up trading posts and recruits local collaborators to advance its interests, expands into a monopoly, gradually acquires political and military functions, finds a traitor or set of traitors who are ready to betray the local ruler, leading to the defeat of the latter while an apathetic elite and populace looks on, with the multinational ending up in establishing an empire that exploits the population for the next couple of centuries, and all this is supposed to have been accomplished in a mythic fit of absentmindedness.
4. *Hindu*, 18 November 1997. The results are based on a survey conducted in Mumbai, Delhi, Chennai, Calcutta and Bangalore. ITC ranked 11; among the fully owned Indian companies, Amul took 13th place, Dabur 15th, and Raymond 16th. Indian companies fared somewhat better in the durable goods sector: BPL, Titan, Asian Paints, MRF, Maruti, Philips, Motorola and Ericsson.
5. Several episodes of takeovers or attempted takeovers are discussed in some detail in Nayar (1998: 2453–68).

6

The United Front and Economic Reforms, 1996–98: Policy and Performance under Democratic Coalitions

After presiding over the momentous economic policy reforms of 1991–96, the Congress Party was defeated in the 1996 elections. With no political party commanding a majority and thus unable to form a single-party government, India entered a period of governance through coalitions in the post-reform period. This raised a profound question about the survivability of the reforms already undertaken and the continuity of the reform process. For, governance through coalitions seemed to compound the already apparent constraints that democracy imposed on the reform process. Since larger social and political forces beyond the narrow confines of government are involved in policy-making under democracy, reform of economic policy depends on its acceptability to key groups in society on whom the government relies for political support. The essential dilemma that democracy represents for reform-minded decision-makers revolves around the question of how they can impose sacrifice and loss on key groups and then turn around and expect, in the absence of war or crisis, these very groups to vote them back to office. At the same time, the requirement to win electoral support from a wide enough popular base to form government can lead to policy distortions through having to provide economic incentives or pay-offs, even as conflict among diverse decision-makers can make for policy stalemates. This more general dilemma in relation to economic policy reform in a democracy seems to become especially sharp in situations where representation leads not to rule by a single, cohesive majority party but to governance based largely on shifting coalitions among a number of separate political groups.

The theoretical case for the dysfunctionality of coalition governments for sound economic policy and management rests on two related features of such governments: short life and heterogeneity, often exacerbated by polarization. More than a century ago, Lawrence Lowell put it down as 'an axiom in politics that, except under very peculiar circumstances, coalition ministries are short lived compared with homogeneous ones' (cited in Dodd 1976: 6–7). Since then, coalition government has become synonymous with lack of government durability and, therefore, with political instability.[1] The two features of short life and heterogeneity impede and distort attempts by coalition governments at economic policy reform, especially in the area of fiscal deficit, the reduction of which is often a central issue in reform. Because of the expectation of lack of durability of coalition governments and equally the uncertainty over which partners will remain in any successor government, coalition governments tend to have a short *time-horizon*. They are likely, therefore, to opt for policies which provide quick pay-offs for their partners even if there is damage done to the economy over the longer run, rather than for policies that assure gain over the long haul even if they impose short-term pain. Indeed, coalition governments can be said to encourage fiscal profligacy. As Alesina and Tabellini (1990) point out in relation to public debt, 'uncertainty about who will be appointed in the future prevent the current government from fully internalizing the cost of leaving debt to its successors.... By leaving debt to the future, today's government can force its successor to "pay the bills"'.

Drawing on game theory, Roubini and Sachs (1989) underline the way heterogeneity and rapid turnover combine to prevent cooperation within coalition governments and, thus, to undercut sound economic policy and management: 'The shorter is the expected tenure of the government, the more difficult it may be to achieve cooperation among the coalition partners'. As in *prisoner's dilemma*, though the partners may see merit in cooperation the absence of a coordination mechanism results in the pursuit of particular interests by them, with almost every partner having a veto. The transience of coalition governments further attenuates the possibilities of developing cooperation over policy, since 'the enforceability of cooperation depends heavily on the repeated-play aspects of decision-making. To the extent that the rapid turnover of governments reduces the time horizon for the repeated play among coalition members, their incentives to cooperate are reduced'. Empirically, Roubini and Sachs demonstrate that 'in several countries, the slow rate at which the post-1973 fiscal deficits were reduced resulted from the difficulties of political management in coalition governments. During the period 1975–85, there is a clear tendency for larger deficits in weaker governments.... The greatest difficulties appear to arise because small coalition partners have veto power over changes in the status quo'.

To a certain extent the infirmities attributed to coalition governments are not altogether absent in majority governments in a democracy. For, the very notion of majority entails considerable heterogeneity in government, especially in large countries like India, while all such governments are subject to constitutional or statutory requirements that mandate facing an electoral contest in four or five years at the most. There are thus limits to homogeneity and time-horizon in any democratic government. What is true nonetheless is that for coalition governments 'the problems are typically exacerbated by the need to mesh the interests of many parties in a single government. An individual majority party has many crucial powers and constraints that allow it to come closer to enforcing "good behaviour"' (Roubini and Sachs 1989: 926).

The literature thus makes obvious a fairly plausible hypothesis: Coalition governments are likely to be unstable and short-lived and therefore will tend to be poor performers in respect of economic policy reform, especially compared to majority party governments. However, the question arises whether this general proposition on the handicaps of coalition governments in economic policy reform holds true of individual cases, in this particular instance, India. If not, why not? If so, are the causes the same general ones, or are they specific to India? The focus in the examination here is on the coalition government that succeeded the Congress Party in 1996. Even though the hypothesis singles out coalition as the key determinant in performance, it should be readily acknowledged that in the actual course of social and political affairs, there are likely to be other determinants as well, both structural and idiosyncratic, not all of which can be kept constant in comparison. However, before a comparison can be made with the record of the Congress Party, it is necessary first to determine the performance of the coalition government. Toward that end, this chapter looks at: (1) the political aftermath of the 1996 elections and the formation of the United Front coalition government; (2) the programmatic compact among the coalition partners about economic policy reform; (3) the dynamics of conflict within the coalition and programme implementation; and (4) a comparative assessment of the coalition's performance in respect of reform.

The 1996 Elections and the Formation of the Coalition Government

The major political actors in the opposition took the results of the 1996 elections to be a rejection of the Congress Party and what it stood for and they were, therefore, determined not to allow it to form the government, with or without a coalition. However, the elections provided no clear verdict for an alternative government since no party emerged with an absolute majority. As the party emergent with the largest number of seats (162), though far removed from a majority in a house of some 540 seats, the Bharatiya Janata Party (BJP) was the first to form the government, but it could not sustain itself in office for more than 13 days. In the alternative, the United Front coalition—consisting of several major regional parties and the Left Front of the communist parties—assumed office on 1 June 1996 under the clarion call of a secular but non-Congress government. However, with its meagre numbers, the United Front (UF) was compelled to come to terms with the Congress Party (140 seats) for support from the outside, quietly burying its past hostility to being associated with a party identified with corruption and economic liberalization. Among the 13 constituent groups of the UF coalition, though not necessarily of the government, the key political parties were: the Janata Dal (46 seats); the Communist Party of India (Marxist) or CPI(M) (32 seats); the Tamil Maanila Congress (TMC), a regional Tamil break-away faction from the Congress Party (20 seats); the Dravida Munnetra Kazhagam (DMK), the reigning regional party in Tamil Nadu (17 seats); the Samajwadi Party, representing the ascendant middle agricultural castes, largely in UP (17 seats); Telugu Desam Party, the ruling regional party in Andhra Pradesh (16 seats); and the Communist Party of India (CPI) (13 seats). The CPI(M) stayed out of the government on the ground of its principled opposition to participating in any government where it could not have decisive influence on policy formation on the basis of its own legislative strength.

From the perspective of economic policy reform, the key portfolios went to H.D. Deve Gowda (Prime Minister), P. Chidambaram (Finance Minister), and Murasoli Maran (Industry Minister). All three favoured reform, an orientation explained by their personal history and political background. Deve Gowda had been chief minister of the state of Karnataka, where he had pushed economic reforms at the state level, regardless of Janata Dal's opposition to reform at the national level. Chidambaram himself and his party TMC, which had broken away from the Congress Party, shared the reform orientation of the dominant faction of the Congress Party; indeed, he had been a major force for reform in the previous Congress government. With his commitment to reform stemming from personal conviction, he was the most ardent, consistent and persistent activist for reform within the government and also the Front's most visible and articulate public spokesman in behalf of reform.

The United Front represented a largely centre-left coalition which had come together on the single issue of a secular but non-Congress government in opposition to the BJP. But on the issue of economic policy reform, it was ideologically polarized between Chidambaram and Maran on one side and the Left Front on the other, with the other parties willing to be persuaded by either. The Left Front was ably led by CPI(M) general secretary Harkishen Singh Surjeet, who emerged as a critical power-wielder in the internal politics of the United Front even as his party stayed out of the government. He played out his decisive role in the steering committee, which was set up to reach decisions before the government finally enacted them into policy. If Chidambaram and his colleagues had become disillusioned by the economic policy regime of the 1950s, 1960s and 1970s, the Left sought precisely to protect and deepen the legacy of that regime. Ironically, that regime was a product of what the Left had trenchantly attacked over a long period as the landlord-bourgeois state but whose legacy was now seen as representing nationally established policies. The two sides represented graphically the opposed forces of economic globalization, and by extension liberalization, on the one hand, and economic nationalism on the other; in its economic nationalism vis-a-vis the outside world, the Left Front was, objectively, not much different from its ideological antagonist, the BJP. The reformers were miffed by the overbearing and aggressive attitude of the Left and resented what they believed to be its two-faced or schizophrenic posture—being part of the coalition and at the same time stridently critical of coalition policies, adopting liberalization in the states where it ruled, such as West Bengal, and shrilly attacking it at the centre. Surprisingly, despite this division, the United Front government started out with the two sides coming together on a jointly agreed programme on economic and other issues.

The Programmatic Compact and its Contents

Over the years since the reform process was accelerated in 1991, the Janata Dal and, especially, the Left Front had been bitter critics of economic liberalization. They were hostile to the opening up of India's economy to globalization in terms of trade and investment and to the shrinking of the state in the economy through industrial delicensing and halting the relentless expansion of the public sector. They particularly attacked any moves toward privatization of the public sector. The opposition of the CPI and CPI(M) to liberalization was based not only on their ideological preference for an interventionist state and a planned economy, but even more on their intent to protect the material interests of labour in the public sector, where their trade union arms, All India Trade Union Congress (AITUC) and Centre of Indian Trade Unions (CITU), respectively, were powerful. The opposition of the Janata Dal was more community-based, rooted in its aim of advancing the interests of the ascendant rural intermediate castes ('other backward classes' or OBCs) against the upper castes through quota reservations and subsidies by an interventionist state. Indeed, some of its leaders believed liberalization, with its thrust of shrinking the state and expanding the role of the private sector at the cost of the public sector, to be a conspiracy on the part of the upper-caste middle classes precisely to undo the recent success of the OBCs in snatching from the state extensive reservations in personnel recruitment in the government and public sector. The Janata Dal and the Left Front had vowed, therefore, to overthrow the economic policy reforms if they came to power, thus threatening the Congress Party's cultivated public posture to the outside world that the reforms were here to stay since they were based on a national consensus. While there is little hard evidence for the position, some declared the election results to be a verdict against the Congress government's policy of liberalization.[2]

As the nascent United Front crystallized during the 1996 election campaign, the partners adopted a 'common approach' and formulated a joint programme promising a strengthened public sector and an expanded public distribution system to provide 14 essential commodities to the poor at reasonable prices. In releasing their joint programme, CPI(M) general secretary Surjeet declared that no privatization would be allowed as the public sector was the foundation of the country's industrialization and had a continuing vital role to play (*Economic Times*, 19 April 1996). As political power came within the reach of the United Front, however, it compelled a certain degree of moderation, at least formally, in the position of these political parties. To begin with, the United Front was not united on economic policy; if it were to come to power, neither the Janata Dal nor the Left Front could simply impose their will on the others without some compromise. More importantly, the United Front was dependent on the Congress Party for support in order to come to power or stay in power, and the Congress Party was not eager to become a partner in destroying or diminishing what it saw as its singular policy accomplishment during its last period in office. The Congress Party let it be known to the United Front leaders that they could not simply take its support for granted for any kind of anti-BJP coalition, and that a necessary pre-condition for such support was continuity of the economic reforms. That message was apparently received seriously. A top CPI(M) leader acknowledged, 'How can we expect the Congress (I) to support us if we were to undo the policies its government had initiated'. Similarly, a senior Janata Dal leader voiced the need for a pragmatic approach to economic policy, stating, 'This is the price we have to pay for preventing "communal" forces from taking over the Centre' (ibid., 12 May 1996). These considerations sealed the fate of any plan to overthrow the liberalization policies of the previous Congress government, and assured the continuity of its reform legacy.

Acceptance of what had already been done was one thing, proceeding further with reforms was altogether another. Here, what emerged was in some eyes a patchwork solution which only spelled conflict in the future, and in other eyes a genuine statesmanlike compromise in developing a national consensus. Regardless, the agreement on economic policy—known as the Common Minimum

Programme (CMP)[3]—constituted an important initiative. It seemed to transform the United Front from what appeared to be a heterogeneous cabal cobbled together to opportunistically grab power into an apparently cohesive group organized around a new vision. The document heralded the new government to be not simply a replacement of one set of rulers with another, but as one that marked 'the beginning of an alternative model of governance based on federalism, decentralization, accountability, equality and social justice, economic and political reforms'. In one sense, the CMP in so far as its signatories included the earlier opponents of liberalization, put the imprimatur of legitimacy on liberalization and removed the threat of its overthrow. It was, therefore, highly welcome to the private sector, especially foreign investors.

Surprisingly, in some respects, the CMP went substantially farther than the earlier liberalization. Through it, the United Front committed itself to faster economic growth as a route to elimination of poverty and unemployment, and established a target of 7 per cent annual growth rate in GDP and 12 per cent annual growth in industry. More importantly, it forthrightly acknowledged the necessity of foreign investment for the country, and made a dramatic and ambitious break with past rhetoric and practice by laying down an annual target for foreign investment at the astounding level, for India, of $10 billion. At the same time, the United Front recognized 'the role of the corporate sector in building a strong and modern India', and assured it 'a level playing field' in facing global competition. Significantly, it committed itself to 'the goal of bringing India's tariffs in accord with world levels'. The United Front affirmed the importance of the public sector and its intent to make it strong and competitive, but it also averred the need for efficiency and profitability and, to that end, for reforming and restructuring it. In addition, the United Front promised to appoint a Disinvestment Commission to render advice on the withdrawal of the public sector from non-core and non-strategic areas, and to implement further reforms in the financial sector so as to increase substantially the flow of domestic and foreign funds to the infrastructure sector. Especially remarkable was the United Front's pledge in respect of fiscal management:

It is recognized [the] world over that fiscal prudence is the key to low inflation, stable price levels and rapid growth. The United Front is committed to bringing the fiscal deficit to below 4 per cent of GDP. The management of the fiscal deficit will, therefore, enjoy the highest priority.... All inessential and unproductive expenditure will be eliminated.

That this aim of fiscal restraint would be hard to achieve was evident from other promises that the United Front made in the CMP in the pursuit of its motto of 'growth with social justice' in regards to employment, public distribution system, and education. Besides, for a government that was essentially a coalition of regional parties, there would be the perennial but insatiable appetite of the states for central funding. For the time being, nonetheless, the CMP received a ringing endorsement from most quarters. The *Times of India* (6 June 1996) noted that it 'reads a lot like the manifestos of the two major political formations, the Congress Party and the Bharatiya Janata Party.... It is reassuring to see the vast common ground between all the national and regional parties on issues of central concern to the people of India'. The *Economic Times* (6 June 1996) was more effusive in its editorial 'Good Script, Act on It': 'The United Front has just supplied Dr. Manmohan Singh's answer to those who had raised sceptical eyebrows at his assertion of broad national consensus on economic reform. Continuity is the hallmark of the United Front government's economic policy, as enumerated in the Front's common minimum programme'. Later on 20 July, it noted optimistically that India had worked out its own way to developing a consensus on economic reform, one not to be found in the prescriptions of the IMF and World Bank: 'Put the critics in power and let them face the same challenges as the ruling party'.

Coalition Dynamics and Reform: Contention and Cooperation

The UF government took over power in the midst of euphoric proclamations by its leaders and their supporters in the media and academia that the days of one-party dominance were over and that coalitions were the wave of the future. Many declared, indeed, that coalitions were a superior instrument of governance and accordingly to be preferred. They believed that coalitions were an effective mechanism for the empowerment of states against the overbearing centralising thrust fostered by decades of dynastic rule under the umbrella of the Congress Party. They claimed as well that the coalition partners had already learnt their lesson from the earlier experience with unstable coalitions and that the present government would, therefore, last its full term. However, the working and the short life of the new UF government, as it actually occurred in practice, belied these claims.

Conflict among the coalition partners surfaced soon after the UF government came to power. There were, no doubt, differences, serious ones for that matter, over the course of economic policy notwithstanding the apparent consensus in the CMP. In the contention over economic policy, the advocates of liberalization were ranged against the Left Front led by the CPI(M); the persistent conflict between them made reform a painful and draining process. Other issues also threatened the working of the coalition, such as factional divisions, representation in the ministry, and corruption. But beyond these conflicts, the real threat that hung over the life of the coalition was its dependence on the Congress Party for survival. Long used to holding power, the Congress leaders were eager to get back into office, even if only as part of a larger coalition. At the same time, the Congress Party, now under the leadership of Sitaram Kesri, began to suspect that Prime Minister Deve Gowda was conspiring to split and marginalize the Congress Party in order to consolidate the coalition. Regardless of whether the arguments put forward were specious or not, Kesri at the end pulled the rug from under Gowda at the end of March 1997, hardly 10 months after the coalition came to power. However, the entry of the Congress Party into the coalition was not acceptable to the coalition partners, and it had to simply settle for the same government with a new, perhaps more amenable, prime minister—Inder Kumar Gujral, an urbane intellectual without an independent political base.

A more fatal blow was struck by the Congress Party some six months later. Unhappy with its situation of being without any share in power, the Congress Party under Kesri decided to drive home the vital point that the government was dependent on it for survival by asking for the ouster of ministers belonging to the DMK on the pretext of an adverse report from the commission investigating the assassination of Rajiv Gandhi. The coalition saw the demand as an opening gambit in a show of strength which, if accepted, would only trigger more demands, and it firmly refused to comply. The curtain then finally fell on the coalition with the Congress withdrawing support, and in early December 1997 the Lok Sabha was dissolved, and new elections were held in the first quarter of 1998.

It is apparent that in its short life of less than two years, the UF government constantly encountered political conflict, uncertainty and instability. It is precisely in this situation that the coalition government had to formulate and enact economic policy reforms. The reforms encompassed a substantial number of measures. In the treatment that follows, these measures are grouped under three major headings: (1) fiscal management; (2) liberalization, more accurately internal liberalization; and (3) globalization, that is, external liberalization or integration with the world economy. The slotting of reform measures in this manner, however, fails to do justice to those occasions when an overall view is taken by the government to advance economic policy reform. One such important occasion is the presentation of the annual budget, which compels the government to provide a statement of its larger policy aims. The UF government had the opportunity to present two budgets, one in July 1996 and the other in February 1997, which are briefly reviewed here.

The importance of the first regular budget for 1996–97 presented by the UF government in July 1996 lay essentially in the fact that it represented continuity with the reform orientation of the previous Congress government, making manifest in the process that the reforms by that government were, indeed, irreversible. This continuity had already been presaged in the official survey of the economy that normally precedes the budget by several weeks, setting out the major trends, the emergent problems, and the possible policy options. The previous Congress government had presented in February 1996 an interim budget for 1996–97, which had followed the publication of the *Economic Survey 1995–96*. Before the UF could present the regular budget for the year 1996–97, the left partners of the coalition made an issue of the authenticity of the earlier survey, charging that it had been drafted with an eye to attracting votes; in any case, they felt that it did not accord well with the commitments made in the new Common Minimum Programme (CMP).

In response, the ministry of finance under the new dispensation provided, instead of a wholly new full-scale review of the economy, a shorter *Economic Survey 1995–96—An Update*. Interestingly, much to the expressed chagrin of the left parties, the *Update* offered an even more positive assessment of the impact of the economic reforms carried out under the previous government. Even as it noted that 'a great deal more remains to be done', it stated: 'the economic reforms of the past five years have brought about a strong recovery in the growth of production and employment, restored the health of our external sector and ushered in far-reaching changes in agriculture, industry, the financial sector, capital markets and the tax structure' (*Economic Times*, 20 July 1996). Thus, notwithstanding a UF government consisting of parties, most of whom had earlier opposed the Congress Party and its economic programme, the new economic review and the subsequent budget provided confirmation of the essential continuity in regard to the posture on liberalization. The *Economic and Political Weekly* (20 July 1996) editorially charged that the government was 'a Congress government by proxy'. That would seem to be too simplistic a view, however; for, as will soon be apparent, while continuity was apparent in respect of what had already been accomplished, pushing new initiatives to completion was a different matter.

The 1996–97 budget of the UF government was in line with the thrust of the *Update*. Its hallmark was continuity with the earlier reforms; indeed, it denoted their consolidation and underlined their irreversibility. Commentators typically called it 'a Manmohan Singh budget plus or minus two per cent' (*Economic Times*, 23 July 1996). There were no new bold initiatives, but no reversal of policy either; any changes made were incremental and were interpreted for now to be a sign of reassurance rather than a disappointment, with liberalization legitimized by approval from all the political parties. The changes were in consonance with the 'social justice' plank of the CMP, and were designed largely to keep the fragile coalition together through increased subsidies that were really meant to serve the interests of rich farmers and the lower middle class. For the most part, the finance minister made promises to attack the many problem areas in the next budget.

By contrast, boldness dominated the 1997–98 budget. That budget signalled that the reforms were back on track; it made radical changes in the areas of taxes and tariffs with a view to moving India in the very near future, if not immediately, to correspond to the pattern prevailing among ASEAN countries in regard to integration with the world economy. It met with wide euphoric acclaim in the business community and among the upper and middle classes; it was proclaimed as a 'dream budget' and Finance Minister Chidambaram was invidiously hailed by some as an even greater reformer and liberalizer than Manmohan Singh. The budget, however, almost fell through, since in the midst of its consideration the Congress Party withdrew support from the UF government until a prime minister more satisfactory to its desires was appointed. The new UF government under Prime Minister Gujral, in essence the same government except for its head, hurriedly pushed the budget through Parliament. The passage of the two budgets, especially the later one with its bold initiatives, plus some other reforms, were testimony to the cooperation that did take place among the UF partners despite their sharply divergent views. However, apart from taxes and tariffs, many of the promises made in the budget and the CMP remained largely unfulfilled because of contention within the coalition and its short life in power.

Fiscal Management

While fiscal management involves several tasks for the government and becomes manifest in many issues in public life, fundamentally it boils down to the single issue of managing fiscal deficit. Whatever may be said about the alleged power of the IMF and World Bank in coercing developing countries around the world into enforcing structural adjustment programmes, it has not been particularly effective in persuading India to reduce the fiscal deficit to a reasonable level. There has occurred considerable backsliding in achieving targets. The Congress Party left behind the legacy of a fiscal deficit/GDP ratio in 1995–96 of 5.5 per cent. Little wonder that the UF's CMP had promised that 'the management of the fiscal deficit will, therefore, enjoy the highest priority'. More importantly, it pledged: 'All inessential and unproductive expenditure will be eliminated'. However, the very first attempt to attack the problem of fiscal deficit by the UF's minister of finance through controlling expenditures, encountered severe problems.

The Failed Austerity Drive

With the UF hardly two weeks in power, one of the very first initiatives of P. Chidambaram as finance minister was to issue a multipronged directive to various ministries to eliminate non-essential and unproductive expenditures of the central government in an effort to bring down the fiscal deficit to below 4 per cent of GDP. The immediate objective of the various measures included in the directive was to reduce annually of what amounted to a nominal sum of Rs 30 billion in a total budget of some Rs 2,000 billion. Despite the small amount, the austerity package covered a wide net of measures, many of them relating primarily to strict monitoring of expenditures and more effective cash management. However, one was politically sensitive since it asked for reducing manpower sharply and quickly and freezing pay and allowances in real terms for government personnel from the fiscal year 1997–98 onwards, though not from 1996–97.

The immediate response to this set of austerity measures was outrage on the part of the coalition partners, placing the UF government under severe strain soon after its installation. The CPI(M) and CPI and their trade union arms mounted an attack against the finance minister, denouncing the directive as 'anti-people' and contrary to the spirit of the CMP. The CPI(M)'s stand underlined the diametrically different views within the coalition; it chastised Chidambaram: 'Instead of tapping the big monopolies and landlords for resource mobilization, the finance minister has declared a war on the hard earned earnings of the public and the working class'. In a logic different from that of the finance minister, P.K. Ganguly, secretary of CITU, the labour front of CPI(M), declared: 'We will fight to fill up the two lakh [200,000] government posts which have been lying vacant over the last decade. If the government is serious about its commitment to creating employment, how can it not fill up these vacancies' (*Economic Times*, 19 June 1996; *Frontline*, 12 July 1996: 7).

Shaken by the wave of protests, the prime minister intervened to pacify the left parties and the trade unions. He assured them that all austerity measures that were considered to run counter to the rights and privileges of workers and government employees would be deferred, and that the left parties would be taken into confidence on any other austerity measures. In an unusual move, stemming from the exigencies of coalition politics, the finance minister met with trade union leaders to consult with them on the budget, and reversed himself on the austerity drive, assuring the unions of no retrenchment and no wage freeze (*Economic Times*, 19 to 23 June 1996). In brief, the pressures of the left partners scuttled the austerity drive.

Increases in Prices of Petroleum Products

Even as India moved to a greater role for the market in the economy during the early 1990s, it continued to retain an important role for the state in a variety of important activities. These activities included the system of public distribution of a number of essential commodities and the system of administered prices for a variety of goods. Among the latter were petroleum and petroleum products, such as aviation turbine fuel (ATF), diesel, kerosene, and liquid petroleum gas (LPG). Their prices were revised periodically—usually prior to the presentation of the budget—taking into account the movement of world oil prices. There was cross-subsidization under this 'administered pricing mechanism'; prices for petroleum and ATF were fixed high because of their use in means of transport catering to the upper classes while the prices for diesel, kerosene and LPG were kept low in the name of helping the poor, though in actual fact this populist measure subsidized consumption largely by the middle classes. The system of cross-subsidization was handled through an oil pool account, and the three public sector oil companies shared the account. The account needed to be kept in some sort of balance if the oil companies were to pay for the purchase and import of crude oil and petroleum products, and to recover their costs for processing and marketing.

The last time the prices had been raised by the government under the Congress Party was in February 1994, after which it refrained from doing so in order to win favour with the important groups that would be affected and, more generally, to keep inflation under control in view of the upcoming elections in several states in 1995 and the general elections in 1996. The petroleum ministry had warned in May 1995 of the worsening oil pool deficit, but the Congress government refused to act because of electoral considerations. By the time the UF government came to power, the oil pool deficit was headed for a steep rise, and was projected to reach a massive Rs 117 billion by the end of the fiscal year 1996–97 (*India Today*, 31 July 1996: 62). The UF government faced a crisis situation that it described as a 'mess' inherited from the Congress Party. Suddenly, on 3 July 1996, after deliberations in the cabinet but not in the steering committee, the UF government took what was considered to be a courageous step by announcing a hefty increase in the prices of all petroleum products except kerosene with the aim of making the oil pool account self-balancing. The very long delay in raising prices meant that the hike when it finally took place needed to be steep. The significant aspect of the measure was, apart from increasing the price of petrol and LPG, the complete removal of the subsidy for diesel.

The hike in fuel prices, which seemed eminently rational in view of the oil pool deficit, was greeted with a collective outcry, however. Opposition groups organized demonstrations and disrupted railway traffic while taxi unions warned of taking their vehicles off the streets. As expected, the BJP condemned the price increase as 'uncalled [for], unjustified and anti-people', and threatened to launch a countrywide agitation, even though during its short 13-day tenure in power in May it had acknowledged that a hike in fuel prices was inevitable. The Congress Party also expressed opposition as did the chief ministers of states whose ruling parties were coalition partners. But, surprisingly, the CPI which had taken part in the cabinet deliberations on the decision also joined in the condemnation. However, the most vociferous criticism came from the CPI(M), which was angered by not having been consulted on the decision and at the issue not having been discussed in the steering committee. The divisions within the coalition were thus out in the open despite the recent euphoric promises about providing a cohesive and stable government. In the wake of such opposition, the government made a quick but only partial retreat. Within three days of the initial decision, it cut into half the hike in the diesel price, making India's diesel about the cheapest in the world. The government bought peace, but the consequence was an additional subsidy of Rs 19.8 billion, a gap in the oil pool account balance that was left unmet by any other compensating increase.

The price increase failed to resolve the oil pool deficit issue, however. As international oil prices continued to rise, the deficit mounted daily in large amounts. Apart from higher international prices, accelerating local consumption and increased oil imports because of falling domestic oil production were the main culprits behind the ballooning deficit. The situation demanded another price increase, but the government was in no mood to oblige, especially so soon after the previous increase. Having burnt its fingers once, the government wanted to develop a consensus in the coalition. However, as one month passed into another for almost a year, while the oil pool deficit swelled at the rate of around Rs 300 million a day, no consensus could be developed. The left parties, particularly the CPI(M), would not agree to another hike.

As the crisis over the deficit mounted, the coalition seemed paralyzed even as it recognized the inevitability of increasing prices. In the circumstance, after about a dozen inconclusive meetings, the UF steering committee left the decision to the prime minister's personal discretion. Finally, after almost a whole year had passed since the crisis first became manifest, the government announced a package of measures at the beginning of September 1997 in the very propitious circumstance of unusually low inflation. The package was ingeniously designed so as to inflict little pain and largely to postpone it to the future. There was a modest increase in the price of petrol while the subsidy on diesel was eliminated and that on LPG was reduced. Kerosene prices were, however, left untouched. It was assumed that the higher prices for petrol and ATF would be adequate to cross-subsidize kerosene and LPG. An important element of the package was to gradually phase out the 'administered pricing mechanism' over a four-year period beginning in 1998–99 and to shift to the market by 2002 with domestic prices of most fuels reflecting international prices. Given the uncertainty surrounding the future of the coalition, this decision merely left implementation to another subsequent government. The accumulated oil pool deficit and consequently the large outstandings owed to the oil companies were partially handled through issuing about Rs 130 billion worth of five-to-seven year oil bonds at the below-market interest rate of 10.5 per cent.[4]

The long delay on political grounds in coming to a decision, while the necessity of increasing fuel prices was patent to all political players, can only be ascribed to the divisions within the coalition. Even after the decision was made, there followed the repetition of the spectacle of all political parties rising to condemn the decision. Curiously, however, the public did not stir; for one thing, the price increase was modest and therefore tolerable, but for another the long drawn-out debate on the issue had apparently convinced it of the necessity of a price increase. Notwithstanding the long delay and the opportunistic games of the political parties, however, it is noteworthy that the decision did eventually take place despite an otherwise divided coalition.

Harmonizing Taxation

At one time, India had confiscatory rates of taxation on income, amounting to over 90 per cent of income. With the beginning of liberalization in the mid-1970s, taxes on individual and corporate income began to be reduced. With the acceleration of liberalization in the early 1990s, the process of reduction was stepped up and by 1995–96 the maximum marginal tax rate on income had been brought down to 40 per cent (GOI 1997: 30). As the first budget of the UF government for the year 1996–97 was largely marked by continuity with the earlier regime, no radical changes were evident; only minor changes were made. The 1997–98 budget was different. Hailed as bold and visionary, the budget met with a roar of approval from industry and the middle classes. It was described as marking a 'great leap forward', 'leapfrogging into history', 'a psychological, economic and political coup' (Economic Times, 1 March 1997; Business Standard, 8 March 1997). The secret of the finance minister's success in winning such acclaim really lay in his slashing taxes, both income and corporate.

Finance Minister Chidambaram lowered tax rates across the board, replacing the previous rates of 15, 30 and 40 per cent by 10, 20 and 30 per cent for the three income brackets of Rs 40,000–60,000, 60,000–150,000 and over 150,000. The finance minister and his team had apparently turned into believers in the Laffer curve and counted on tax reduction to lead to buoyancy in revenues and thus bring the fiscal deficit down to a targeted 4.5 per cent of GDP. But equally important was the comparative thrust to their stance; they wanted to bring India into line with the ASEAN countries. Similar was the case with corporate taxes. The finance minister completely removed the surcharge on companies after having reduced it to half in the previous budget. More importantly, he reduced corporate tax rates for domestic companies from 40 to 35 per cent.

This venture into supply-side economics created a euphoria in the media, controlled largely by industry and managed and accessed by the middle classes, precisely the groups which were the beneficiaries of what were for the finance minister growth-oriented policies. The enthusiasm for the budget altered the popular expectation of coalition instability, and momentarily put the Congress Party on the defensive in its effort to destabilize the UF government. What is more surprising is the acquiescence of the left partners of the coalition to the slashing of taxes, even though their rhetoric attacked the finance minister. In any case, the government avoided the hard decisions on cutting subsidies, on pushing privatization, and on enacting an exit policy in the hope that the softer option of slashing taxes would make for rapid growth, which would then facilitate raising the prices of petroleum products subsequently even as it would provide revenues for the extra expenditures that the finance minister had promised on subsidies for food and fertilizer. It was a high risk strategy, where everything depended on the economy picking up.

Wage Settlements

Contrary to its declared aim of reducing the fiscal deficit, the coalition government during its second year in office ended up putting additional pressure on the deficit through an excessively generous wage settlement for the over 4 million employees of the central government. The occasion for the government's generosity was the submission of the much-awaited report of the Fifth Central Pay Commission. And the reason for the generosity was division within the coalition and the strategic position occupied by the left in that coalition.

The 1600-page report of the Commission was wide-ranging, seeking to reform and restructure administration in order to raise productivity in government work. It significantly raised salaries but, recognizing that this would put enormous pressure on the government's budget, the Commission recommended measures that would reduce the draft on the budget even as they would enhance productivity; chief among them were the abolition of 350,000 positions that had been lying vacant and the reduction of the workforce by 30 per cent over a 10-year period. The report was immediately attacked by various interest groups; the severest criticism came from the trade unions representing the lower-level clerical and support staff. For its part, the government simply accepted, without putting up much resistance, virtually all the principal demands of its employees. More noteworthy is the modality whereby this result was achieved. The government appointed a group of ministers, headed by Home Minister Indrajit Gupta—who not long before had been the head of CPI's labour front AITUC—to negotiate with the unions. Instead of standing up to the unions, he put pressure on the finance ministry to oblige. Meanwhile, key leaders of the United Front encouraged the employees in their demands by showing up at their demonstration in front of the finance ministry. Not unsurprisingly, one trade unionist commented: 'They almost acted as our comrades in arms'. The trade union leaders were themselves amazed at how swiftly the government caved in before them (*Business India*, 22 September–5 October 1997: 47–48).

The final settlement more than doubled the increase in the wage bill that the Commission had envisaged. One Commission member, Suresh Tendulkar, called it 'fiscal suicide'. But the impact of the concessions to the central government employees carried more far-reaching implications than the increase of 0.5 percentage point in the fiscal deficit, for it could not but generate pressures among the over 7 million employees of the state governments, several of which already had salary bills higher than their revenues. The explanation for the generous wage settlement lay in the weak and divided nature of the government in power. Tendulkar believed the government to have been 'an irresponsible, unprincipled and unethical negotiator' (*Business India*, 22 September–5 October 1997: 224). It was a bizarre affair, and angered by it and other populist measures of the UF government, economic columnist Prem Shankar Jha accused the UF coalition partners of 'ensuring that by the time this government departs the Government treasury will be wrecked for all time to come' (*Hindu*, 4 November 1997). Jha's target was not just the wage settlement, but also the whole issue of subsidies.

Subsidies

Apart from increasing the administered prices for petroleum products, the UF government attempted to make a contribution to the process of educating the public about the serious impact of subsidies. The ministry of finance under Chidambaram brought out in May 1997 a discussion paper on 'Government Subsidies in India' with the purpose of stimulating an informed debate on the subject. The paper underlined the spectacular growth of *explicit* subsidies provided by the central government. Before the 1970s, subsidies had been only a minor presence in the central budget, but the 1970s and 1980s saw rapid expansion in subsidy expenditures. That made for persistent fiscal profligacy, which in turn led to the economic crisis of 1991. The reforms of 1991 did not call a halt to the expansion though they perhaps slowed its pace somewhat. The aggregate figure for explicit central subsidies included in the 1997–98 budget (revised estimates) stood at Rs 196.44 billion as against a bare Rs 1.4 billion in 1971–72. The bulk of the central subsidies have gone to food and fertilisers, with these two items accounting for three-fourths of the subsidy expenditure in 1997–98 (GOI 1998: 21–24). However, explicit subsidies hardly scratch the surface of the issue. More importantly, the paper estimated total subsidies, both explicit and implicit, at the state and central levels and came to the astounding figure of 14.4 per cent of GDP.

More substantively, the UF coalition government deserves credit for restructuring, if only partially, the Public Distribution System to serve the interests of the poor. Under the two-tiered pricing of the revamped and retitled Targeted Public Distribution System, which was put into effect in June 1997, families below the poverty line were made eligible for 10 kg of foodgrains a month at half the central issue price. The left was not satisfied with this quantity of additionally subsidized foodgrains and demanded the allocation to be increased to 30 kg. However, it was not successful in its demand. Some may regard the action on further subsidizing food for the poor, numbering some 320 million, as another mark of fiscal profligacy. However, it needs to be remembered that, when the midday meal scheme was launched in the schools of Tamil Nadu in 1982, it was attacked for its fiscal irresponsibility only to be lauded some years later for its contribution to the improved health of children. Where the restructuring of the Public Distribution System can be faulted is that the targeting was incomplete in that it did not withdraw the subsidy from those above the poverty line, especially the well-to-do. However, no political party is willing to risk losing the support of the middle class and the organized working class. In the absence of that, subsidies will continue to add to the burden of the fiscal deficit.

Failure on Fiscal Deficit

Shortly before the 1997–98 budget, Finance Minister Chidambaram had declared that 'My first concern is fiscal deficit. Fiscal correction, therefore, is high on the agenda' (*India Today*, 28 February 1997: 56). Despite the brave proclamations on the part of the UF coalition about reducing the fiscal deficit at the centre, the end result was failure on that front. Instead of bringing down the fiscal deficit to the targeted 4.5 per cent of GDP, it ended up elevating it to 6.1 per cent, the second highest level since economic reforms were instituted in 1991–92. The *Economic Survey 1997–98* acknowledged that 'the process of fiscal consolidation received a setback during 1997–98' and that the fiscal year 'saw a major deterioration of the fiscal deficit' (GOI 1998: 8, 17). The setback is conveyed more vividly by the actual amounts; the fiscal deficit for 1997–98 had been budgeted at Rs 654.54 billion but had overshot the target by 32 per cent to Rs 863.45 billion (revised estimates). A major cause of the rise in the fiscal deficit was the shortfall in tax revenue by Rs 142.36 billion. This shortfall was despite the fact that, as the worsening fiscal situation—particularly after the concessions on the wage settlements—became apparent, the finance minister had, besides cutting Plan and non-Plan expenditures by 5 per cent, made a mid-term post-budget fiscal correction in September 1997 by instituting an increase of 3 percentage points in the special duty on customs on non-oil imports. Apparently, the very feature of slashing taxes that had led the 1997–98 budget to be called a 'dream budget' had made for fiscal deterioration. It confirmed the critics in their view that the finance minister had gambled on a high growth rate and lower taxes to lift up revenue intake, only to emerge unfortunate on both counts. The end consequence was that the UF bequeathed an economy to the successor government in a far worse shape than the one it had inherited from the previous government.

Liberalization

As a general proposition, it would seem that during the rule of the UF coalition it was easier to enact reforms in those areas where authority for decisions was a matter of executive discretion. Not that it was entirely easy, for issues were often discussed within the steering committee that was paralyzed between the left and the reformers. It mattered a great deal, therefore, how committed a particular minister was to reform within his jurisdiction and what support he brought from his constituency in the coalition. Also, wherever legislative approval was necessary, reform was more problematic, for not only internal divisions within the coalition could defeat reform but reform was also hostage to other political parties since the coalition constituted a minority government. To that extent, it would be accurate to say that India's economic policy reform under the UF government lacked depth.

A considerable number of minor changes did take place but largely within areas that were a matter of executive discretion. That meant that on the really important issues, stalemate was generally the outcome. Indeed, internal liberalization was the major casualty of the coalition. No doubt, there was a lot of activity but it culminated in little of major substance. No reform of the labour markets could even be contemplated, no privatization of the public sector could be advanced, no legislation on patent rights could be revived, and no opening up of the insurance sector could be pushed through. Some of the seemingly weighty pronouncements amounted to mere statements of intent while others simply postponed implementation into the future when the coalition may or may not be around to handle reform. Still, a number of serious studies, such as on small-scale industries and banking, were undertaken and several pieces of important legislation drafted, even if not enacted, and they could be of value to a successor government.

Deregulation

In the area of deregulation, Industry Minister Murasoli Maran, an obvious enthusiast for reform, reduced the number of industries that required prior licences from the central government. Despite the radical reform it undertook, the previous Congress government had left behind 15 industries that were still subject to licensing by the central government. Initially, the UF government delicensed consumer electronics and then another five industries were exempted from licensing; as a consequence, only nine industries—such as drugs and pharmaceuticals, petroleum, sugar, and alcohol—continued to require licences. The Congress government had also left six industries reserved for the public sector. The UF government opened coal and lignite mining to the private sector. However, while the UF government was formally willing to open up additional industries to the private sector, individual ministers and ministerial bureaucracies endeavoured, even where areas had already been opened to the private sector, to protect the interests of specific public sector enterprises (PSEs) under their charge from competition from the private sector (such as by refusing the Tatas to set up an airline).

An important initiative of the coalition government was the setting up of the Telecom Regulatory Authority of India as an independent agency to regulate all telecommunications operators, both government and private; it started functioning in early 1997. As already seen, the UF government in 1997 decided to phase out the administered pricing mechanism for petroleum products though its implementation was left to the future. The government also decided to repeal the Urban Land (Ceiling and Regulation) Act, so as to remove restrictions on land holdings in urban areas, but the government fell before it could bring forward legislation toward that end. Earlier, it failed to get legislative approval for opening the insurance sector to the private sector.

Privatization

In the area of privatization of the public sector, the coalition government's attitude was somewhat different from that of the preceding Congress government. Despite being frustrated in its plans, the Congress government was attracted to the prospect of radical disinvestment in most PSEs to the level of 49 per cent, probably as a way station to further privatization. Given its divisions, the UF incorporated a variety of remedies for the predicament of the public sector; in a sense, no alternative was excluded, but it was inclined more to restructuring than to privatization.

The CMP incorporated a positive view of the public sector even as it recognized its weaknesses. Accordingly, the United Front was determined 'to make the public sector strong and competitive'. Instead of coming to terms with the fact that, barring a few PSEs, the profitability record of most PSEs was dismal and they had proven recalcitrant to improvement through administrative reform, the UF continued to express faith in the proposition that 'the public sector requires to be reformed and restructured'. What is more, it promised to 'identify public sector companies that have comparative advantages and will support them in their drive to become global giants'. At the same time, the CMP promised to carefully examine 'the question of withdrawing the public sector from non-core and non-strategic areas' provided the interests of workers were safe-guarded. To assure transparency in the decisions made and imple-mented in respect of disinvestment in the public sector, the UF agreed, quite innovatively, to establish a Disinvestment Commission.

The UF government took several actions in accord with the provi-sions of the CMP. The industry minister designated nine out of some 250 PSEs at the centre as *navaratnas* ('the nine [crown] jewels'), which were to be built up as global giants; this group of nine was accorded greater autonomy in the areas of mobilization of capital and entering into joint ventures and strategic alliances; their boards were made more broadbased by inclusion of non-official profession-als. Besides, the UF government subsequently designated another 97 profit-making PSEs as 'mini-ratnas' and also granted them opera-tional autonomy. Though these attempts to endow greater auton-omy on PSEs were well-meaning, they could not be expected to really surmount the deep-rooted structural and cultural constraints on efficiency and competitiveness that resulted from the PSEs being in the ultimate analysis simply subordinate wings of the ministries.

The appointment in 1996 of the Disinvestment Commission, con-sisting of members who were highly regarded for their competence and probity, was an innovative measure of the UF coalition. Under its capable chairman, G.V. Ramakrishna, it submitted a series of ex-cellent reports, which recommended substantial disinvestment for a dozen PSEs and strategic sales of another score, even as they endor-sed measures to safeguard the interests of labour. However, a turf war erupted between the industry ministry and the commission over who should handle the actual disinvestment. In the event, little reve-nue could be generated through disinvestment; the 1997–98 budget had hoped to raise Rs 48 billion from disinvestment, but the short-fall amounted to Rs 38.93 billion (GOI 1998: 19).

In brief, in terms of internal liberalization, there was considerable noise and apparent activity but little of consequence took place; per-haps the only action of some significance was the setting up of the Telecom Regulatory Authority to oversee and regulate the telecom-munications sector.

Globalization

In contrast to internal liberalization, the UF's record on external lib-eralization was extensive and far-reaching. The period saw dramatic moves towards the integration of India into the world economy. This was evident both in lowering tariff barriers and in facilitating entry of foreign investment. Significantly, the key actors in these two areas were, respectively, Finance Minister Chidambaram and Industry Minister Maran. Moreover, action in these areas was not dependent on special legislation; rather, it either entailed only executive decision-making or it was part of the budgetary exercise.

Lowering Tariffs

The successive rounds of trade reform since mid-1991 had removed the all-embracing licensing requirements for most imports except for consumer goods, imports of which were nonetheless considerably liberalized. By the time the UF government came to power in 1996, trade reform had brought the maximum tariff down to 50 per cent from over 300 per cent and the average import-weighted tariff down to 27.2 per cent from 87 per cent.

Finance Minister Chidambaram was cautious in his first budget for 1996–97, and he retained the peak tariff rate. Supporters of tariff reduction were disappointed. However, they were enthused by the 1997–98 budget, which cut the peak tariff rate sharply to 40 per cent; economic columnist S.S.A. Aiyar remarked: 'This constitutes a global vision, a considered strategy to integrate India with the global economy' (*Economic Times*, 1 March 1997). Mid-way through the fiscal year, however, there was a reversal in the trend toward greater trade liberalization. As the fiscal deficit target seemed threatened, the finance minister increased the special customs surcharge of 2 per cent on all non-oil imports to 5 per cent. In the event, the import-weighted average tariff for 1997–98 increased to 25.4 per cent after having come down to 24.6 per cent in 1996–97 (World Bank 1998: Annex Table 10). Significantly, the government reached agreement with important trade partners over gradually phasing out quantitative restrictions on the remaining items of consumer goods imports.

Foreign Investment

When the CMP first came out, the item that attracted the most attention concerned foreign investment. While the United Front counted on domestic savings to meet industry's requirements, it held that 'at the margin, the country cannot do without foreign investment'. It was a surprise that CPI and CPI(M) could formally subscribe to such a position even though the CPI(M)-led state government in West Bengal had for some years been actively soliciting foreign investment. Even more surprising was the scale on which foreign investment was envisaged: 'The nation needs and has the capacity to absorb at least $10 billion a year as foreign direct investment'. This stand is significant because in the previous year, 1995–96, foreign direct investment (FDI) was only $2.1 billion. There was a caveat, however, in the CMP that the bulk of the investment would be directed to the core and infrastructure sectors while 'entry of multinational companies into low priority areas will be discouraged through suitable fiscal and other measures'. In the event, foreign investment was one area in which the UF displayed substantial achievement notwithstanding the fear about political instability. Total foreign investment climbed from $4.9 billion in 1995–96 to $6.0 billion in 1996–97 only to fall back, under the impact of the East Asian economic crisis, to $4.8 billion in 1997–98. More significantly, FDI showed a consistent rise from $2.1 billion in 1995–96 to $2.7 billion in 1996–97 and $3.2 billion in 1997–98 (World Bank 1998: Annex Table 10).

It is not surprising why the UF could demonstrate success in this area. Foreign investment does not entail any immediate social and political costs in terms of resource mobilization within the country while it allows the government to move forward in achieving its goal of more rapid economic growth and thus greater employment and, consequently, poverty alleviation. This calculation was nothing new; indeed, liberalization had been from the beginning premised on foreign investment resolving India's problem of lack of adequate financial resources to achieve its economic goals. No doubt, it may affect domestic industry adversely but then industry did not control a large vote bank as did the peasantry, the middle class and labour in other areas of reform.

The entry of portfolio investment is substantially dependent on the state of the capital markets, but the government was sensitive to its concerns. As events warranted it, the government relaxed restrictions on the level of equity that foreign institutional investors could severally and jointly hold in Indian companies. However, it is the encouragement of FDI that attracted the most energy and effort of the government. Here, Industry Minister Maran proved to be an open and active enthusiast for FDI. Maran was not squeamish about his enthusiasm for foreign capital, and he expressed it repeatedly: 'It is essential. We have a gap between our savings and investment rates. The gap can only be filled by foreign direct investment. Whoever comes to power will have no other go than to fill the gap with foreign investment.... If we lose the race [on foreign investment], we will be pushed into a limbo of stagnation' (Business World, 16–28 February 1997: 37).

Three sets of measures were involved in assuring an expeditious flow of FDI. First, under Maran's energetic leadership, the Foreign Investment Promotion Board (FIPB), the agency responsible for case-by-case processing of foreign investment proposals, speeded up the clearance of such proposals. Maran himself took a liberal view of the areas into which foreign investment would be allowed. Second, the government deepened the process of external liberalization by revising the existing rules which allowed automatic approval by the Reserve Bank of India (RBI) of proposals for FDI up to 51 per cent in respect of 35 industries. Later, the RBI route of automatic clearance was extended to proposals for FDI up to 74 per cent of equity for nine categories of industries, including power generation, construction and maintenance of roads and ports, and semi-finished iron and steel. Besides, 13 other industries were added to the existing list of 35 industries for automatic clearance of foreign equity up to 51 per cent while three industries in the area of mining were now made eligible for RBI automatic clearance for foreign equity up to 50 per cent (GOI 1998: 109–13). Third, to provide an element of transparency to the work of the FIPB, the government for the first time issued guidelines on FDI, spelling out levels of foreign investment permitted in various industries. Near the end of the short term of the UF government, Maran suggested that the FIPB should be abolished, and that foreign investment should be allowed to come in automatically under clearly-established guidelines.

Capital Account Convertibility

This was a cherished goal of Finance Minister Chidambaram, but he was unsuccessful in this regard. That was partly due to the government's premature fall, but more importantly because his hopes of bringing down the fiscal deficit faded. Further, the economic crisis in

East and Southeast Asia, starting in 1997, put an end to talk of capital account convertibility, for the lack of controls on capital movements was now held to be a key cause for the crisis.

Concluding Assessment

That the UF coalition government proved to have a short life, about a year and a half, and that too characterized by constant internal conflict and even breakdown in midstream, is consistent with the general proposition about the brevity of coalition governments. To that extent, the coalition theory is vindicated by the experience of the UF. But can the same be said of the performance of the government in the area of economic policy reform? Does the UF government's performance correspond to the proposition of weakness, indecisiveness and paralysis?

Assessing performance in relation to economic policy reform for a specific government, short-lived at that, can be a highly subjective undertaking, for several determinants are at work and they cannot all be held constant in comparison. An initial question arises as to what the comparative reference point ought to be for performance assessment, for an assessment cannot be made in the abstract. No doubt, in India's brief experience with economic policy reform the only likely comparison could be the performance of the preceding Congress government, which initiated and presided over the period of economic adjustment. While at first blush this would seem fair procedure, in fact a strong argument could be made that it is not. For, the Congress Party came to power as a minority government at the peak of an economic crisis of substantial proportions, which necessitated going to the IMF and World Bank for assistance in economic adjustment. The economic crisis resulted in a paradigm shift in economic policy. The public and the polity recognized the need for stern measures in the context of the crisis. However, the economic crisis was largely overcome in 20 months, or at the most in two years. With that, there occurred the restoration of normal politics. It seems fairer to make the subsequent post-crisis period of normal politics, even as there continued to be a large unfinished agenda for reform, the reference point for comparison in evaluating the performance of the short-lived UF government from 1996 to 1998.[5]

What is noteworthy about the second half of the Congress Party's five-year term in office from mid-1991 to mid-1996 is that, notwithstanding its known enthusiasm for reform, the passion for reform waned as the economic crisis passed even though the party had in the meantime acquired, whether through persuasion or economic incentives, a majority in the Lok Sabha. The reform process had essentially come to an end by mid-1993. Even in relation to the reform that had been actually pushed through earlier, what is remarkable is that it did not affect any significant group adversely; it was essentially economic adjustment without pain. Basically, the Congress Party relied on foreign investment to foster economic growth and manage India's balance of payments problem.

Although Finance Minister Chidambaram of the UF had made a positive endorsement of the Congress Party's reform accomplishments, as evident in the *Economic Survey Update*, the same *Update* referred to a considerable unfinished agenda for liberalization, which the Congress Party had also recognized: capital account convertibility, removal of quantitative restrictions on consumer goods imports, restructuring and privatization of the public sector, dereserving the small-scale sector, reforming the labour market, strengthening the financial system, opening the insurance sector to competition from the private sector, and reduction of subsidies. What is more, the fiscal deficit seemed recalcitrant to scaling down. Indeed, there had been a severe deterioration in fiscal management, which issued out of populistic responses by way of launching welfare programmes and refusal to increase in time the administered prices of petroleum products or the issue prices of foodgrains in the public distribution system. Populistic considerations also lay behind keeping inflation down through a policy of paring capital expenditures to the barebone in the public sector and a highly restrictive monetary policy which, with its accompanying high interest rates, constrained business investment. These policies of the Congress years, in turn, led to the economic slowdown which chronologically emerged in mid-1996 just as the UF started its term in office.

At the root of this record of performance in the second half of the Congress Party's term in office were electoral compulsions. Almost every year there were elections in one or more states. Elections at the state level had repercussions for economic policy at the national level. The failure of the Congress Party to revive its electoral fortunes in UP and Rajasthan in 1993 started alarm bells ringing about the future electoral prospects of the party, and induced caution. As the seasoned economist, D.R. Pendse (1996), had noted: 'Alas, come the 1994–95 budget and we saw the government had decided not only to keep on hold any further major reforms: but actually undertook a reverse journey towards fiscal indiscipline. Their election pundits obviously felt reforms would not mix with elections'.

However, it was the defeat of Congress governments in the state elections in Andhra Pradesh and Karnataka in 1994 that proved to be a bombshell and, therefore, consequential in calling a halt to liberalization. It demonstrated the efficacy of competitive populism, for the opposition had won by promising cheaper food and larger subsidies while labelling liberalization as a policy for the rich. The shock of electoral defeat sparked a serious debate within the Congress Party, which put the reformers on the defensive. Then in 1995, the party suffered major electoral blows in the western region with the loss of the important states of Maharashtra and Gujarat. The impending national elections in 1996 further persuaded the Congress Party to adopt policies to appease the electorate and key groups within it—restraint on administered prices and on public investment in order to control inflation, even as outlays on subsidies and the social sectors were expanded.

It would be futile to speculate whether the Congress Party would have reverted to its earlier liberalization course if it had won, but the record of the UF government in its brief tenure, despite all the conflicts and the delayed and stretched-out decision-making, seems in comparison to be superior to that of the second half of the Congress Party's period in office. After all, the UF government was decisive in raising foodgrain prices and in the first round of increase in petroleum prices. Even in regard to the second round of increase in petroleum prices, it finally did arrive at a decision, overruling opposition from the left. It was decisive, again, in dramatically lowering taxes and tariffs, and thus in changing expectations about harmonizing and integrating with the global economy. And it made a valiant effort to bring down the fiscal deficit and even met the target in the first year. Perhaps, there is exaggeration in one businessman's assessment of the UF government that, 'It achieved much more than the Congress in terms of financial reforms, budgetary proposals and continuing the reforms process', and may be there is greater merit in the position of another businessman that 'Given all the limitations of a 13-member coalition, I feel they did a good job in continuing the reforms process'.[6] Still, the UF coalition's record stands in considerable contrast with the later period of the preceding Congress government.[7] It would be easy to cavil at the fiscal profligacy of the UF in respect of subsidies and trade union demands, but the Congress Party had been no more immune to taking to soft options in this regard.

The intellectual puzzle that arises, given the position of coalition theory on the issue, is as to why a minority coalition government, riven by divisions and polarized between reformers and opponents of reform, uncertain about its continuance in office and dependent on outside support for sheer survival, should have been able to perform at all in the area of economic policy reform.

The answer, it would seem, lies in the fact that a coalition government is in the contemporary era subject to strong pressures for economic policy reform. These pressures emanate from several major sources. First, there are *state-centred pressures*. There is no doubt that the specific nature of India's political structure in the form of representative democracy throws up social and political forces that inhibit or retard reform. But, paradoxically, the same system also generates pressures that push it in the direction of reform. If it be granted that modern governments are under political compulsion to promote economic growth (Lindblom 1977) and that, during the 1980s and 1990s, the overall intellectual and political ethos[8] has overwhelmingly favoured economic liberalization as a means to promoting growth, then coalition governments are also under pressure to prove their capacity at performance in pushing liberalization. What is more, they are under a time constraint to prove such capacity; ironically, there is evident here a reverse 'time-horizon' advantage for reform lying precisely in the very shortness of life of coalitions. Not being sure of its tenure in office builds up pressure in a coalition for quicker decisions to pile up a record. It is not surprising then that the short period of the UF coalition in office was more action-packed and more hectic-paced than the second half of the preceding Congress government in respect of economic reform.

Besides, there are other institutional pressures at work within the democratic framework. The requirement of presentation of an annual budget for legislative approval focuses the attention of the government on economic policy reform and creates a momentum for reform, especially when that government is keen to be vindicated on being better at performance than the preceding government. Similarly, the political requirement for the executive to be responsive to demands of interest groups favouring reform, such as the apex business associations like FICCI, CII and Assocham, and for it to be visible through high-level officials, including the prime minister and ministers for finance, commerce and industry, at the annual meetings of these organizations, and further for it to justify the performance record of the government in the area of reform, and also to promise new initiatives—all this creates an updraft for pushing reform. Again, the mass media, especially the press which is known for its vitality and assertiveness, keeps the government constantly under the limelight, compelling it to publicly prove its performance and how it compares with earlier governments.

Second, there are *market-centred pressures*. For one thing, although a major economic crisis may be unusual, the market in the present epoch confronts the government constantly with mini-crises that require policy changes. Such crises arise perpetually in the areas of exports, balance of payments, banking, industry, and agriculture. The very fact of partial liberalization generates new pressures for further liberalization. More importantly, the stock market provides as it were a running commentary on government policy, and consequently stimulates policy responses. Until the mid-1980s, when Prime Minister Rajiv Gandhi's economic policies activated capital markets in the Indian economy, government was largely immune to market behaviour and sentiment. Since then, however, the stock market serves to force the government to own up to the impact of its policies on the real economy and the financial sector, and to modify or adopt policies that are responsive to market sentiment. As one authority (Sharma 1997) has argued:

> In the bigger picture, the most significant aspect of the budget is the extent to which the markets have played a role of disciplining policy-makers. Last year when the stock market collapsed in the aftermath of the [1996–97] budget, the same set of policy-makers arrogantly dismissed the market reaction as inconsequential. The capital markets then went on to behave in such a nasty manner that the effects clearly began to be transmitted to the real economy. The finance ministry was made to care and the end-result is that the present [1997–98] budget is a very market-sensitive, if not market-savvy, budget. The markets are acting as the disciplinarians and this is very much a global phenomenon. Why the market's verdict matters so much is because it is bound to be closest to reality as market participants put their hard-earned money where

their mouth is. Indian policy making is aligning with global policy making.

Third, there are pressures from *the global system*. The Indian state has to be sensitive to comparison with other states which are said to have performed better economically because of more effective liberalization. Thus, the finance minister can, under certain circumstances, make the open economies of Southeast Asia the standard to which Indian policy should conform. Also, the imperative to push forward reform is drilled into the ears of Indian policy-makers by a stream of visiting foreign votaries of liberalization, such as World Economic Forum's chairman Claude Smadja. Again, attendance by Indian officials at Davos creates pressures to make decisions in advance which can be shown off there; note, for example, the comment: 'there's little doubt that the finance minister wants to create the impression before the international business community at Davos that the reform programme is alive and kicking.... "Chidambaram is pulling all the ministries together before Gowda and he go to Davos"' (*Business World*, 1–15 February 1997: 32). More significantly, there is a constant barrage of authoritative and leveraged advice, demands and pressures from international organizations, such as the IMF, World Bank and WTO, for the Indian government to act in the area of fiscal deficit, removal of quantitative restrictions on consumer goods imports, reduction and better targeting of subsidies, restructuring of state electricity boards, and strengthening of the financial system. Market-driven fluctuations in foreign trade and current account balances also compel government to come up with policies.

To be sure, coalition governments have countervailing pressures against reform as is apparent in the main analysis above, but what the immediately preceding discussion demonstrates is that the situation is not altogether one-sided. In a sense, it is precisely because the situation is not one-sided that whatever has been done by a government in favour of liberalization has proven to be irreversible, even with the change of government. No doubt, democracy slows down reform but that is not equivalent to no reform. In the situation of a functioning representative democracy, progress toward economic policy reform is necessarily gradual and halting, in brief incremental, slowing down at one time and picking up at another. Nothing different could be expected within a democratic framework. For, democratic governments must hold 'a balance between conflicting preferences and interests, so the pace of reforms reflects tradeoffs between present and future consumption and between the costs to one group versus the benefits to the rest' (Mohan 1998b). In India's case, the reality is that while there is a national consensus it is, as the *Economic Times* (12 November 1996) put it, only on 'muddled reform', for 'reform in India has been driven not by ideology (which would have meant less muddle)' but by contingent need.

In India's democratic framework, the threshold for tolerance of an economic, and therefore political, crisis is extremely low, especially one foisted by radical changes in policy, and governments can inflict such crises only at their own peril. Even the left performs a useful function in slowing down reform, and forcing government to rethink its policies and priorities before acting. The conception of liberalization as a once-for-all measure to be achieved at one blow, as prescribed by the advocates of the 'Big Bang' or shock therapy, is a misconceived one; it is, indeed, incompatible with democracy and requires a different type of political system. Liberalization is a process, not an end-stage to be achieved in the here and now, and incrementalism seems the appropriate method for policy in a democracy. As often, the point was most effectively expressed by a practitioner of Indian politics, Murasoli Maran (*Business World*, 16–28 February 1997: 26):[9]

Reform is not a one-time thing; you cannot do it at one go, as was done in the erstwhile Soviet Union and eastern Europe. Secondly, we are not an authoritarian state like China, so that we can push it further. We are the largest functioning democracy in the world. So some people may accuse us of going slowly. It is wrong to do so. We are going cautiously because we have to take the people along with us. And also we are a coalition government; so we have to consult other parties. Every step forward is always taken with a lot of caution, with a lot of analysis of the situation. We want to be careful that reforms are painless. Besides, in the meantime, actual economic trends, as revealed in the economic crisis beginning in 1997 in East and Southeast Asia and the economic turmoil in the 1990s in Russia have given rise to scepticism even among economists about rapid full-scale liberalization as an appropriate prescription for developing countries. These only underline the virtues of caution and gradualism.

Notes

1. The myth of short-lived coalition governments has, however, come under attack in the face of some evidence—not of overwhelming statistical power—of coalition stability in some countries (Dodd 1976: 208–09). The formation of stable coalitions in Dodd's analysis is dependent on restrictive requirements—such as stable, depolarized, and only moderately but not excessively fractionalized party systems—that are likely to be rarely met, especially in the developing world.

   'Coalition government' is not a homogeneous concept, however. Dodd distinguishes between (1) minimum winning cabinets, (2) oversized or greater-than-minimum winning cabinets, and (3) undersized or less-than-minimum winning cabinets (that is, minority governments); he holds the first type to be quite durable and the other two to be more transient. Other key elements entering into the prospects of stability of coalition governments pertain to attributes of the party system: cleavage conflict or polarization; fractionalization (the number and relative strength of parties within parliament); and party system stability (the continuity over time in the identity and relative strength of parties). See Dodd (1976: 17–18, 54–70).

2. One commentator on the left asserted: 'The deeply retrogressive nature and aims of the economic reform programme, drawn up for India by the IMF/World Bank combine, already stands exposed among the people and they voted against it firmly and unambiguously' (BM, in *Economic and Political Weekly*, 15 June 1996: 1434–35). Note, however, the results of a systematic study based on rigorous polling of voters under the auspices of the Indian Council of Social Science Research and the Centre for the Study of Developing Societies: 'Coming more specifically to the recent shifts in economic policy, only a fifth [of the sample] had heard about them. And of these, over half approved of the changes. One can thus legitimately doubt the assertion that the electoral debacle of the Congress party can be traced to the new economic policy' (Singh and Yadav 1996).

3. Citations from the CMP hereafter are from: United Front (1996).

4. See *India Today*, 15 September 1997: 54; *Business India*, 8–21 September 1997: 9–10; and GOI (1998: 106).

5. It may be objected that the comparison is unfair since, failing to take the particular stage of the electoral cycle into account, it compares the second half of the five-year term of the Congress Party in office—when the government had to keep the impending elections in view—with the 18 months or so of the UF government right after the elections. However, it is important to note that the UF government from the very beginning lived under the constant threat of being overthrown.

6. Wockhardt chairman Habil F. Khorakiwala and Larson & Toubro managing director S.D. Kulkarni, in *Business World*, 22 December 1997: 21.

7. However, the public may still consider a stable majority government a desirable end in itself. Besides, it may find the political instability under coalition governments intolerable for other undesirable consequences it may generate, such as political uncertainty and deterioration in law and order. The function of government is to govern, and instability may prevent it from doing that.

8. Economic policy is often influenced by dominant ideas of the particular time—such as Keynesianism, development economics, or the new economic orthodoxy—though no doubt filtered through concrete interests.

9. This preference for gradualism is treated more systematically by Agarwal and Sengupta (2000) in their analysis of the differences between incremental reform, as exemplified by India and China, and the shock therapy approach as evidenced in East Europe.

7

The Limits of Economic Nationalism: Economic Reforms under the BJP-led Government, 1998–99

The national elections in 1998, following the collapse of the United Front government, resulted in a new coalition government, this time led by the Bharatiya Janata Party (BJP) under the leadership of Prime Minister Atal Behari Vajpayee. The installation once again of another coalition government, even though led by a different party, aroused renewed concerns about political stability. In the event, these concerns proved valid since the government lasted in office a bare 13 months and the country had to face elections again in 1999. Beyond the issue of political stability, however, the coming into power of the BJP, even if only at the head of a coalition of 18 parties, raised crucial concerns of a different order altogether. These concerns stemmed from the nature of the origins and affiliations of the BJP, for the BJP is a successor to the Bharatiya Jana Sangh. The Jana Sangh had been founded in 1951 as a political front of the Rashtriya Swayamsevak Sangh (RSS), a cadre-based cultural organization openly dedicated to Hindu nationalism, an element that stood outside the accepted value structure of the country's political system at the time.[1]

The BJP regards itself as a distinctive party, 'the party with a difference', since it rejects the larger normative consensus among the other political parties regarding secularism. For, it views such secularism pejoratively as only pseudo-secularism in the conviction that it is not genuine and only a mask worn by opportunistic political parties for the appeasement of minorities in order to secure their votes during elections. Again, the party avers itself to be particularly different from other, presumably soft-minded, political parties in the arena of national security. It sees itself to be single-mindedly dedicated to building a strong India that has its rightful share in influence in the world order and stands up to those whom it looks upon as international bullies. But the BJP considers itself distinctive as well in economic affairs. It rejects the developmental model followed by the Congress Party, whether the earlier one of Nehru's which invested the commanding heights of the economy in the state or the more recent one since 1991 of Narasimha Rao's which drastically shifted the emphasis from the state to the market, allegedly at the behest of the international financial institutions. More broadly, the BJP rejects both communism and capitalism, because of their foreign origins which, according to its view, render them out of harmony with India's own cultural traditions. Rather than mimic foreign models, it opts forthrightly instead for an organicist model of a well-integrated economy and society that supposedly draws upon India's own indigenous traditions. A key feature of its economic programme is *swadeshi*, which can be loosely translated as economic nationalism.

The question that emerges as of interest here is whether, rhetoric apart, there was in actual practice anything distinctive about the BJP's economic policy in contrast to that of the Congress Party or that of the United Front. To some extent, perhaps, the question is premature for a definitive answer, for the BJP was in power for only a brief period, and that too as part of a coalition. However, both the fact that it was in power through the mechanism of a multiparty coalition and the further fact that it was the dominant partner in that coalition are in themselves highly significant in that they evidence both the limits and the possibilities of implementing the BJP's economic programme. The BJP's period in office, even if brief, provides nonetheless an opportunity to assess its policy behaviour against its stated ideology.

The empirical proposition that emerges from a review of the actual record of the BJP in office, as against the stated ideology, is that there is nothing really distinctive about the BJP governance in relation to economic policy; that is, there is little to set it apart from the Congress Party. This is a significant finding in view of the BJP's emphatic perception of itself as a distinctive party as also equally the characterization of it as such by its antagonists. This raises the important question as to why there should be little to differentiate the BJP in office from the Congress Party, or for that matter from the United Front. The explanation for the phenomenon of similarity in economic approach during governance seems to be two-fold. First, it lies, *internally*, in the centrist tendency of Indian politics in the context of the country's immense social diversity and the considerably institutionalized nature of its political framework of democracy. Second, it lies, *externally*, in the nature of the modern international system, primarily in terms of the substantial incentives to participation in a highly, though certainly asymmetrically, interdependent world economy, but as well, to some extent, in the pressures of real-politik associated with politics among nations. In the treatment of the empirical proposition and the explanation, this chapter is divided into the following four parts: (1) the centrist tendency of Indian politics and the incentives to globalization and liberalization; (2) the centrist tendency in BJP's long march to power; (3) the BJP's economic agenda and the centrality of national interest; and (4) economic policy reforms under the BJP-led government. The presentation of the analysis here reverses the usual order of description followed by explanation for the sake of providing a better comprehension of the dynamics of politics and policy-making under the BJP-led government.

The Centrist Tendency and International System as Explanation

The Centrist Tendency in Indian Politics

Certainly, the most impressive fact about the Indian polity among the larger developing countries is its uniqueness in sustaining a democratic political framework for more than half a century, justifying claims to Indian exceptionalism (Weiner 1989: 21–23). Over this period, political groups in India have thus confronted a political system in which the ballot box is the final arbiter in their quest for power. Despite the deterioration in the level of its institutionalization after the first quarter-century following independence, the system has still proven sturdy and resilient enough to bar seizure of power through violence or the possession of the means of violence; putschist politics has simply not been possible. The mainline communist parties have since the early 1950s had to conform to the political requirements of the overarching democratic framework, while no Hindu nationalist group has ever contemplated seizure of power through violent means.

Coalition-building is an integral part of the process of acquiring state power within a democracy. However, in India's case it is particularly reinforced as a requirement for power acquisition by the immense social diversity of the country. In India, every group is in practical terms a minority. To be sure, with 85 per cent of the population, the Hindus constitute an overwhelming majority, but that majority is only notional since it is itself fragmented by divisions based on language, caste, sect and class. In their effort precisely to overcome these divisions, the Hindu nationalists have but ended up creating some additional fresh ones of their own. The diversity of India, springing from its horizontal and vertical cleavages, is further raised to a monumental scale by the vast size of its political unit, comparable to that of Europe minus the former Soviet Union.

In a unique development in India's history, the nationalist movement as organizationally expressed in the Congress Party built a grand political coalition in its long drawn-out struggle to overthrow colonial rule. That coalition, constructed in the name of the Indian nation, encompassed the urban middle classes and the rich and middle peasantry of the rural areas belonging to the upper and middle castes. The Congress success was only partial, however, since its nationalism had appeal primarily for the Hindus. The Muslim minority, then about a quarter of the subcontinent's population, largely though not universally chose to stay out of the coalition in the pursuit of a separatist path which finally led to the formation of Pakistan. The Congress coalition was organized around a broad consensus on the moderate platform of nationalism, democracy, the secular state, economic development, and an autonomous foreign policy, a platform that was carried over into the period after independence and remained dominant until the end of the 1970s. With the breaking down of the Congress coalition in the late 1960s under the pressure of competitive outbidding among its constituents and of the social mobilization of new groups as a result of the very operation of political democracy, India entered a long transitional process of forging new, but in the event only short-lived, ruling coalitions out of its numerous social and political groups, a process that is still under way.

Narrowly-based political groups are likely to make for extreme positions in politics, whether in regard to ideology and policy or intergroup relations. On the contrary, coalition-building for a winning majority, whether in national politics or in the legislature, is likely to make for moderation in politics and policy. That tendency is strengthened by India's immense social diversity. More than 200 years ago, James Madison in *Federalist* Number 10 had recommended extending the size of a political unit as a means, through encompassing greater diversity, to achieving the aim of moderation in politics and policy. What Madison intended to accomplish through political engineering has, however, been structurally given in India, especially for the centre, by its vast diversity. Interestingly, the impact of India's diversity to advance moderation has been apparent to Hindu nationalists also; Lal Krishan Advani, the BJP's preeminent party organizer and theoretician, underlined the point in 1980:

> *Advani:* In India, a party based on ideology can at the most come to power in a small area. It cannot win the confidence of the entire country—neither the Communist Party nor the Jana Sangh in its original form.
> *Journalist:* However, despite its ideological anchorage, the Jana Sangh's appeal was steadily increasing.
> *Advani:* The appeal increased to the extent the ideology got diluted. Wherever the ideology was strong, its appeal diminished (cited in Jaffrelot 1996: 314).

Functional as diversity may be in some respects, it can also have adverse consequences for politics. In the area of policy-making, it often leads to policy stalemates, which then require a crisis for decisional breakthroughs. More seriously, diversity has another impact, which has long been recognized and looms large in the literature—that of aggravating tensions and conflict in society as a result of the appeals by political parties to ethnic groups. Diversity thus sets in motion two opposing processes: ethnic mobilization and coalition-building. No party is immune to either process, and all have to develop strategies to cope with both even if at different levels of the political system.

The situation is, however, also pregnant with tension for relations within political parties, principally between the parliamentary or government wing and the organizational wing along with its associated interest groups. The parliamentary wing is likely to be oriented to the wider political environment with the aim of acquisition of power within its constraints, while the organizational wing is likely to be more oriented to the interests, material and ideal, of its membership and related interest groups. Take, for instance, the relationship between the RSS as the sun or mother, as it were, and the BJP as the satellite or child, with cadres from the former constituting a large part of the membership of the latter. The RSS as a cultural organization is exclusionary in its membership and approach, intent on advancing the interests of the Hindus as a nation. On the other hand, politics and the quest for power in the context of a diverse and divided society demand that the BJP as a political party be inclusionary and compel it to seek coalitions with other political groups. For, in the alternative, the cost for the BJP is to remain permanently in the political wilderness as a political untouchable, precisely the position which it has consistently struggled to overcome and one to which most other parties have largely endeavoured to consign it. By the same token, if the BJP is compelled to be broad-based in the pursuit of power, it cannot necessarily be taken to be monolithic after the assumed model of the RSS. Rather, diversity within the party is likely to make for internal differences over policy, necessitating some compromise. Indeed, the compulsions of politics may even give rise as a result to occasions where divergence emerges in strategy and policy between the BJP and the RSS. How to resolve the resulting tension between the BJP and the RSS, and within the BJP between its parliamentary and organizational wings, is the most formidable challenge for the BJP leadership.

In brief, India's institutionalized political structure dictates that power can be acquired only through the democratic process. That process, particularly as reinforced by India's social diversity, further dictates that political groups engage in coalition-building. In turn, coalition-building requires compromise among narrowly-based political groups and the moderation of their narrow and extreme political positions towards a centrist stance. The BJP cannot be and is not immune to that process, at least over the longer run.

The Incentives to Globalization and Liberalization

Even though at one time an anathema in Indian politics, economic liberalization—incrementally, if not rapidly—has in the contemporary era of globalization become an aspect of the centrist position in relation to economic policy. No doubt, the advantages of openness in trading and investment among the world's economies have long been argued theoretically by economists since Adam Smith. However, the recognition by national decision-makers of the need to open their economies more widely has been a more recent phenomenon since the 1980s. Behind this recognition has lain the new-found awareness that, even though the gains from participation in the world economy are unequally distributed in favour of the already strong, that is, the developed countries, shrinking away from active participation in it carries penalties by way of slower economic growth and therefore retardation of employment and poverty alleviation. It is precisely this awareness that lay behind the United Front coalition, most of the constituents of which had earlier been opposed to liberalization, coming around to accepting, even if without enthusiasm, its necessity. That behaviour of the coalition was testimony to a changed mindset.

Two dominant facts relating to economic performance that became starkly apparent at the end of the 1980s have been critical in making evident to national decision-makers the gains from participation in the world economy through trade and investment. On the one hand, negatively, the economic collapse of the countries in the Soviet bloc laid bare the failure of the contrasting closed economy model. The subsequent opening up of these countries to the world economy as the only possible option available has been a potent lesson to economic nationalists in the developing countries. On the other hand, more positively, there has been equally obvious the high growth experience of the East Asian economies, including China, which opened their economies to foreign trade and investment. To some extent, this positive assessment of the performance of the East Asian economies has been tarnished by the economic crisis of the late 1990s. Still, the disparity in levels of per capita income between the relatively closed economies like that of India and the open economies of East Asia, even after the impact of the crisis has been factored in, makes it highly attractive for national decision-makers to open their economies, even if only gradually in order to avoid economic disruption. In this fashion, developing countries have in recent years been led to following the single model of economic liberalism. In other words, there are powerful incentives for national decision-makers to follow similar policies in respect of liberalization and globalization. The BJP in office is no more immune to these incentives than are other governments.

Realpolitik and Economic Policy

Politics and economics are highly interrelated, not only domestically but internationally as well. The process of liberalization has been at times additionally pushed forward by the application of coercive pressures by the developed countries—directly and through the various international economic regimes that they have erected and dominate—in order to advance the interests of their multinational corporations searching for new markets. This is, of course, a commonplace assumption in respect of international economic relations, where the powerful exert pressure on the less powerful. But economic policy is also influenced by pressures springing from strategic impulses. For example, whether loans are extended to Russia is not simply a function of negotiations over strictly economic matters but depends on how the US and its allies view Russian foreign policy behaviour in relation to events in Europe and elsewhere. Similarly, developing countries may adopt more open policies that accommodate the economic demands of one or more developed countries as side-payments to bridge or smooth over strategic differences. The BJP as a ruling party is not immune to such political calculations or the earlier-mentioned coercive pressures.

The Centrist Tendency in BJP's Long March to Power

Given the BJP's continued linkage to the RSS, through the party's considerable reliance on the RSS cadres for staff and assistance in political mobilization, discussions about it often bristle with characterizations such as communal and sectarian, fascist and semi-fascist, and with accusations of having a hidden agenda to convert India into an authoritarian and theocratic Hindu state. For long, most other political parties treated the BJP as a political pariah even as they readily used, when convenient, its political support in their own drive to power.

In the most thorough and insightful treatment to date of the politics of Hindu nationalism, Christophe Jaffrelot (1996) takes a somewhat different view of the BJP, interpreting its development in terms of oscillation between a strategy of ethnic mobilization and a strategy of moderation and alliance-building. The oscillation theory is an attractive one, but it still tends to place the dynamic for change in the internal structure of the party, where the cadres are oriented towards the RSS and the party leadership is oriented towards the larger political system. However, another but different reading of the historical material, as taken here, suggests a unilinear direction in change in party strategy towards moderation and coalition-building—under the external stimulus of the structural features of India's democratic framework and social diversity—but one which was seriously interrupted, and partly disrupted, by antagonist political forces external to the party. It tends to downplay somewhat the within-party tension in favour of the structural features in determining the longer-run direction of the BJP.

This different reading can be indicated here in only the briefest of outlines so as to have the analysis remain focused on its principal concern with recent economic policy. As the Jana Sangh, founded in 1951, took part in the country's political process, it came to moderate its political stance and engage in forming alliances with other political parties. Eventually, in 1977, it merged itself into the hastily-created Janata Party, which came to power at the centre in that year following the electoral defeat of the Congress Party. The Janata coalition collapsed in 1979. The former Jana Sangh leaders were not the cause of the collapse even though they were made the pretext for it in the factional infighting; indeed, they tried hard to have the party stay united. The bitter and humiliating experience at the hands of some of the coalition partners resulted in the revival of the Jana Sangh in 1980 in the new incarnation of the Bharatiya Janata Party, but on the moderate platform of secularism and Gandhian socialism. The BJP's moderate path was disrupted in the 1980s by forces external to the BJP rather than from within. Faced with threats to national unity on the part of religious-based movements, the Congress Party had turned to a softer position on Hindu nationalism in order to attract political support for itself. At that point, the BJP took to a militant course to prevent the erosion of its exclusive constituency. However, this course was soon exhausted, while the political process drove home the lesson that power at the centre, or even in the states, could not be obtained or retained except on a wider and more inclusive political base. By the mid-1990s, the BJP had moderated its position and turned to an alliance-building strategy. It is noteworthy that, when the BJP finally succeeded in achieving power at the centre in 1998, it did so as a part of an 18-party coalition. Significantly, to arrive at this coalition arrangement, the BJP placed a moratorium on core issues of its agenda in order to create a common platform for the coalition.

BJP's Economic Agenda and the Centrality of National Interest

Since the BJP is often identified as a revivalist party of the Hindus, whose religion predates the Christian era, there is a tendency to assume that its economic programme must represent a reversion to some archaic, antediluvian form of economic thinking. While its prescriptions may be presented under traditional nomenclature and one may not necessarily agree with them, they represent, in fact, an intellectually cogent and balanced, rather than ideological, position. They have honourable intellectual precursors in the mercantilism of Alexander Hamilton, Friedrich List, the advocates of managed trade in the West, and the contemporary practitioners of preferential trading blocs in the garb of free trade areas.

As the Congress government under Prime Minister Narasimha Rao initiated the acceleration of liberalization in 1991 and as the economic question moved to the forefront of the political debate, even though it was temporarily overshadowed by the Ayodhya issue, the BJP began to develop a more coherent economic programme of its own, going beyond mere criticism of the government. The first outcome of this effort was an elaborate 54-page Economic Policy Statement in 1992. After that, the party's economic proposals were embodied in the election manifesto of 1996 and 1998. The election manifesto for 1998 remains the latest and the last statement of the BJP's economic programme, since the party decided to forego a separate manifesto for the 1999 elections in favour of a single manifesto for the BJP-led National Democratic Alliance. This manifesto is the more relevant document for consideration since it immediately precedes the formation of the BJP-led government in 1998. It is the most elaborate among the manifestos of all the parties, and it has the most coherent viewpoint underlying its various chapters.

The starting point for the BJP's thinking on economic policy is that the solution to the country's economic problems lies not in foreign models but rather within the country itself. Rejecting both communism and capitalism, the BJP offers an organismic or communitarian approach which is stated to be derived from India's national heritage. Homage to a model supposedly derived from tradition aside, the key impulse that underlies the BJP's economic programme is really 'the vision of every patriotic Indian to see our beloved country emerge as a strong, prosperous and confident nation, occupying her rightful place in the international community'. The vision, no doubt, mandates freedom from hunger, unemployment, fear and corruption, but also importantly 'to see India, the world's oldest cradle of civilization, transform itself yet again into a benign global power' in order to contribute to saving the world from 'the gathering civilizational crisis' (BJP 1998: 2). No exaggerated chauvinism need be attributed to the party here. For, there is the firm conviction that India's aspiration to be a great power is fully justified by its size, capacity and civilizational background. Towards the end of assuring a strong and prosperous nation, the BJP wants to build a modern economy—not restore some traditional subsistence economy based on old and outdated technology—and endorses rapid economic development. The guiding principle that is central to the BJP in determining economic policy is not dogma, but entirely 'considerations of *national interest* and what is appropriate for us'. Older technology may be more appropriate for a labour-surplus economy, but the attraction lies in its functionality, not in its age.

In the underlining of the national interest as the guiding principle for economic policy-making, the BJP is motivated by the strong belief that that is what all nations, in fact, do:

> Every nation advocates free trade in all global fora but, in practice, they compulsively resort to quotas, tariffs and anti-dumping measures to protect their national interests. Whether it is the USA which resorts to Super 301, anti-dumping and high tariffs, or it is Japan whose market is very difficult to access even now, the story is the same. While the declared agenda is free trade, the undeclared, but actual, agenda is economic nationalism.

Accordingly, 'India, too, must follow its own national agenda', and 'the broad agenda of the BJP will be guided by Swadeshi or economic nationalism'. The BJP places this concept in a universal context and does not consider it as something idiosyncratic to India: 'Swadeshi simply means "India First". This is the governing principle of all nations' (BJP 1998: 10–11). The concept is not to be understood simply in the narrow sense of protectionism: 'By Swadeshi one means that the local resources and talents have the full *scope* for development in national interest and the benefits therefrom should primarily flow to the people. Integration into a global economy should not mean obliteration of national identity and predominant sway of powerful economic forces from the outside' (BJP 1992: 8).

The BJP as well as its predecessor, Jana Sangh, had for long been against excessive state intervention in the economy characteristic of the Nehru model. While 'urging a liberal economic regime in which the full creative genius of the Indian people could flower', the BJP indicted the Nehru model rather severely for having given rise to centralization, economic inefficiency, suppression of entrepreneurship, and corruption. With the liberalization undertaken by the Narasimha Rao government in 1991, the liberalization part of the BJP plank had been snatched away, as it were, by the Congress Party. Those who feared that the BJP may, if it came to power, undo liberalization were assured by BJP representatives that the party was the original liberalizer in India and that the Congress was only a late convert.

The preempting of the liberalization model by the Congress Party did not leave the BJP without a line of attack, however. That line, while accepting the general direction of the policy of liberalization, set out a distinctive path that was consistent with BJP's philosophical position. The BJP rejected the conception of liberalization as a single homogeneous policy, and distinguished between 'internal liberalization' and 'external liberalization' or globalization. The central question then became of sequencing. Its principal critique against the Congress government was that it had opened up India to the ruthlessly competitive world economy without first making sure that Indian firms were competitive. In its view, India should have first allowed local firms, which had been throttled for nearly four decades by state controls, to learn to compete among themselves over a period of 10 to 15 years before forcing them to confront foreign competition. In not doing so, the Congress government had undermined the national economy by facilitating its being overwhelmed by foreign multinationals. The BJP would have, instead, followed a policy of internal liberalization first, only then external liberalization. The overall prescription by the BJP (1998: 11) was:

[to] evolve a consensus on the time span required to enable our industries to adjust to the exacting demands of international

competition. It means rapid, large-scale internal liberalization, but calibrated globalization so that the Indian industry gets a period of seven to ten years for substantial integration with the global economy. On the basis of this consensus, the Government and the industry should work out a strategy to create an atmosphere of international acceptability and manage external relations, particularly with the WTO.

India must move carefully and gradually towards integration with the global economy and even as it so does, it must act in a manner that suits its national interest. This strategy recognizes that Indian industry needs a period of transition before it can compete with global players. All policies of tariff reduction and lifting of quantitative restrictions will be formulated taking the above facts into account, but the objective will be to protect the national economy and national interest like all nations do and not to indulge in economic isolationism.

Just like the BJP is not for economic isolation, so it is not simply opposed to foreign investment as such. Instead, the BJP is, again, guided in its position by what it considers to be in the national interest. It believes that economic development in India has been and should continue to be financed primarily by local capital, with foreign capital playing only the role of supplementing the national effort. Accordingly,

Policies will be framed consistent with the national interest in respect of FDI [foreign direct investment]. The BJP Government will ensure that FDI flows into such priority areas and not in areas where the domestic industry is functioning well. The BJP Government will frame policies to restrict FDI in non-priority areas. FDI will be encouraged to promote exports rather than target the domestic market. FDI is welcome in a non-predatory role in joint ventures rather than in 100 per cent subsidiaries. Generally, the role of foreign capital should be in harmony with and advance the nation's economic objectives, as also in line with other Asian countries. Again, until the Indian economy reaches a level of global strength, takeovers of existing Indian companies by foreign companies will not be encouraged and suitable, transparent rules will be framed to give effect to this policy. Even developed nations like France, Germany and Switzerland have restrictions on the takeover of domestic companies (BJP 1998: 14).

While eager to open the insurance sector to competition 'by involving Indian private sector in the insurance business', the BJP was averse to opening it to foreign companies. It wanted foreign companies also to stay out of the consumer goods sector and to focus instead on high technology areas and the infrastructure ('computer chips yes, potato chips no'). In regard to foreign trade and patents, it was highly critical of WTO:

> The major task facing our country in the economic sphere is the preservation of a measure of autonomy in the management of the national economy, which the Congress Government surrendered meekly by accepting without resistance the highly prejudicial WTO conditionalities.... This would be the foremost objective of our party to restore the desired autonomy.... The agreement on services, particularly financial services, would be monitored in respect of powerful foreign interests in our country.... The patent system, in particular, would not be allowed to become an import monopoly and working of a patent and dissemination of technology would be ensured by an effective and strong 'license of right' and 'compulsory license' regime (BJP 1998: 20–21).

The BJP's outlook on the world economy is embedded in a broader economic approach which accords special importance to the interdependence of industry and agriculture in the national economy and gives a critical role to small-scale industry. The BJP promises 'to reverse the process of economic, social and political marginalization of India's rural population and effectively fight the elitist, anti-kisan [farmer] Congress mindset', and to that end 'earmark 60 per cent of Plan funds in the budget for agricultural and rural development'. It sees housing construction as a critical social need and a means to generating employment. In line with its nationalist posture, but contrary to policy projections based on its allegedly high-caste middle class social base, it makes rapid advance in health and education a key aim. It commits a future BJP government to providing potable drinking water to all villages and slums, increasing state spending on education to 6 per cent or more of GNP in five years, and giving priority to free primary education.

Even though in the working out of the joint National Agenda for Governance with its allies the BJP gave up what were regarded as contentious issues or extremist measures, its economic agenda on

India's relationship with the world economy seems to have been largely acceptable to its allies. In other words, there was little difficulty in arriving at a consensus on economic nationalism. Besides promising primacy for removal of unemployment, high priority for infrastructure, allocation of 60 per cent of plan investment to agriculture in order to increase the purchasing power of the people, accelerated investment in the social sectors, particularly housing and education, the brief document on the joint agenda (reprinted in Bhambri 1999: 224–30) summarily stated:

> We will continue with the reform process, give it a strong Swadeshi thrust to ensure that the national economy grows on the principle that 'India shall be built by Indians'.... We will carefully analyze the effects of globalization, calibrate the process of it by devising a time-table to suit our national conditions and requirements so as to not undermine but strengthen the national economy, the indigenous industrial base and the financial and services sectors.

Despite the claims to novelty about BJP's economic policy on the basis of a philosophy based on India's national heritage, not much credence need be placed on them. Protectionism is no virtue or vice of the right or communalism. It is equally identified with socialism; as an authority on the subject (Burnell 1986: 37, 78, 209) points out: 'Economic nationalism is, then, in some versions and some accounts actually subsumed under socialism'. Indeed, while economic nationalism initially developed in India as part and parcel of the struggle against colonialism, in the post-independence period it had progressive origins insofar as it formed the central thrust of economic planning launched by Nehru in his vision of India's march towards a socialist society. Interestingly, despite their disavowals to the contrary, Nehru and his planners aimed to build a largely autarkic economy through self-sufficiency in metal-making, engineering and capital goods industries. What is more, the underlying aim of Nehru's economic strategy was precisely the same as that of the BJP—to make India into a great power. Essentially, what seems to have happened is that the BJP snatched away the flag of nationalism, including economic nationalism, from the Congress Party when the latter tended to lose sight of Nehru's national vision amidst the widespread corruption and the pressures of the great powers. Remarkably, on the specific issues addressed by the BJP in its economic agenda in relation to the world economy, there is hardly any difference to be found from the position taken by the communist parties and their trade unions.

Since both the BJP and the Congress Party after 1991 largely agree on internal liberalization, the real test of BJP's performance in relation to its claims to a distinctive economic policy pertains to the external liberalization aspect. To be sure, the BJP also places greater emphasis on agriculture and the informal sector, and on an accelerated privatization of the public sector, but these aspects can be easily accommodated within the economic agenda of the Congress Party. Briefly, from the stated position of the BJP, one would expect it to be more restrictive than the Congress Party had been in relation to trade policy, foreign direct investment, the opening of the insurance sector to foreign companies, and patents policy. However, in case the BJP should find that the compulsions of power require it to shift its position closer to that of the Congress Party, an interesting question would arise for investigation, viz., whether it would have the autonomy to undertake such a shift and, if so, what the repercussions would be on its relationship with the RSS and its affiliates, who hold even stronger views on these issues.

Economic Policy Reforms under the BJP-led Government

Any assessment of the performance of the BJP-led government must take into account the fact that the government was in power for only a short time, just 13 months. It did not have a normal term of five years. Even over this short period, its record was not spread evenly. The period can be divided into two phases; the first phase of about four months, indeed the first eight months, which proved to be an absolute disaster in terms of economic policy and management of the economy, and a second phase that demonstrated a great deal of movement and showed considerable promise but which was not fulfilled, for the government soon lost majority support in the Lok Sabha.

Legislative and Economic Mismanagement and the Steep Learning Curve

During the first phase, especially the first four months of it, the economy which had been on a downslide for nearly two years was allowed to drift, with serious consequences for the reputation of the government and therefore doubts about its continuance in power. Three important factors underlay the dismal performance. The first of these concerned the nuclear tests in May 1998 after the government had been in power for hardly two months. The nuclear tests had a two-fold effect on the economy and economic policy. On the one hand, the government perforce became completely preoccupied with the diplomatic fallout of the nuclear tests, as the western coalition under the leadership of the US sought to isolate India politically and to punish it economically. The government was simply bogged down in trying to cope with the diplomatic situation. On the other hand, while the tests were overwhelmingly popular with the public, they made the government politically vulnerable. To begin with, the economic sanctions and the diplomatic isolation that followed the tests aggravated an already deteriorating economy that the government had inherited from the previous administration, and escalated economic uncertainty. International credit rating agencies downgraded India's credit status. Meanwhile, the razor-thin majority of the government made it risk-averse, and it was reluctant to undertake any important, and therefore controversial, initiatives in the economic field that would run counter to its nationalistic outlook or undermine the support of its cadres and its affiliate organizations.

The second factor which deepened fears about political instability had to do with the perils of coalition-management in a government comprising 18 partners, especially from the exceedingly recalcitrant and obstreperous Ms J. Jayalalitha. She eventually defected and brought about the downfall of the government. Until then, the government remained preoccupied not only with the diplomatic fallout of the nuclear tests, but also with the constant pulls of allies that perpetually threatened the survival of the government. Thus, with survival as its constant preoccupation, major initiatives in the economic arena could only take second place. The BJP cannot be particularly faulted for the perils involved in coalition-management, for that situation has been willed by the electorate and forms a political parameter within which this or any other party has had to work since the end of the single dominant party system. Rather, it is remarkable that, with the exception of the case of Jayalalitha, the BJP government leadership in the main showed great agility and adaptability in managing the coalition, which observers thought it would be incapable of doing in view of its ideological orientation and suspected authoritarian inclinations. However, the allies were not the only source of problems for the government; so, too, were the BJP organization and the RSS. At the very beginning, the RSS seems to have vetoed Vajpayee's initial selection of Jaswant Singh as finance minister (who later went on to make a name for himself as special envoy and foreign minister for the government) because of his more favourable attitude toward the multinationals. Vajpayee then chose Yashwant Sinha as finance minister, who cannot be blamed for holding the grudge of having been a second choice. The RSS veto served to undermine, to some extent, Vajpayee's capacity to manage the government and the coalition by showing him up to be a weak leader who could not stand up to the RSS bosses. Nor was the government helped much by the BJP organization; with a rather provincial background, Kushabhau Thakre, who replaced Advani as president of the BJP, proved to be a poor choice as the leader of a national party, especially in a supportive role to the government.

The fallout of the nuclear tests and the perils of coalition-management were bad enough for the government. A third factor that affected the functioning of the central government adversely was the lack of experience on the part of most of the ministers from the BJP and its allies. The BJP leaders had for most of their lives been participants in an opposition movement, with little expectation of some day taking charge of running a government. The lack of experience resulted in making the ministers dependent on the bureaucracy. However, 'without the advantage of having been in power for any length of time before, the Vajpayee government had neither any rapport with the right bureaucrats nor the ability to manage them' (Burman 1998). The consequence was incapacity on the part of the government to push through new initiatives during the honeymoon period of the new dispensation. Some, indeed, suspected worse, believing that the bureaucracy was basically loyal to the Congress Party, whose return it expected imminently since obituary notices about the new government had already started appearing.

The Fiasco of the First Budget

The annual budget is the most important statement on the government's economic policy, but the reception of the budget by the public and economic actors depends on their prior expectations. In the case of the budget for 1998–99, the Finance Minister's task was a formidable one in view of the state of the inherited economy and the excessive expectations over the budget. Especially since mid-1996, the economy had been on a severe downturn. It was in tatters when Yashwant Sinha took over as Finance Minister. The gravity of this economic situation was compounded by the economic fallout of the nuclear tests. The US imposed economic sanctions against India while the US-led western alliance sought to isolate India politically, affecting market sentiment. World Bank loans were no longer available except for humanitarian projects, while foreign investors were understandably hesitant to rush in. Foreign investment (especially foreign portfolio investment [FPI]) had already—perhaps because of turbulence in Asian markets and political uncertainty in India—seen a considerable decline from $6,008 million (FPI $3,312 million) in 1996–97 to $5,025 million (FPI $1,828 million) in 1997–98. During April–December 1998–99, essentially the period after the nuclear tests, it fell from $4,253 million (FPI $1,742 million) in the comparable period in 1997–98 to $880 million (FPI $ –682 million). In other words, rather than bringing in money, foreign portfolio investors were selling off their holdings and taking money out of the country. In the process, they hammered down the stock markets; the Sensex fell steeply from 4,006 in April 1998 to 2,810 in November 1998.

It was in this situation of a growing economic crisis that Finance Minister Sinha had to develop his budget. The challenge for him was how to get the economy out of its depressed state and how to overcome the decline in foreign aid and loans as a result of the economic sanctions. The expectation was that Sinha would present a tough budget which would show the world that India meant business in the post-nuclear period. Some counted on, as one commentator had expressed it, a 'mother of all reforms' budget. Such exaggerated hopes were to show the actual budget in much poorer light than it perhaps merited. The expectation seemed to be that the Finance Minister would, under the pressure of the economic sanctions and the country's political isolation, suddenly reject the BJP's platform of economic nationalism and make a giant leap to globalization; in a sense, it reflected the desire of the globalizers to use the lever of the predicament of the nuclear sanctions to open up the Indian economy to foreign multinationals.

However, the budget came as a major disappointment to investors, especially foreign investors, though Indian industry gave it a warm welcome. The immediate epithet that was applied to it by the usually liberal-oriented financial press and journals was that it was a swadeshi budget. The reasons for the choice of that epithet were basically two. First, Sinha did not extend any special welcome to foreign investors, insisting that the existing incentives were sufficient and that the problem lay in the hassles of red tape, which he intended to remove; he promised clearance of foreign investment proposals within 90 days. Sinha himself shrugged off the sanctions as of little consequence for the Indian economy, and therefore not deserving of any extraordinary counter-measures on his part. More significantly, the budget manifested a deeper sentiment that reliance for investment requirements needed to be placed on local business and Non-Resident Indians (NRIs) in the belief that they were more loyal to India and more sensitive to its needs than foreign investors could ever be. Any NRI could now purchase up to 5 per cent of the total equity of domestic companies (compared to the earlier limit of only 1 per cent), while the upper limit for total NRI investment in a domestic company was raised from 5 to 10 per cent. To overcome the constraint on foreign funds as a result of the stoppage of new World Bank loans and the decline in foreign investment, the Finance Minister launched the scheme of Resurgent India Bonds for purchase by NRIs. Contrary to the doubts of most commentators, that scheme turned out to be highly successful, mopping up $4.3 billion. The success of the scheme was the equivalent of the Indians thumbing their nose at the economic sanctions, mocking at the international credit rating agencies for downgrading India's credit rating, certifying the correctness of India's cautiousness in opening up to the world in response to the sanctions, and improving India's bargaining power by showing its capacity to cope with the sanctions. Further, the Finance Minister, in order to assure Indian business of a level playing field, placed a special additional duty on imports.

Second, with huge increases of the order of 19 per cent in Plan allocations for investment with a view to kick-start the economy, most analysts and opposition critics believed that the budget would be inflationary since it was based on erroneous premises; they feared a return to the days of double-digit inflation. It was alleged that the Finance Minister had been inveigled by the bureaucracy into buying a rosy picture of the economy in the coming year, during which GDP growth was expected to grow at 6.5 to 7 per cent. Since the critics doubted that the economy could grow at that rate, the consequence would be a shortfall in the estimated government revenues. Again, the Finance Minister was presumed to have been unduly optimistic on mobilizing resources from privatization of the public sector. It was feared that the likely result would be that the fiscal deficit, already a very serious problem, would end up going out of control and generating higher inflation. It also seemed that the Finance Minister was not bothered by the fiscal deficit, with his priority being to prevent the economy from continuing to be depressed. The government had apparently bought the argument of the left on the crowding-in effects of public investment and it viewed with concern the paring of public capital expenditures to the bare bone by the previous governments since 1991 (*Business Today*, 4 January 1999: 98–101).

Beyond these aspects of the budget, what emerged as really disturbing was the management of the budget after its presentation. That turned out to be a veritable bungle, partly as a result of the political compulsions of a fragile coalition and partly because of bureaucratic errors. As a consequence, budgetary calculations were thrown into further disarray, and the government faced acute embarrassment within less than 24 hours. The Finance Minister had announced a hike of one rupee (Re 1) per litre in the price of petrol, plus an increase of 15 per cent in the excise duty which was not supposed to be passed on to the consumer. However, the bureaucrats at the ministry of petroleum issued instructions overnight, instead, for an increase of Rs 4 per litre. There was public outrage. Immediately the next day, the government retracted and changed the increase back to Re 1. Again, the government had also made a justifiable increase of Re 1 per kg in the price of urea. However, the next day, after protests from its coalition partners in the Punjab and Haryana, it cut the increase to half; later, after the opposition parties attacked the government for even this reduced increase, the government eliminated it altogether.

Still again, the Finance Minister had imposed a special additional duty of 8 per cent on about one-third of the imports in response to a persistent demand of the Indian industry for a level playing field. The industry's plea was that it had to pay local sales taxes and municipal octroi, amounting to about 8 per cent, from which imported goods were exempt, and that these taxes placed the local industry at a disadvantage. However, the moment the demand was conceded, a substantial part of the industry protested that the additional duty had increased its input costs and made it less competitive with imported goods. Besides, for many, the extra duty was excessive since the real rate would turn out to be not 8 per cent but more like 11 to 16 per cent, because it would be computed on the aggregate of assessed value and other duties. Moreover, such an increase in the level of protection was no longer justified because of the depreciation of the Indian currency. In view of the attacks from different quarters, the Finance Minister cut the additional duty into half. These frequent changes made the whole budgetary process into one big mess. Critics both in Parliament and outside began to refer to the Finance Minister mockingly as 'Rollback Sinha'. One economic columnist charged that the government had turned 'from saffron to yellow' in the face of bullying by different lobbies (*Times of India*, 7 June 1998). The government seemed clueless and, in the context of the frequent changes made to the budget, the pertinent question seemed to be not whether the BJP had a hidden agenda, as often charged, but whether it had any agenda at all.

The question arises whether the Sinha budget was really swadeshi notwithstanding the consensus about that characterization among the liberal-oriented financial press and the partisan political opposition. Actually, it would seem, there is little basis for such a characterization of the budget, particularly as it was finally passed. There were really slim pickings for the swadeshi lobby. The special additional duty was halved when a part of the industry protested against it. Even with the extra duty, India remained fully compliant with its commitments to WTO. The Finance Minister's anxiety for Indian industry stemmed from his assessment that previous ministers had rushed into slashing tariffs much beyond what India was committed to and this had unnecessarily put Indian industry at risk. The additional duty was simply a countervailing duty aiming to net out the effects of local taxes. Sinha was unapologetic about his intent to offer protection to local industry:

> I will be quite upfront and tell you very clearly that I have no doubt in my mind that the Indian economy would not progress by destroying Indian industry and Indian entrepreneurship. The strength we have built over a period of time must be protected, and we should build from there. I'll give time, say two years, and from there I'll ask Indian industry to swim or sink (*Economic Times*, 4 June 1998).

The Resurgent India Bonds, which relied on NRIs to rally behind the country, were no innovation of Sinha's; Congress governments in 1988 and 1991 had launched similar bond schemes for mobilization of funds from abroad. Nor was the special additional duty on imported goods any different in its effects from the special import duty of 5 per cent imposed by Finance Minister P. Chidambaram the previous year. It seems that the charge of swadeshi was made against Sinha because he had refused to hastily lay out the red carpet to foreign investors with new incentives, which the advocates of globalization wanted. It was really excessive expectations, and not substance, that led to the budget being described as swadeshi. In the final analysis, the budget was swadeshi not for its content but simply for having been presented by the BJP. Nothing had been taken away from foreign investors; indeed, the Finance Minister intended to double FDI in the next two years and FIIs (foreign institutional investors) were now allowed to invest in unlisted debt, while there was no increase in taxes on domestic or foreign companies. Interestingly, political partisanship first forced changes in the budget and then used the outcome to underscore the incompetence of the government. As a result, the label of ineptitude in the management of the economy stuck to the BJP-led government and it could not shake it off. In the end, the budgetary process proved to be a disaster area for the BJP and its reputation in governance.

In the midst of the perception of ineptitude, some of the positive aspects of the budget were ignored. The BJP's determination to deepen reforms was manifest in the bold decision to open up the insurance sector to private enterprise, albeit only Indian enterprise for the time being; in so doing, the BJP went further than the proposals of any earlier government. Also radically different was the increase in the Plan allocation for agriculture of the order of 58 per cent (as against the cut of 12 per cent in the previous year's budget). Critics charged that the Finance Minister was trying to spend his way out of the recession. However, the hefty increase was based on the government's belief that a healthy rural economy is good for the long-term health of the national economy. Taking a barb at the English media, which is largely focused on globalization as the panacea, Sinha pointed out: 'This budget takes care of the rural economy and neglected areas like small industries. These are areas which do not have lobbies in the English press' (*Economic Times*, 4 June 1998). The BJP-led government believed that, with prosperous agriculture as the base and a flourishing small-scale industry as a leading sector, the economy could be pulled out of the recession. The budget also increased the allocation for education by 50 per cent; this was in part-fulfilment of the determination to take expenditure on education to 6 per cent of GDP. Again, the budget embodied a radical decision by the government to bring its share in the equity of non-strategic public sector enterprises down to 26 per cent, besides the delicensing of coal, lignite and petroleum. In the light of these initiatives, Sinha objected to the charge that his budget showed no vision, no big ideas, and that it was merely inclined to tinkering. His response was that he had taken a balanced approach rather than emphasize one or two issues to the exclusion of others.

Deepening of the Economic Crisis and the Electoral Shocks

It was Sinha's misfortune that he had to present his budget in the context of enormous turbulence in the world economy, particularly in East and Southeast Asia, and a decline in India's agricultural production during the preceding year. After the presentation of the budget, the financial markets were in continuous turmoil with the Sensex plunging sharply. Some predicted an economic meltdown. It may not have been the case that the budget caused the fall in the stock markets, but it undoubtedly failed to reverse the free-fall resulting from change in market sentiment under the impact of the economic sanctions, the contagion of the Asian economic crisis, and political uncertainty. Similarly, the rupee continued to depreciate.

Prices rose sharply; the rate of inflation based on the consumer price index for industrial workers more than doubled from 8.2 per cent in April to 19.7 per cent in November 1998; that based on the index for agricultural labourers more than quadrupled from 4.6 per cent to 18.3 per cent. However, the impact of the price rise was especially marked in particular sectors. First the heat-wave conditions and then the excessive rainfall had damaged crops and vegetables in northern India. Food prices shot up. The price of onions came to dominate the price scene; normally in the range of Rs 6–12 per kg, it increased multifold to Rs 45 in October and November, and even Rs 60 on some days. Clearly, there was weather-inflicted misfortune for the BJP-led government, but there was government bungling as well. While onion prices were going up, the government procrastinated on banning their export. Later, it had to rush in imports of onions at much higher prices. The ruling party appeared to the public as callous, uncaring and seemingly helpless. The public in the capital was further angered by power outages for extended periods and by shortage of water supply in the sweltering heat of Delhi. The rise in crime did not help the image of the BJP as incompetent and ineffective in governance. The problem was not so much authoritarianism or fascism of the BJP, as had been predicted, but rather its inability to exercise authority at all. Clearly, the management of the economy turned out to be another disaster area for the BJP. The label of ineptitude here in the case of economic management, as in guiding the budgetary process, stuck to the BJP. The resulting public anger spilled over into the state elections, which turned out to be a referendum on the onion crisis.

Elections to the state legislative assemblies were scheduled for November 1998 in three important states—Delhi, Rajasthan and Madhya Pradesh. Normally, the anti-incumbency factor is supposed to operate in Indian elections, reflecting an inbuilt tendency for the Indian electorate to vote against the incumbent party in control of the government, given that there is no way any government in India can meet all the demands and aspirations of the public. In these three state elections, it was expected that the BJP would lose in Delhi and Rajasthan where it was the governing party, but that it would succeed in ousting the Congress Party from the government in Madhya Pradesh. However, in the event, the BJP lost in all three states; it was a stunning blow to the party. The debacle of the 'onion elections' was not simply a judgement on the performance of the state governments; the comprehensive sweep of all the three states by the Congress Party was a resounding pronouncement on the performance of the BJP government at the centre in what amounted to a semi-national election. The election results signalled a resurgence of the Congress, an ominous development for the BJP; it led to the belief that the BJP-led government's days were numbered as the coalition would soon disintegrate. The elections underlined that ideology was not enough, and that performance in governance mattered to the electorate, even in the BJP's citadel in the capital. In the view of the public, governance was another disaster area for the BJP.

BJP's Conversion to the Globalization Paradigm

After the fiasco of the first budget of the BJP-led government, Vajpayee became concerned about the public image of the government as a doddering coalition and, more substantively, about the continuing decline and turbulence in the economy. He became determined, therefore, to take a direct hand in economic management and economic reforms. However, it would be a mistake to think that until then the government had done nothing in that direction. In fact, quite a few initiatives had been undertaken in different areas, with individual ministers eager to establish a record for themselves.

Liberalization Before the Budget

Several ministers were particularly active in the area of economic policy reform. Indeed, it would seem that the liberalizing face of the BJP was already manifest, only it had been overshadowed by the caricaturing of the budget as swadeshi and by the foreign criticism of the nationalism evident in the nuclear tests. Soon after taking charge as Finance Minister, Sinha declared that the 1991 reforms had been 'a step in the right direction', assured multinationals that they 'have nothing to fear' from BJP's policy of economic nationalism, and vowed to 'deepen, broaden and accelerate reforms' (*Times of India*, 21 and 26 March 1998). In what was the first major economic policy pronouncement of the BJP-led government, Commerce Minister Ramakrishna Hegde inaugurated the second generation of reforms in April 1998 by boldly moving faster than India's commitments to WTO on phasing out quantitative restrictions on imports, including consumer goods, and hastening the process of integrating the economy with the global economy. The move did not go unnoticed. Under the title 'Swadeshi Liberalism', the *Times of India* (15 April 1998) observed: 'For all its swadeshi rhetoric, the BJP-led government has shown itself in practice to be eminently pragmatic and progressive'. The *Economic Times* (14 April 1998) agreed, commenting 'Mr. Hegde has risen above the pettiness of swadeshi and pushed for a more liberal trade regime', while *India Today* (27 April 1998) in a piece entitled 'Blow to Saffronomics' thought Hegde's dramatic move 'might embarrass those who had written off a BJP-led government as swadeshi fanatics'.

A similar trend was obvious in industry, where the government early on decided against the BJP's longstanding commitment to institute a 'negative list' of non-priority areas, especially consumer goods, from which foreign investors would be barred. The *Economic Times* (4 April 1998) thought that the decision was evidence that 'the sobering realities of governance have overtaken swadeshi'. Industry Minister Sikandar Bakht emphatically declared that there will be no reversal of reforms and no discouragement of foreign investment (*Economic Times*, 17 April 1998). Paradoxically, the assertion of nationalism through the nuclear tests quickened the pace of government approval of foreign investment proposals in an endeavour to compensate for the fall in official aid flows and to strengthen the business lobby abroad against the sanctions. The effort drew the comment from the *Times of India* (19 May 1998) that 'one of the first casualties of Shakti [code name for the nuclear tests] has been swadeshi'. As a signal to foreign investors, Bakht also amicably resolved the dispute, inherited from the previous government, between Suzuki and the government, the two equal partners in the automobile giant Maruti, over management control. The government also quickly signed counter-guarantees for several power projects.

In perhaps the most important piece of economic reform legislation brought forward until then by the BJP-led government, Power Minister P.R. Kumaramangalam introduced a bill in Parliament in June 1998 to set India's state-owned electricity supply industry in order. His bill aimed to convert the state electricity boards into independent state electricity commissions, which would have removed them from the control of state governments, and thus to rescue them from their bankrupt position through establishing commercially viable power tariffs. The bill was an indicator of the reformist intent of the government. It is a different matter that it had to be diluted in the face of strident opposition from some of the coalition partners and the other political parties, all of whom wanted no interference in the practice of supplying highly subsidized or free electricity to farmers. What was designed to be mandatory was then made optional at the discretion of the state governments. In another area, Housing Minister Ram Jethmalani brought considerable dynamism to his ministry. With determination, he pushed for the repeal of the Urban Land (Ceiling and Regulation) Act, a deterrent to investment in housing, even though success came only in the next year. In sum, the reformist inclinations of the BJP-led government were already manifest.

Liberalization After the Budget

Placed on the defensive by the nuclear tests and the experience of the budget, the government's drive for reforms had stalled.

Recovering its balance after the passage of the budget in July but fearing that it may face a no-confidence motion during the coming winter session in November, the government entered a more assertive phase, and 'the pendulum ... now swung towards a new activism on reforms'. The continuing economic slowdown created pressure on the government to move decisively in the economic arena. Like Narasimha Rao, Vajpayee made the economy his priority. At a series of meetings, the cabinet reviewed ways 'to launch a steady stream of policies and initiatives that would enable the ruling coalition to drastically improve its image, and prepare it for the polls if necessary' (Goswami 1998; Mohan 1998a). The coming independence anniversary also provided a stimulus for new policy initiatives. The government then unveiled a far-reaching time-bound plan for the information technology sector, which was received with enthusiasm by the computer industry. A definite indication of the government's determination to move forward along a broader front came with a major bureaucratic shuffle and the strengthening of the Prime Minister's Office.

There then followed the appointment of two blue-ribbon advisory councils, one consisting of eminent economists and the other of top business leaders, to advise the prime minister on economic policy. This caused some bitterness in the BJP because the members appointed to these councils could as well have all been appointed by the Congress Party. Two of the BJP's resident economists, known for their enthusiasm for economic nationalism—Jay Dubashi and Jagdish Shettigar—were ignored because it was felt that they were too ideological. Also excluded was Rahul Bajaj, the foremost exponent of economic nationalism in Indian business and a charter member of the Bombay Club. Later, a series of policy moves by the government cumulatively added to the BJP shifting its centre of gravity to the globalization agenda of the previous governments of the Congress Party and the United Front. The government delicensed the sugar industry, and decided to join the Paris convention of intellectual property rights.

In its determination to signal that the government had an outward-looking orientation, the cabinet decided, in what was for the BJP an extraordinary step, a veritable volte face, to bring forward two pieces of highly important legislation that had earlier been approved in one form or another by the previous governments but that had so far not received legislative approval—the Patents Bill and the Insurance Regulatory Authority Bill (IRA). The BJP's decision to make the IRA bill its own was momentous for two reasons. First, the BJP had prevented the introduction of the bill by the United Front government the previous year when it was in opposition. Second, unlike the draft of the United Front government which only provided for the appointment of an insurance regulatory authority, though with the unstated intent of subsequently opening up the insurance industry to private competition, the BJP's amended bill was far more radical in that it allowed foreign companies to invest and did so at the high level of 40 per cent of equity (including 14 per cent by NRIs). This represented a remarkable somersault in BJP's posture on globalization, even though the passage of such a bill remained a questionable proposition.

The electoral setbacks in the state elections did not deter the BJP-led government from proceeding with the new globalization agenda but added to its determination to stick with it. Apparently, the government was of the view that, if it had eventually to go, it better go out with a record of performance behind it, rather than remain paralyzed. However, for some who were from the BJP it was a moment of truth, for their world had just been turned around. Initially, Human Resources Minister Murli Manohar Joshi, a former president of the BJP, had taken a hardline position against the opening up of the economy, but finally came around. Home Minister Advani, deemed to be close to the RSS, forthrightly accepted the new line. With his usual no-nonsense pragmatism, he took the position that one cannot just keep on holding to old positions and that being in charge of government made a difference: 'When we were not in the government, we felt that opening up of the insurance sector to Indian private entrepreneurs would suffice. But in government, with a determination to make as much progress as we can in the field of infrastructure, we felt that a different approach was called for'. More broadly, he added: 'No economic philosophy should become a dogma. The BJP believes in swadeshi, which in essence means that India has to develop on its own. It certainly does not mean xenophobia or belief that everything foreign is bad'. (*Economic Times*, 9 December 1998). Similarly, Finance Minister Sinha realized: 'There's a big difference between being in the government and outside the government. In government, you have access to a great wealth of information which could change your opinion. I don't see why ideas should not be changed and modified over the years' (*India Today*, 23 August 1999: 41).

For the BJP ministers in the government, the opening up of the insurance sector was no longer considered antithetical to swadeshi. Indeed, swadeshi was now given a new interpretation to make it consistent with globalization, with Sinha maintaining: 'Swadeshi actually means competition, going out to the world and winning' (*Economic Times*, 11 September 1998). Subsequently, in a long interview, Sinha elaborated on this sentiment, in the process making globalization the best means to swadeshi:

It all depends on how you perceive swadeshi. Nuclear tests were swadeshi because they made India powerful. Now, India must be a powerful economic nation to match its military might, and the only way you can become an economic power is by being able to test your strengths against others. Which means going out into the world and competing—or letting the world come in and compete. It is not from hiding from the world, but by going out and meeting the world that we can compete.... I understand swadeshi basically as a concept which will make India great. And India can be great only when we become an economic superpower.... We can be great by being able to compete. I think competition is the essence. I am a great believer in competition. We are willing to face it abroad and here. After the nuclear tests, to think that we will go the East India Co. way, or that transnationals will come in and take over, or that they will exercise undue influence, that foreign investment should be resisted—these are all concepts which are not valid any more. And therefore, swadeshi, globalizer, and liberalizer are not contradictions in terms. I personally think that globalization is the best way of being swadeshi (*Business Today*, 22 January 1999: 98–101).

Sinha may or may not have been a closet liberal, but Vajpayee had all along been the liberal face of the BJP. Some, no doubt, had described him as a mask for the party, and even for the RSS, which would be discarded the moment the BJP acceded to power. Here, now, he had revealed the mask to be the real face. However, he could not have single-handedly persuaded all of his BJP ministers on reform. What the episode disclosed was that there was, indeed, always a substantial liberal wing in the BJP that had now taken charge of the government, and that it had been responding to the requirements of coalition-making in the Indian situation. S. Swaminathan Aiyar relates his experience with Vajpayee during the 1998 elections when Vajpayee seemed to be distancing himself from what Aiyar thought was the historical position of the BJP:

> I asked you at the time, is this not dilution of policy? Not at all, you replied. When the Jana Sangh started, it had to cater to the aspirations of a small section of society. As the party grew and grew, it had to cater to the aspirations of several other sections of society. This, you declared, was not dilution but evolution (*Times of India*, 10 January 1999).

However, such an evolution in a centrist direction and in joining the mainstream was not acceptable to all in the Hindutva family.

The Hindutva Empire Strikes Back

The reaction to the shift by the government on globalization was not too long in coming, and it came from the RSS and its other affiliates as well as from the BJP organizational wing and a segment of its parliamentary wing. The most strident assault on the government's position came from SJM—Swadeshi Jagran Manch (Front for the Mass Awakening of Economic Nationalism)—and it was quickly echoed by other RSS affiliates. The special clout of SJM derived from the presence on its steering committee of K.S. Sudarshan, a top functionary of the RSS who later became the supreme leader of the RSS, and Dattopant Thengadi, a highly-regarded aging RSS leader who had founded the SJM and the trade union arm Bharatiya Mazdoor Sangh (BMS). That lent SJM's pronouncements the imprimatur of the RSS itself.

Normally, the expectation would have been that the entire RSS family would discuss things quietly and privately, and bring the government into line. But the government did not seem to be amenable, for a two-day meeting of the SJM's steering committee at August-end in 1998 brought the dispute definitively into the open with a stinging resolution warning the government 'not to give in to vested interests and business lobbyists' and 'not compromise with national interests'. It urged the government 'to refrain from allowing FDI directly or indirectly in the insurance sector'. Its attack was wide-ranging, raising serious objection to retaining bureaucrats 'who are habituated to compromise national interests' and appointing persons on advisory committees 'who are hostile to the very idea of swadeshi'. The SJM softened its stand for a while, but then charged into the government with renewed vigour after the BJP's losses in the state elections, which were attributed to the BJP government having gone back on its swadeshi platform. At November-end, 25,000 BMS workers from all over India protested in front of Parliament against the government's economic policies; Thengadi accused the government of proposing the insurance bill under American pressure and asked it to 'desist from taking an anti-national course'. Interestingly, the left parties welcomed the SJM resistance to FDI in insurance.[2]

Soon, the SJM was joined in its opposition by the BJP organizational wing. BJP president Kushabhau Thakre underlined the contradiction between the party's rhetoric and the government's plan on insurance, complaining: 'The party was given no indication that this was in the offing. Till yesterday, we were saying something, and now our government is doing just the opposite'. In similar vein, Jay Dubashi, member of the BJP national executive, underlined in an open letter to the BJP president:

> The government has suddenly made an about-turn and is now following an agenda of its own, which not only differs markedly from ours but is in many respects diametrically opposed to it.... The government's stand is diametrically opposed to the party's long-standing position on these issues.

Several seasoned members of the BJP's parliamentary wing expressed their opposition to the government's plans. The attack on the government turned into an avalanche. Most critically, the RSS pitched in, after a rarely-held study session, with a resolution strongly censuring the government's conduct as 'improper' in allowing FDI in insurance. RSS strongman Sudarshan held a veiled threat to the BJP and the government by declaring that the RSS had never aligned itself with any particular political party, but that it only supported those parties that reflected its overall views (*Economic Times*, 7 December 1998 and 26 February 1999; *Times of India*, 15 December 1998). There was evident in the RSS a sense of having been betrayed by the government, worry about the 'Congressization' of the BJP (*Economic Times*, 10 January 1999), and its straying away from the RSS. The relations between the two had plummeted, and one commentator thought 'the scale of RSS attack this time is truly phenomenal' (Subrahmaniam 1999).

Vajpayee and Government Stand Firm

Despite the rising tide of criticism and protest from the RSS and its other affiliates, Vajpayee refused to yield. This development was unlike the past when the political party would normally fall in line after being reprimanded by the RSS to mend its ways. It was also unlike the occasion at the beginning of the BJP-led government when Vajpayee let the RSS veto his appointment of Jaswant Singh as Finance Minister. Now, he inducted him as Foreign Minister, a sheer defiance of the RSS. Vajpayee also brought the BJP organizational wing into line with the government. At the meeting of the national executive of the BJP at Bangalore in early January 1999, which was a turning point in the relations between the government and the BJP, Vajpayee stood firm and refused to subordinate himself to the party organization, asserting the primacy of the prime minister and government: 'widest consultations are desirable, but decisions of the government are final'. Vajpayee seemed determined to disengage the BJP from the RSS. Eventually, the party had to accept the position that 'government knows best'.

Nor would Vajpayee concede specifically on his economic policy reforms, and he considered it an embarrassment that the party instead of being supportive was adding to the government's problems. The party finally had to give in; the economic resolution, in the words of the *Hindu* (6 January 1999), 'all but disavowed the mindset of economic nationalism', aiming 'to silence the strident swadeshi lobbies among the Sangh Parivar'. After the Bangalore meeting, the BJP rallied to the defence of government policies against the attacks of the SJM and its allies. This definitely marked a change in the relationship of the BJP to the RSS; the equations within the family seemed changed; it was the party that appeared to have acquired primacy. The resulting consequences for policy covered a wide arena, including treatment of minorities. In due course, a sort of truce developed within the family in view of the threat to the stability of the government from the Congress and other parties, but significantly the truce was on the BJP's terms.

Vajpayee and his government pushed forward with economic policy reform. However, their success depended on cooperation from the Congress Party, since the government lacked a majority in the upper house Rajya Sabha. Such cooperation was forthcoming only for the Patents Bill, apparently because the Congress Party was the one that had made international commitments for it when in office and non-passage would have meant penalties for India for which the Congress Party would have been held responsible. However, the IRA bill was a different story. The Congress Party proved to be devious about extending support; one financial columnist (Bhalla 1998) thought the BJP to be naive in expecting cooperation from the Congress because the credit for the most important globalization measure since the reforms of 1991 would then have gone to the BJP. Indeed, the Congress Party became desperate to oust the government precisely when it saw the BJP finally getting its act together along a wide front, including foreign relations, and becoming adept at governance. Even as it failed to get the IRA bill and other measures enacted because of non-cooperation of the Congress Party and the blocking tactics of the other opposition parties in Parliament, the BJP had by its actions before its downfall made abundantly clear the shift in its outlook on globalization.

Beyond economic policy reform, which was also manifest in other areas—such as buy-back of shares, innovatively amending telecommunications policy, opening internet services to the private sector, moving more boldly on phasing out quantitative restrictions on imports—the government had learnt to manage the economy better, with some help from nature. The government's second market-friendly budget for 1999–2000 was marketed better and it triggered a boom on the stock market to reach record levels; there were no roll-backs this time. Meanwhile, the GDP growth rate for 1998–99 increased to 6 per cent; agricultural production reached record levels; industrial recovery was under way; and inflation was at its lowest in some two decades. Subsequently, despite the war-like conflict with Pakistan over Kargil, which added immensely to Vajpayee's stature as a mature and responsible statesman, inflation remained low and the Sensex remained largely stable. The BJP's continued commitment to reform was subsequently confirmed by its pressing on with reform-oriented legislation after the return of the coalition to power following the elections in late 1999.

Conclusions

The structural features of India's society and polity, in terms of its immense social diversity and the considerable institutionalization of its democratic political framework, have had a significant impact on the behaviour of its political parties. They have, to be sure, meant an enormous political fragmentation, making the reaching of decisions difficult except in a situation of crisis. But they have also meant that over the long run political parties, whose purpose is to attain power, tend to become centrist, notwithstanding their initial ideological positions, and they tend to enter into alliance-building, especially at the centre, and moderate their extreme or ideological positions.

In its interaction with social diversity, politics has a double effect. In the arena of political mobilization, it accentuates tension by encouraging appeals to ethnic identities. But at the level of organizing for power, it attenuates tension and advances a centrist tendency. No party is immune from either tendency. While the dichotomy of secular forces and communal forces is a handy instrument in the struggle for power, no party has been above using the communal card or above making alliances with its earlier antagonists when it has served its purposes. At the same time, no party has been immune to the centrist tendency either. Because of the tension between the two processes, the centrist tendency does not emerge smoothly but by fits and starts, but it does emerge. Along with it, there takes place the erosion of ideology. Unlike religion, the social sciences deal only with tendencies, not absolutes and certainties. Nonetheless, the centrist tendency is visible in the experience of the BJP.

The centrist tendency in Indian politics was apparent earlier in the political career of the Jana Sangh, leading to its merger in the Janata Party. It was apparent, again, in the beginning years of the BJP. The tendency was disrupted, not by forces internal to the BJP, but forces external to it. As the Congress Party oriented itself favourably towards Hindu communal forces in the context of threats to national unity on the part of religious-based movements, the BJP changed direction to reclaim and protect an earlier exclusive constituency. But the compulsions of power-seeking made the BJP once again moderate its position and launch an alliance-building strategy. It is significant that the BJP came into power as part of a larger coalition, in the formation of which the BJP had to give up its extremist planks. The experience of the BJP, if sustained, would not be unique; similar changes have been commonplace under democracy. Witness the transformation of Britain's Labour Party under Tony Blair in respect of both ideology and the control over the party by the central trade unions. Witness also the change in Israel's Likud Party, which had a much more radical and violent past compared to the BJP, and yet was agreeable to a peace accord with Egypt.

The learning experience as a result of being in charge of government has further induced moderation in the BJP and made it largely into another version of the earlier Congress Party. This moderation of a 'new BJP' is equally evident in the area of economic policy where its earlier strident position on economic nationalism has been discarded in favour of a stance that is in practice convergent with that of the Congress Party and the United Front (now defunct). The centrist tendency generated by India's political system is the principal explanation for the change in the BJP's turn to moderation; the acceptance of economic liberalization is the specific manifestation of the centrist tendency in the contemporary era of economic globalization.

Notes

1. On the RSS, see Andersen and Damle (1987). Fundamentally, in its organization and ideology, the RSS has been, in part, reflective of an emulative strategy of 'semitization' of Hinduism through selectively borrowing from those whom it perceived as its very adversaries—Muslims and Christians—such features as it believed to have contributed to their power and enabled them to conquer India and to dominate the much more numerous Hindus. (See Jaffrelot 1996: 51, 76, 78.) In this sense, the RSS is only a copy, Islam and Christianity are the original models.

2. See *Economic Times*, 11 September 1998; *Times of India*, 1 September 1998; *Organizer*, vol. 50, no. 7 (13 September 1998): 11, and vol. 50, no. 20 (3 December 1998): 3.

8

Summary and Conclusions

In the continuing interaction between globalization and nationalism, representing markets and states, respectively, a new stage of
acceleration in globalization has been evident in the second half of
the twentieth century and it is that which has given rise to the need
for economic policy reform. The new stage of globalization is the
latest in the series of challenges that states have faced from markets
since their largely contemporaneous origins some four centuries ago.
In this new stage of accelerated globalization, states have a choice
whether to insulate against it or to adapt to it, rather than be overwhelmed by it, but the fact of globalization itself cannot be wished
away. The principal issue in economic policy reform is that of the
respective roles of the state and market in the management of the
economy. Notwithstanding the acceleration in globalization, it is significant that in the whole process of expanding the role of the market in the contemporary era, it is the state itself that has served as the
midwife while crisis has been critical to the enactment of reform.

In the Indian case, the need for a wider opening to the market has
arisen from the fact that India has had, prior to the reforms of the
1990s, the most controlled and the most insulated economy outside
that of the communist regimes, and for that it has had to pay the
price of a slow growth rate of the economy and, therefore, higher
economic deprivation. When the balance between states and markets is inappropriate in that it violates their different logics and functioning in the particular contexts in which they are located, it affects
adversely the opportunities for growth and development and for

protecting national security and mass welfare. The starting point for India in economic policy reform has not been an already liberal economy where globalization threatens the survival of the state, but rather the excessive command and control over the economy in the hands of the state which need to be loosened in favour of a more appropriate balance between state and market.

How the excessive domination of the state over the market came to be created in India is related to Nehru's vision, in turn partly reflective of the nationalist movement, of a distinctive non-revolutionary path to a socialist society in order to overthrow the colonial legacy of a backward and exploitative economy. Within that socialist vision, nationalism was an integral component. The strategy of building a largely autarkic economy, on the base of a local heavy and capital goods industry in the hands of the state, was intended to advance India's strategic independence, that is, to provide for its *national security* and *economic autonomy*. However, the strategy soon created serious economic imbalances and disequilibria, particularly in respect of agriculture. Under Nehru's successors, India faced many years, especially during the 1960s, of food crisis, balance of payments problems, shortages of basic necessities, industrial overcapacity, and inflation. A correction was at first sought to be applied through devaluation and economic liberalization, but this was done largely under the pressure of foreign aid donors. The foreign authorship of the corrective measures served to undermine the legitimacy of the government and provoked a nationalist reaction. The resulting lurch to the left escalated the role of the state through large-scale nationalization of important sectors of the economy even as restrictions were placed on the corporate sector. When the adverse consequences of these measures became evident in economic stagnation and shortages of food and consumer goods, there followed a disenchantment with the left course, particularly with the lack of efficiency and profitability of the public sector. With this home-grown, rather than foreign-inspired, realization of the impact of the radical path, there occurred in the mid-1970s a halt to further nationalization and a slow movement towards economic liberalization.

Notwithstanding the shift away from the inward-oriented economic strategy in the 1990s, that strategy need not all be viewed entirely negatively. For one thing, any assessment of it needs to take account of its bearing on the structural adjustment undertaken in 1991. At the time of the launching of the adjustment programme, a senior economic planning expert, S.P. Gupta (1993: 5, 19), stated that 'the most painful process is the transition from initial imbalance to a phase of stabilization [and] is mostly reflected in terms of the social cost inflicted by a contractionary economy'. On the basis of a study of the experience of 30 countries that had undergone structural adjustment programmes under World Bank auspices, he concluded that in low-income and poverty-stricken countries which had started their stabilization in the face of a heavy balance of payments disequilibrium, as was the case with India, 'the transitional pain over the contracting period is likely to be prolonged and more intense'. He reiterated that 'almost no low-income country could avoid a contractionary period of less than 4 to 6 years.... With the heavy foreign exchange constraints and import compression and a relatively unfavourable international scenario, India will have to go through a *painful prolonged period of adjustment*'. Well-known economist, C.T. Kurien (1994: 121), readily agreed with this assessment and, citing the already apparent rise in poverty and unemployment during the first year of stabilization, warned that 'the indications are that what was recognized as a crisis in 1991 may well turn out to be a calamity by 1995 or even 1994'. In contrast to these expectations, the most remarkable aspect of the endeavour at economic adjustment was that not only did India make a quick recovery, with minimal economic pain and political turmoil, but also that it took to a higher growth path.[1] This performance is quite unlike the experience of many developing countries undergoing stabilization, which have often witnessed recessions of long duration. Certainly, credit for this performance must go to the economic team which managed the adjustment with extraordinary dexterity and smoothness. However, it has also been suggested that the performance was related precisely to the self-reliant economic base built by Nehru and Mrs Indira Gandhi.[2]

More importantly, the inward-oriented economic strategy was part of a much larger 'grand strategy', the principal aim of which was to ensure the economic, political and foreign policy independence of India and its acquisition of a major power role in the world over the long run. The economic part of that grand strategy was designed to equip India with the necessary economic and military capabilities. No doubt, Nehru as the architect of non-alignment was an ardent advocate of international cooperation, but as the author of the economic strategy he also understood that the international system was a harsh place in which nations had to survive as independent entities. He was not wrong in that view, for even before the nuclear tests of 1998 India had become a target of sanctions applied by foreign nations against its nuclear, space, defence and electronics agencies. By the same token, if India had acquired substantial autonomous capabilities in these areas that were regarded as deserving of such targeting, it bears recognition that those capabilities were fundamentally the result of Nehru's economic strategy launched in 1956. The underlying impulse in Nehru's strategy is of enduring significance, for the world in which India must function continues to be defined by power. There was undoubtedly a price to be paid for the strategy, but Nehru was acting on the basis of a social rationality with a longer time-horizon, which must remain an essential complement to individual rationality that serves as the basis for economic liberalization. As Selig Harrison (1978: 326) has expressed it: 'The Indian development experience cannot be meaningfully judged in a narrowly economic context. For the implicit rationale underlying Indian policies has been a nationalist rationale, a readiness to bear inordinate costs, if necessary, to maximize the independent character of the industrialization achieved'. Not all aspects of the assumed social rationality of economic nationalists always turn out to be functional in the actual scheme of human affairs. Perhaps the heavy industry strategy could have been less onerous in terms of cost if it had not had the additional burden of the industries being located in the public sector, or if it had not been planned on as massive a scale, or if it had not neglected to make greater use of opportunities offered by the world economy, or if its protectionism had not been so severe. But these aspects were all tied as it were in a seamless web in the holistic world view and economic architecture to which Nehru and his associates were intellectually and socially committed.

The crawling liberalization that was initiated in the mid-1970s was stepped up in the mid-1980s but soon became stalled. Later, under the impact of an economic crisis in 1991, a paradigm shift took place in economic policy in the early 1990s. At first blush, the break in economic policy in 1991 seems to mark a disjuncture in the government's earlier integration of the goals of national security and economic autonomy into the very design of Nehru's economic strategy (Mukherji 1999). However, the relationship of national security and economic autonomy to economic policy is more complex, and is not limited to a single variant and certainly not for all time. In part, the break in economic policy itself was a consequence of the fact that Nehru's economic strategy, while no doubt laying a substantial base for a defence-oriented and self-reliant economy, also led to a considerable marginalization of India on the international economic scene in that India fell far behind many other developing countries which had started out from a similar economic base but with a different economic policy. India's economic performance was starkly unimpressive in terms of per capita income, alleviation of poverty, and share in the world output and exports. The implications of this economic performance were, as Paul Kennedy would have predicted, profoundly inimical to national security, for it led to a gross imbalance between India and other major powers in national capabilities. In this state of affairs, no major power role could be gained, and no national security could be assured. A flourishing economy was essential to national security, to economic autonomy, and to an adequate international role. In contrast, the country's economic performance in the 1960s and 1970s aggravated the political and military vulnerabilities of the nation. Within less than a decade between 1962 and 1971, the country faced three wars, all of which were initated by other powers. The economic performance crippled the nation from asserting itself on the international scene. Its vulnerabilities in terms of food and aid dependence, compounded by internal threats to political stability and national unity, made the country cautious in pursuing its foreign policy aspirations for fear of alienating the chief aid donors.

India's economic marginalization on the world scene was an important stimulus to economic policy reform. Though this was articulated primarily in economic terms, the disquiet over its implications for security and autonomy was not far from the surface. It is significant that it is in the context of the higher economic growth following the economic reforms of the 1990s, which added to the resources and self-confidence of a new political elite in power, that India took the decision to defy the major powers to go in for the nuclear tests in 1998 in the assurance that with an improved economy, combined with its self-reliant base, it could take the resulting economic sanctions in its stride. It is evident that national security can not be disassociated from economic performance and, therefore, from economic policy, though the form in which the relationship manifests itself may change.

By and large, the economic policy reforms that India undertook to resolve its problems of relative economic stagnation and marginalization have been gradual and incremental. That feature has been a consequence of the requirements of *legitimacy* under India's political structure of representative democracy, which dictates that decision-makers must be elected through a system of adult franchise. The fact that decision-makers are, in the ultimate analysis, responsible to an electorate constrains them from imposing sacrifice on key groups in society. Consequently, governments under democracy are led to follow a more moderate course in reform. At the same time, the reforms that have been adopted have been consolidated under a variety of governments, because they have represented a home-grown realization of the shortcomings of the earlier economic regime.

The economic policy reforms since 1991 represent some relaxation of the controls on the market by the state, but the state has been the master actor in charge of the liberalization process. Embedded in society, the state has been responsive to internal impulses from society, rather than to the advice of international financial institutions except as it fit with its own assessment. To the extent that the central government may be more hampered in the exercise of its powers in the contemporary period has less to do with globalization than with the regionalization of politics within as a result of the working out of the electoral process in a federal polity set in a socially diverse society. Ironically, economic liberalization—which is supposed to have the perverse effect of shrinking the state—has enabled the Indian state to enhance its capabilities for national security and made possible an assertion of nationalism in relation to the outside world, as evident in the nuclear tests.

The state has been pivotal to economic policy reform, both to the extent that it has taken place and to the extent that it has not. The agenda for further reform is vast, particularly in respect of the fiscal deficit, privatization, consolidating a national market by knocking down barriers to internal trade, carrying out reforms at the state level, and, most importantly, to lift one-third of the population out of poverty and illiteracy. The problem here is not knowledge, but action. There is no lack of considered policy packages, given the highly skilled and sophisticated nature of the country's numerous elites, both in the government and outside. However, action has been slow and halting by virtue of the very nature of the state. There is no denying at the same time the extraordinary achievements of the Indian state in running, howsoever inadequately, a continental polity of daunting diversity and complexity, and in managing the transfer of power through democratic processes, even if too frequently. It has also displayed considerable capacity for social learning and self-correction. So far, crisis has been well nigh necessary to push reform. But leadership continues to make a difference, both nationally and regionally. The necessary equivalent for crisis can be a vision on the part of the state leadership that enables it to mobilize political forces behind reform, thus overcoming the extreme political partisanship characteristic of the party system that blocks reform.[3]

The state will continue to be pivotal to reform. For, in the ultimate analysis, markets cannot regulate themselves; they need an agency outside of them with legitimate authority to set the rules of the game and to enforce compliance. That authority is the state. The state and market are, however, not alternatives; both are needed, in proper measure, to manage economic affairs in cooperation rather than in contention in a harshly competitive world. A strong state remains a prerequisite for a strong market. Besides, markets, whether internal or external, cannot be left to their own devices, for they can have destructive consequences for society. Also, domestic economic players in any developing country need to be assured of an even playing field in a fundamentally unequal world, and they need to be assisted in world competition by an adequate social and economic infrastructure at home. Accordingly, for all these reasons, any project for economic policy reform must go beyond economics and have as an essential component the enhancement of the regulative and transformative capacity of the state.

Notes

1. Figures for GDP growth rates have been frequently revised. One of the more recent reports of the World Bank (2000: 98) gives, as against the average growth rate of 5.7 per cent for 1981–90, the rates for the crisis years of 1990–91 and 1991–92 as 5.4 and 0.8 per cent, respectively. The corresponding figures for the subsequent seven years are: 5.3, 6.2, 7.8, 7.6, 7.8, 5.0 and 6.0 per cent.
2. Conversation with Mohit Sen, former CPI leader, in New Delhi, January 1998.
3. In his discussion of the models of the political economy of reform, Arjun Sengupta (2000) suggests that sustaining the reforms requires the leadership to go beyond (1) a coalition of elite groups that, in a democracy, advances reforms by stealth through attempting to win popular support from non-elite groups by appeasing them with subsidies and public distribution schemes, to (2) fostering mass participation in politics and economic development through a programme that is genuinely beneficial for the poor and unemployed.

Bibliography

Agarwal, M. and D. Sengupta (2000), 'Comparing Transition Economies: India & China', *China Report* (forthcoming).

Alesina, Alberto and Guido Tabellini (1990), 'A Positive Theory of Fiscal Deficits and Government Debt', *Review of Economic Studies*, 57: 403–14.

Amsden, Alice H. (1989), *Asia's Next Giant: South Korea and Late Industrialization* (New York: Oxford University Press).

Andersen, Walter K. and Shridhar D. Damle (1987), *The Brotherhood in Saffron: The Rashtriya Swayamsevak Sangh and Hindu Revivalism* (Boulder, Colorado: Westview Press).

Apter, David E. (1963), 'System, Process and Politics of Economic Development', in Bert F. Hoselitz and Wilbert E. Moore (eds) *Industrialization and Society* (Paris: UNESCO-Mouton).

———. (1966), *The Politics of Modernization* (Chicago: University of Chicago Press), ch. 7.

Associated Chambers of Commerce and Industry of India (1997), *Report of the Committee to Review Issues Relating to Foreign Direct Involvement and MNCs: Foreign Investment* (New Delhi).

Bailey, David, et al. (1994), *Transnationals and Governments: Recent Policy in Japan, France, Germany, the United States and Britain* (London: Routledge).

Baker, Dean, et al. (eds), (1998), *Globalization and Progressive Economic Policy* (Cambridge: Cambridge University Press).

Basu, Kaushik (1993), 'Structural Reform in India, 1991–93: Experience and Agenda', *Economic and Political Weekly* (27 November), 2599–2605.

Bates, Robert H. and Anne O. Krueger (1993), *Political and Economic Interactions in Economic Policy Reform: Evidence From Eight Countries* (Oxford, UK: Blackwell).

Bhaduri, Amit and Deepak Nayyar (1996), *The Intelligent Person's Guide to Liberalization* (New Delhi: Penguin Books).

Bhagwati, Jagdish (1997), 'Bhagwati on Trade: Fast Track to Nowhere', *The Economist* (18 October), 21–23.

Bhagwati, Jagdish and Sukhamoy Chakravarty (1969), 'Contributions to Indian Economic Analysis: A Survey', *American Economic Review*, LIX, no. 4, part 2 (September), Supplement, 2–73.

Bhalla, Surjit S. (1998), 'Don't Cry For the Congress', *Economic Times* (18 December).

Bhambri, C.P. (1999), *Indian Politics Since Independence* (New Delhi: Shipra Publications).

BJP [Bharatiya Janata Party] (1992), *Economic Policy Statement 1992: Our Commitment to Antyodaya—Humanistic Approach to Economic Development (A Swadeshi Alternative)* (New Delhi).

———. (1998), *Vote BJP, Vote for a Stable Government, Vote for an Able Prime Minister: Election Manifesto 1998* (New Delhi).

Bowles, Chester (1971), *Promises To Keep: My Years In Public Life 1941–1969* (New York: Harper and Row).

Burman, Rachna (1998), 'Instability No More a Concern for Industry', *Times of India* (18 May).

Burnell, Peter J. (1986), *Economic Nationalism in the Third World* (Brighton, Sussex, UK: Wheatsheaf Books).

Byres, Terence J. (ed.) (1994), *The State and Development Planning in India* (Delhi: Oxford University Press)

———. (1998), *The Indian Economy: Major Debates Since Independence* (New Delhi: Oxford University Press).

Cafruny, Alan W. (1987), *Ruling the Waves: The Political Economy of International Shipping* (Berkeley: University of California Press).

Chakravarty, Sukhamoy (1987), *Development Planning: The Indian Experience* (Oxford, UK: Clarendon Press).

———. (1993), *Selected Economic Writings* (New Delhi: Oxford University Press).

Chandra, Bipan (1966), *The Rise and Growth of Economic Nationalism in India: Economic Policies of Indian National Leadership* (New Delhi: People's Publishing House).

Chelliah, Raja J. (1996), *Towards Sustainable Growth: Essays in Fiscal and Financial Sector Reforms in India* (New Delhi: Oxford University Press).

Chopra, Ajai (1995), *India: Economic Reform and Growth* (Washington, D.C.: IMF).

Communist Party of India (1977), 'Communist Party in the Struggle for Peace, Democracy and National Advance', in Mohit Sen (ed.) *Documents of the History of the Communist Party of India*, vol. VIII (1951–56) (New Delhi: People's Publishing House), 416–40.

Cox, Robert W. (1993), 'Production and Security', in David Dewitt, David Haglund and John Kirton (eds) *Building a New Global Order: Emerging*

Trends in International Security (Toronto: Oxford University Press), 141–58.

Das, Debendra Kumar (ed.) (1993), *Structural Adjustment in the Indian Economy* (New Delhi: Deep and Deep Publications).

Das, Tarun (1996), 'MNCs: India Strategy Needs Rethink' (Typescript; New Delhi: CII).

Datta, Sudipt (1997), *Family Business in India* (New Delhi: Sage Publications).

Diamond, Larry and Marc F. Plattner (1995), *Economic Reform and Democracy* (Baltimore: Johns Hopkins University Press).

Dodd, Lawrence C. (1976), *Coalitions in Parliamentary Government* (Princeton: Princeton University Press).

Domar, Evsey M. (1957), *Essays in the Theory of Economic Growth* (New York: Oxford University Press).

Evans, Peter B. (1995), *Embedded Autonomy: States and Industrial Transformation* (Princeton: Princeton University Press).

Evans, Peter B. et al. (eds) (1985), *Bringing the State Back In* (New York: Cambridge University Press).

FICCI (1955), *Second Five-Year Plan: A Comparative Study of the Objectives and Techniques of the Tentative Plan-Frame* (New Delhi).

Frankel, Francine R. (1978), *India's Political Economy, 1947–1977: The Gradual Revolution* (Princeton: Princeton University Press).

Gereffi, Gary and Donald L. Wyman (1990) (eds), *Manufacturing Miracles: Paths of Industrialization in Latin America and East Asia* (Princeton: Princeton University Press).

Ghosh, Jayati (1998), 'Liberalization Debates', in Byres (1998), ch. 7.

Gilpin, Robert (1975), *U.S. Power and the Multinational Corporation: The Political Economy of Foreign Direct Investment* (New York: Basic Books).

———. (1987), *The Political Economy of International Relations* (Princeton: Princeton University Press).

GOI (1956), *Second Five-Year Plan* (New Delhi: Planning Commission).

———. (1961), *Third Five-Year Plan* (New Delhi: Planning Commission).

———. (1962), *Papers Relating to the Formulation of the Second Five-Year Plan: 1955* (New Delhi: Planning Commission).

———. (1965), *Report of the Monopolies Inquiry Commission* (New Delhi).

———. (1967), *Economic Survey 1966–67* (New Delhi: Ministry of Finance).

———. (1969), *Report of the Industrial Licensing Policy Inquiry Committee* (New Delhi: Ministry of Industrial and Company Affairs).

———. (1983), *Economic Survey 1982–83* (New Delhi: Ministry of Finance).

———. (1985), *Seventh Five-Year Plan: 1985–1990* (New Delhi: Planning Commission).

———. (1996), *Finance Minsiters' Budget Speeches, 1947 to 1996* (2 vols; New Delhi: Lok Sabha Secretariat).

GOI (1997), *Economic Survey 1996-1997* (New Delhi: Ministry of Finance).

———. (1998), *Economic Survey 1997-1998* (New Delhi: Ministry of Finance).

Goswami, Anupam (1998), 'Powered Shift', *Business India* (24 August–6 September), 50–55.

Gowa, Joanne (1994), *Allies, Adversaries and International Trade* (Princeton: Princeton University Press).

Grieco, Joseph M. (1990), *Cooperation Among Nations: Europe, America and Non-Tariff Barriers to Trade* (Ithaca, New York: Cornell University Press).

Grindle, Merilee S. and John W. Thomas (1991), *Public Choices and Policy Changes: The Political Economy of Reform in Developing Countries* (Baltimore: Johns Hopkins University).

Gupta, S.P. (ed.) (1993), *Liberalization: Its Impact on the Indian Economy* (Delhi: Macmillan).

Haggard, Stephan and Robert R. Kaufman (eds) (1992a), *The Politics of Economic Adjustment: International Constraints, Distributive Conflict, and the State* (Princeton: Princeton University Press).

———. (1992b), 'The State in the Initiation and Consolidation of Market-Oriented Reform', in Louis Putterman and Dietrich Rueschemeyer (eds) *State and Market in Development: Synergy or Rivalry?* (Boulder, Colorado: Lynne Rienner), ch. 11.

Ham, Christopher and Michael Hill (1984), *The Policy Process in the Modern Capitalist State* (Brighton, Sussex, UK: Wheatsheaf Books).

Hanson, A.H. (1996), *The Process of Planning: A Study of India's Five Year Plans 1950–1964* (London: Oxford University Press).

Harrison, Selig S. (1978), *The Widening Gulf: Asian Nationalism and American Policy* (New York: The Free Press).

Hazari, R.K. (1967), *Industrial Planning and Licensing Policy: Final Report* (New Delhi: Planning Commission).

Hirst, Paul and Grahame Thompson (1996), *Globalization In Question: The International Economy and the Possibilities of Governance* (Cambridge, UK: Polity Press).

Huntington, Samuel P. (1993), 'Why International Primacy Matters', *International Security*, vol. 17, no. 4, 68–83.

Jaffrelot, Christophe (1996), *The Hindu Nationalist Movement in India* (New York: Columbia University Press).

Jalan, Bimal (1991), *India's Economic Crisis: The Way Ahead* (New Delhi: Oxford University Press).

Jha, L.K. (1985), 'Liberalizing the Economy', *Business India* (6–19 May), 97–98.

Jha, L.K. (1987), 'Indian Economy in Eighties and Nineties', *Mainstream* (Republic Day), 26.

Jha, Prem Shankar (1980), *India: A Political Economy of Stagnation* (New Delhi: Oxford University Press).

Jog, N.G. (1969), *Saga of Scindia: Struggle for the Revival of Indian Shipping and Shipbuilding* (Bombay: Scindia Steam Navigation Company).

Johnson, Chalmers (1982), *MITI and the Japanese Miracle: The Growth of Industrial Policy, 1925–1975* (Stanford, CA: Stanford University Press).

Joshi, Vijay and I.M.D Little (1996), *India's Economic Reforms 1991–2000* (New Delhi: Oxford University Press).

Kahler, Miles (1990), 'Orthodoxy and Its Alternatives: Explaining Approaches to Stabilization and Adjustment', in Joan M. Nelson (ed.) *Economic Crisis and Policy Choice* (Princeton: Princeton University Press), ch. 2.

Kalecki, Michael (1976), *Essays on Developing Economies* (Hassocks, Sussex, UK: Harvester Press).

Kanter, Rosabeth Moss (1995), *World Class: Thriving Locally in the Global Economy* (New York: Simon & Schuster).

Katzenstein, Peter (ed.) (1977), *Between Power and Plenty: Foreign Economic Policies of Advanced Industrial States* (Madison: University of Wisconsin Press).

Kennedy, Paul (1988), *The Rise and Fall of Great Powers: Economic Change and Military Conflict from 1500 to 2000* (London: Unwin Hyman).

Kitching, Gavin (1982), *Development and Underdevelopment in Historical Perspective: Populism, Nationalism and Industrialization* (London: Metheun).

Krasner, Stephen D. (1978), *Defending the National Interest: Raw Materials Investments and U.S. Foreign Policy* (Princeton: Princeton University Press).

———. (ed.) (1983), *International Regimes* (Ithaca, New York: Cornell University Press).

———. (1991), 'Global Communications and National Power: Life on the Pareto Frontier', *World Politics*, vol. 45 (April), 336–67.

Krugman, Paul (1996), 'Cycles of Conventional Wisdom on Economic Development', *International Affairs*, vol. 72, no. 1, 717–32.

Kumar, Nagesh (1998), *Globalization, Foreign Direct Investment and Technology Transfers: Impacts and Prospects for Developing Countries* (London: Routledge).

Kurian, K. Matthew (ed.) (1975) *India—State and Society: A Marxian Approach* (Bombay: Orient Longman).

Kurien, C.T. (1994), *Global Capitalism and the Indian Economy* (New Delhi: Orient Longman).

Lenin, V.I. (1974), *Imperialism: The Highest State of Capitalism* (New York: International Publishers).

Lewis, W. Arthur (1954), 'Economic Development with Unlimited Supplies of Labour', *Manchester School*, vol. 22, 131–91.

Lindblom, Charles E. (1977), *Politics and Markets: The World's Political-Economic Systems* (New York: Basic Books).

Lowell, Lawrence (1896), *Governments and Parties in Continental Europe* (Cambridge: Harvard University Press).

Maddison, Angus (1995), *Monitoring the World Economy* (Paris: OECD).

Mahalanobis, P.C. (1953), 'Some Observations on the Process of Growth of National Income', *Sankhya*, XII, part 4, 307–12.

———. (1963), *The Approach of Operational Research to Planning in India* (London: Asia Publishing House).

———. (1985), *Papers on Planning*, P.K. Bose and M. Mukherjee (eds) (Calcutta: Statistical Publishing House).

McFaul, Michael (1995), 'State Power, Insititutional Change, and Politics of Privatization in Russia', *World Politics*, vol. 47, no. 2, 221–43.

Mohan, N. Chandra (1998), 'Vajpayee Government Gets Down to Business', *Times of India* (7 August).

Mohan, T.T. Ram (1998), 'Steady As She Goes', *Economic Times* (3 September).

Mukherji, Joydeep (1999), 'Commentary: India Seeks An Economic "Tryst with Destiny"', *Standard & Poor's* (December), 1–6.

Nagaraj, R. (1997), 'What Has Happened Since 1991?', *Economic and Political Weekly* (8 November): 2869–79.

Namboodiripad, E.M.S (1988), *Nehru: Ideology and Practice* (New Delhi: National Book Centre).

Narayan, Sanjoy (1992), 'Industry: Effective Postures, Sceptical Private Reactions', *Economic Times* (1 January).

Nayar, Baldev Raj (1972), *The Modernization Imperative and Indian Planning* (New Delhi: Vikas).

———. (1974), 'The Political Mainsprings of Economic Planning in the New Nations: The Modernization Imperative versus Social Mobilization', *Comparative Politics*, VI, no. 3 (April), 341–66.

———. (1989), *India's Mixed Economy: The Role of Ideology and Interest in its Development* (Bombay: Popular Prakashan).

———. (1990), *The Political Economy of India's Public Sector: Policy and Performance* (Bombay: Popular Prakashan).

———. (1992), 'The Politics of Economic Restructuring in India: The Paradox of State Strength and Policy Weakness', *Journal of Commonwealth and Comparative Politics*, vol. XXX, no. 2, 145–71.

———. (1995), 'Regimes, Power and International Aviation', *International Organization*, vol. 49, no. 1, 139–70.

———. (1998), 'Business and India's Economic Policy Reforms', *Economic and Political Weekly*, vol. XXXII, no. 38 (19–25 September), pp. 2453–68.

Nayyar, Deepak (1996), *Economic Liberalization in India: Analytics, Experience and Lessons* (Calcutta: Centre for Studies in Social Sciences).

Nehru, Jawaharlal (1943), 'India Can Learn From China', *Asia and the Americas*, vol. 43, no. 1 (January), 25–26.

———. (1946), *The Discovery of India* (New York: The John Day Company).

———. (1957), *Planning and Development: Speeches of Jawaharlal Nehru, 1952–56* (New Delhi: Publications Division).

———. (1958), *Speeches: Volume Three: March 1953–August 1957* (New Delhi: Publications Division).

———. (1968), *Speeches: Volume Five: March 1963–May 1964* (New Delhi: Publications Division).

Norman, Dorothy (ed.) (1965), *Nehru: The First Sixty Years*, vol. I (New York: The John Day Company).

Nye, Joseph S. (1990), *Bound to Lead: The Changing Nature of American Power* (New York: Basic Books).

Pani, Narendar (1996), 'When Are Multinationals Desirable?', *Economic Times* (5 April).

Parikh, Kirit S. (ed.) (1997), *India Development Report* (New Delhi: Oxford University Press).

Patel, I.G. (1993), 'New Economic Policies: A Historical Perspective', in Debendra Kumar Das (ed.) *Structural Adjustment in the Indian Economy* (New Delhi: Deep and Deep Publications).

Patnaik, Prabhat (1994), 'Critical Reflections on Some Aspects of Structural Change in the Indian Economy', in Byres (1994), ch. 4.

Patnaik, Prabhat and C.P. Chandrasekhar (1998), 'India: Dirigisme, Structural Adjustment, and the Radical Alternative', in Dean Baker et al. *Globalization and Progressive Economic Policy* (Cambridge: Cambridge University Press), ch. 3.

Pendse, D.R. (1996), 'Economic Reforms', *Times of India* (4 June).

Polanyi, Karl (1957), *The Great Transformation* (New York: Rinehart).

Rao, V.K.R.V. et al. (1973), *Inflation and India's Economic Crisis* (New Delhi: Vikas).

Rapkin, David K. (1983), 'The Inadequacy of a Single Logic: Integrating Political and Material Approaches to the World System', in William R. Thompson (ed.) *Contending Approaches to World System Analysis* (Beverly Hills, CA: Sage Publications): 241–68.

Rodrik, Dani (1997), *Has Globalization Gone Too Far?* (Washington, D.C.: Institute for International Economics).

Rosen, George (1966), *Democracy and Economic Change in India* (Berkeley, CA: University of California Press).

Roubini, Nouriel and Jeffrey D. Sachs (1989), 'Political and Economic Determinants of Budget Deficits in the Industrial Democracies', *European Economic Review*, vol. 33, 903–38.

Rudra, Ashok (1985), 'Planning in India: An Evaluation in Terms of its Models', *Economic and Political Weekly*, vol. XX, no. 17, 758–64.

Ruggie, John Gerard (1983), 'International Regimes, Transactions and Change: Embedded Liberalism in the Postwar Economic Order', in Krasner (1983): 195–231.

Sen, Amartya Kumar (1958), 'A Note on the Mahalanobis Model of Sectoral Planning', *Arthaniti*, vol. I, no. 2 (May).

Sen Gupta, Arindam (1996), 'Paranoid Nationalism?', *Economic Times* (27 March).

Sengupta, Arjun (1995), 'Financial Sector and Economic Reforms in India', *Economic and Political Weekly* (7 January): 39–44.

———. (2000), 'Designing Reforms: No Hope Without Wider Coalition', *Times of India* (6 July).

Sharma, Ruchir (1997), 'Supply-Side Economics', *Economic Times* (2 March).

Sheel, Alok (1986), 'Peasant Nationalism in India in the Gandhian Era', in Amit Kumar Gupta (ed.) *Agrarian Structure and the Peasant Revolt in India* (New Delhi: Criterion Publications): 67–92.

Shenoy, B.R. (1962), 'The Second Five Year Plan: A Note of Dissent on the Basic Consideration Relating to the Plan Frame', in GOI (1962), 15–26.

Singh, Manmohan (1964), *India's Export Trends and the Prospects for Self-Sustained Growth* (Oxford: Clarendon Press).

———. (1992), 'Keynote Address', in ILO-ARTEP, *Social Dimensions of Structural Adjustment in India: Papers and Proceedings of a Tripartite Workshop Held in New Delhi, December 10–11, 1991* (New Delhi), 108–14.

———. (1993) 'New Economic Policy, Poverty and Self-Reliance', in Siddheswar Prasad and Jagdish Prasad (eds) *New Economic Policy: Reforms and Development* (New Delhi: Mittal Publications).

———. (1995), 'India's Economic Reforms: The Experience and Options', in Sinha (1995), 11–22.

———. (1997), 'Interview: Liberalization and Globalization: Where Is India Heading?', *World Affairs*, vol. 1, no. 1 (January–March), 16–42.

Singh, V.B and Yogendra Yadav (1996), 'The Maturing of a Democracy', *India Today* (31 August), 28–43.

Sinha R.K. (ed.) (1995), *India's Economic Reforms and Beyond* (New Delhi: Anamika Publishers).

Sobhan, Rehman and Muzaffer Ahmed (1980), *Public Enterprise in an Intermediate Regime: A Study in the Political Economy of Bangladesh* (Dacca: Bangladesh Institute of Development Studies).

Streeten, Paul (1998), 'Globalization: Threat or Salvation?', in A.S. Bhalla (ed.) *Globalization, Growth and Marginalization* (Houndmills, Basingstoke, Hampshire, UK: Macmillan), ch. 1.

Subrahmaniam, Vidya (1999), 'RSS-BJP Standoff: Straining at the Umbilical Leash', *Times of India* (12 January).

Sullivan, Michael P. (1990), *Power in Contemporary International Politics* (Columbia, South Carolina: University of South Carolina Press).

Swaminathan, S. Anklesaria Aiyar (1996), 'Chidambaram = Manmohan+– 2 percent', *Economic Times* (23 July).

Swamy, Dalip S. (1994), *The Political Economy of Industrialization: From Self-Reliance to Globalization* (New Delhi: Sage Publications).

Tendulkar, Suresh (1997), 'It's Fiscal Suicide', *Business India* (22 September–5 October), 224.

Thakurdas, Purushotamdas et al. (1945), *Memorandum Outlining a Plan of Economic Development for India* (London: Penguin Books).

Tilly, Charles (ed.) (1975), *The Formation of National States in Western Europe* (Princeton: Princeton University Press).

Tordoff, William, and Ali A. Mazrui (1972), 'The Left and the Super-Left in Tanzania', *Journal of Modern African Studies*, vol. X, no. 3 (October), 427–45.

UNCTAD (1998), *Trade and Development Report 1998* (New York: United Nations).

———. (1999), *Trade and Development Report 1999* (New York: United Nations).

UNDP (1999), *Human Development Report 1999* (New York: Oxford University Press).

United Front (1996), 'A Common Approach to Major Policy Matters and a Minimum Programme' (New Delhi: CII).

Vakil, C.N. and P.R. Brahmananda (1962), 'Investment Pattern in the Second Five Year Plan', in GOI (1962), 114–19.

———. (1977), *Memorandum on Inflation Reversal and Guaranteed Price Stability* (Bombay: Vora and Company).

Vakil, C.N. et al. (1974), *A Policy to Contain Inflation with Semibombla: Submitted to the Prime Minister on Behalf of 140 Economists* (Bombay: Commerce).

Venkitaramanan, S. (1997), 'They Put on Trousers, One Leg at a Time', *Economic Times* (5 March).

Vernon, Raymond (1971), *Sovereignty at Bay: The Multinational Spread of U.S. Enterprises* (New York: Basic Books).

Vyasulu, Vinod (1996), *Crisis and Response: An Assesment of Economic Reforms* (New Delhi: Madhyam Books).

Wade, Robert (1990), *Governing the Market: Economic Theory and the Role of Government in East Asian Industrialization* (Princeton: Princeton University Press).

Wadhva, Charan D. (1994), *Economic Reforms in India and the Market Economy* (New Delhi: Allied Publishers).

Wallerstein, Immanuel (1974), *The Modern World System: Capitalist Agriculture and the Origins of the European World-Economy in the Sixteenth Century* (New York: Academic Press).

Weiner, Myron (1989), *The Indian Paradox: Essays in Indian Politics* (New Delhi: Sage Publications).

Weiss, Linda (1998), *The Myth of the Powerless State* (Ithaca, New York: Cornell University Press).

Weiss, Linda and John M. Hobson (1995), *States and Economic Development: A Comparative Historical Analysis* (Cambridge, UK: Polity Press).

Williamson, John (ed.) (1990), *Latin American Adjustment: How Much Has Happened?* (Washington, D.C.: Institute for International Economics).

———. (ed.) (1994), *The Political Economy of Policy Reform* (Washington, D.C.: Institute for International Economics).

World Bank (1996), *India: Five Years of Stabilization and Reform and the Challenges Ahead* (Washington D.C.).

———. (1998), *India: Macro Economic Update* (Washington, D.C.).

———. (2000), *India: Politics to Reduce Poverty and Accelerate Sustainable Development* (Washington, D.C.).

Wriston, Walter B. (1992), *The Twilight of Sovereignty: How the Information Standard is Transforming the World* (New York: Scribners).

Zaidi, A. Moin (1972), *The Great Upheaval* (New Delhi: Oriental Longman).

About the Author

Baldev Raj Nayar is Emeritus Professor of Political Science at McGill University, Montreal. During his distinguished career, he has been awarded several prestigious fellowships such as the Carnegie Study of New Nations Fellowship at the University of Chicago, and the Senior Long-term Fellowship of the Shastri Indo-Canadian Institute. Professor Nayar has published a large number of books including the prize-winning *Minority Politics in the Punjab; India's Mixed Economy: The Role of Ideology and Interest in its Development; The Political Economy of India's Public Sector: Policy and Performance; Superpower Dominance and Military Aid: A Study of Military Aid to Pakistan; The State and International Aviation in India: Performance and Policy on the Eve of Aviation Globalization;* and *The State and Market in India's Shipping: Nationalism, Globalization and Marginalization.*